Embracing the Passion

Embracing the Passion

Christian Youth Work and Politics

Nigel Pimlott

scm press

© Nigel Pimlott 2015

Published in 2015 by SCM Press
Editorial office
3rd Floor, Invicta House
108-114 Golden Lane
London EC1Y 0TG.

SCM Press is an imprint of Hymns Ancient & Modern Ltd
(a registered charity)
13A Hellesdon Park Road
Norwich NR6 5DR, UK.

www.scmpress.co.uk

Unless otherwise indicated, scripture quotations taken from the
HOLY BIBLE, NEW INTERNATIONAL VERSION, 2011 edition.
Copyright © 1973, 1978, 1984, 2011 by Biblica (formerly International
Bible Society). Used by permission of Hodder & Stoughton Ltd,
a member of the Hodder Headline Group.

Written and developed in association with Frontier Youth Trust.
The views expressed are those of the author and do not necessarily reflect
those of Frontier Youth Trust.

This book uses inclusive language, but occasionally gender-specific
references have been maintained when using quotations. The names of some
people referred to have been changed in order to protect their real identities.

British Library Cataloguing in Publication data
A catalogue record for this book is available
from the British Library

978 0 334 05311 8

Typeset by Manila Typesetting Company
Printed and bound by
CPI Group (UK) Ltd, Croydon

Contents

Acknowledgements

It is almost impossible to write a book like this without the help of large numbers of people. I owe a huge debt of gratitude to all the people who took part in the research, especially the youth workers who gave their time so willingly. I remain in awe of the passion and commitment you show to young people in the work you do.

The journey of this book began in earnest with my PhD studies. I am indebted to Staffordshire University, Institute for Children, Youth and Mission and Oasis College for their generous bursary support that enabled me to embrace a passion. I am very grateful to Pete Twilley, David Webb, Nick Shepherd and Paul Fenton for helping keep my studies on track. Thanks also to those who provided helpful critiques of my early book drafts and made constructive suggestions for improvements: Debbie Garden, James Ballantyne, Janey Barrett, Jodie Watson and Adam Akers.

My colleagues at Frontier Youth Trust (FYT) have been continually supportive and encouraging during my writing. I am biased, but I think the work FYT does is awesome. The people I work with and the work they do serves young people unswervingly, and I am full of admiration for them and it. Sadly, two former colleagues are no longer with us. FYT legends Terry Dunnell and Ian Sparks died recently. They were pioneering and inspirational figures, who championed social justice work with young people – authentic activists who made a difference. You taught me much, and I think you might have quite liked what this book has to say . . .

Thanks also to Stephen Timms MP for writing the Foreword and SCM Press for their commitment to this project, especially from Natalie Watson, who patiently guided and supported me.

And finally, special thanks to my wife Sue for putting up with me when my mind was exclusively focused on political matters and for being there and sharing the journey.

Shalom.

Foreword by the
Rt Hon. Stephen Timms MP

We Christians have sometimes separated ourselves from politics, confining our interest to a small number of rather narrow moral issues. As a result, the political influence of Christians has been much less than it should have been.

But today, Christians are increasingly stepping-up to meet growing community need. A million people called on church-led foodbanks last year. There is today in Government and among politicians a new recognition of the importance and the value of faith in our society. I want to see Christians taking advantage of that recognition.

Growing disengagement of young people from politics is very troubling. The position has been made worse by the seemingly casual abandonment in the coalition negotiations after the 2010 election of commitments on tuition fees which many young people cared deeply about. The churches now account for most of the youth work undertaken in Britain, and this book seeks to support the next generation of Christians and young people becoming politically engaged.

I have known Nigel, and the Frontier Youth Trust which employs him, for many years. They have always had a deep commitment to young people, especially to those young people who have not always found it easy in life. Their compassion, advocacy and campaigning exemplify the type of 'stepping-up' on the part of Christians which is so important.

I chaired the Demos Inquiry into Faith, Community and Society.[1] It found that religious people are more active citizens, and that they are more likely to be politically progressive, placing a greater value on equality than the non-religious. It argued that Local Authorities will benefit both financially and through improved community relations if religious groups are brought into service delivery. It also highlighted the importance for politicians of making common cause with faith groups,

---

1 *Exploring the Role of Faith in British Society and Politics*, 2013, edited by Jonathan Birdwell with Stephen Timms MP. London: Demos.

whose active participants in Britain far exceed the membership of all the political parties put together. The early Labour Party had deep roots in the Church. We want to engage today in a proper dialogue with faith groups. We see them instilling, in modern Britain, the values to make politics work.

This book does not offer quick fixes to complex challenges. It establishes a clear theological position from which political work with young people can emerge. It is full of practical ideas to enable church-based activism. It asks questions of all of us. I hope you will read and reflect on it, and act upon what it says, in order to help young people engage in and be more passionate about politics.

This book encourages us all to work together so that young people can build a better society and develop the common good. I warmly commend it.

Rt Hon. Stephen Timms,
MP for East Ham;
Shadow Minister for Employment;
Labour Party Faith Envoy

Religion, Politics and Young People?

Mission without politics is like dinner without vegetables – easier and quicker, but in a few years you'll be pretty unhealthy.

Andy Flannagan, singer–songwriter, rouser of rabble

Certainly in the context I work in, I would say the young people are more interested in 'celebrity gossip' than politics. I think politics is a subject they feel uninformed about and is somehow distant from them and inaccessible to them.

Youth worker

Introduction

I have a bit of a problem: despite common wisdom advising against it, I am passionate about talking about religion and politics. I think religion and politics are the most interesting things in life to talk about. I am not that interested in the type of shoes you are wearing, the style of my hair (perhaps not surprising given my bald head), which celebrity is sleeping with who, the latest app for the newest phone, whether your handbag is a £250 leather designer piece or a £3 plastic charity shop bargain or the myriad of other trends and vogues that come and go. I am very interested in matters impacting the world, communities, the person and the soul of the individual. Religion and politics are at the heart of these.

My problem is accentuated by the fact that many people do not share my missional passion for religion and politics. When I told a family member I was writing a book about Christian youth work and politics, she – despite being a Christian for many years – completely dismissed the idea asking, 'What's politics got to do with it?' Clearly, some seek to divide the functions and practice of faith and politics into separate entities that should never co-exist, let alone bring influence on one another. Others do not always perceive Jesus as a political figure who, I would argue, almost daily appeared to be politically engaged with societal structures, military powers and religious authorities.

There are times when I am asked to tone down my discussions about faith, politics and justice. In family conversations and professional meetings people think I am being negative and grumpy simply because I have a strong view about something. There have been occasions when everybody would prefer I be quiet in the interests of harmony and compliance – this frustrates me. I want people to think about God, Jesus, the world we live in and our responsibilities in that world. Nothing frustrates me more than apathy and lethargy regarding these matters.

The American comedian W. C. Fields is credited with saying, 'Don't work with children and animals.' It thus appears my problems are further exacerbated, because for nearly 35 years I have worked with children – or more specifically, young people in the 11–18 age range. While there are limited references to animals, this *is* a book about young people. The problem here is that we don't seem to like young people very much in the United Kingdom. As I discuss later, we vilify them, accuse them and marginalize them, seeing them as problems to be fixed rather than individuals full of potential and possibility. Furthermore, spending a whole lifetime working with young people might be seen as folly. Some 20 years ago, I vividly remember sitting down with my then church leader to discuss my sense of vocation. He somewhat dismissively said, 'You can't do this [work with young people] for the rest of your life, can you?' Well, here I still am, and I have no plans to stop.

So, this is a book about things it is suggested we should not talk about: politics, religion and young people. From a marketing point of view, this does not sound like a good idea. However, I wish to assert that people who are not engaged in politics and who refuse to consider how politics relates to faith, life and people might be, in the original sense of the word, *idiots*.

The word 'idiot' originates from ancient Greece. The word (*idiōtēs*, ἰδιώτης) was used to describe those people who were self-centred and withdrew from public affairs to the private sphere. Athenians placed great emphasis on participation in their democratic political arenas. Those citizens (who at the time tended to be male citizens with Athenian-born parents) who were able to debate, judge, hold office and vote were expected to do so. Those that didn't were branded 'idiots'.

Clearly, today's democratic political culture and processes are very different to those of ancient Greece, but it is illuminating to see how much emphasis the Greeks placed upon their citizens being politically informed and actively involved. Might there be an argument that people who choose not to be involved in today's context are *idiots*? Various people have helped with research for this book and as one person said, 'You cannot change anything by doing nothing.' In short, if people don't get involved then they have to accept whatever happens to them and society because they have abdicated responsibility to others without seeking to bring influence. As 14-year-old political commentator Isaac Hansen says, many people are 'politically lazy' (2014) in the UK.[1] This might be considered a little idiotic.

Whether this is true or not could be debated for many hours. Whatever the outcome of any debate, we know politics and politicians seem to have a bit of an image problem these days. As I will expand upon in due course, we know young adults are not voting and participating in general and local elections like they once did; people are less enamoured with and don't trust politicians like they used to; membership of political parties is falling; and political scandals appear endemic. Indeed, what has happened in institutional politics is mirrored by what has happened in the institutional church: diminishing levels of young people's involvement; declining trust in the Church and its ministers; falling membership and child abuse and fraud scandals. All causing a crisis of legitimacy for the institutions.

While evidence suggests[2] young people have a declining interest in organized religion, spirituality and politics, they do have strong views on issues, get involved when given the chance and make very positive contributions if space is created for them to do so. I would like to suggest that what young people have rejected about both church and politics is the institutional, hierarchical approaches, which limit the contributions they can make. I do not necessarily believe this means they have rejected either God or politics per se, merely the way both are often presented to them.

Despite these challenges, churches appear to be getting more involved in the public square and undertaking social action with a re-energized sense of activism. They have responded to the current economic crisis by speaking out against injustice, setting up compassionate and practical ministries to alleviate suffering and combat poverty and have been criticized by both media and politicians for doing so.

The thoughts and analysis set out in this book are underpinned by rigorous research. I draw on my PhD investigation into faith-based youth work in a social policy context, a survey of Christian youth workers and ministers I conducted on behalf of my employers, Frontier Youth Trust (FYT), and a consultation day with youth workers and politicians that took place at the Palace of Westminster in 2014. Further details about the research can be found at the end of the book. Quotations from those who took part in my research are used throughout to illuminate

---

1 Isaac runs a political blog: http://fresherperspective.tumblr.com/.

2 See, for example, Pimlott and Pimlott 2008; Collins-Mayo and Dandelion 2010; Collins-Mayo, Mayo and Nash 2010.

and illustrate the points I make. I will also be referring to research undertaken by others and integrating this into my reflections. I also draw upon my own practice experience and reflect upon my own work. There is a risk that in so doing what I say might come across as 'Look what I've done'. If this does happen, then I apologize for it. My intention is simply to highlight practical possibilities rather than brag about my own endeavours.

The research indicates a diverse, fluid and dynamic context. At this juncture, I briefly state that while many Christian youth workers are well informed about politics and social issues, it is clear others are not. Passions often run high in discussions, but Jesus-style confrontations with authority and narratives that substantially challenge religious and political hegemony and institutionalism are often placid in nature, rarely upsetting the status quo. Many workers say they need more resources to help them engage young people and discuss the subject of politics. My hope is this book will be one of these resources, helping Christian workers better tackle the subject. It endeavours to embrace the passion that is politics so we all flourish and enjoy the world as intended. Before proceeding further, I wish to clarify what I am talking about and offer an overview of the terminology and meanings used in this book. I also want to be clear about my own bias, so state my own faith and political positions, before setting out what is in the rest of the book.

Meanings and understandings

Primarily, this is a book for Christian youth workers. Experienced workers will be aware of long-standing debates about what is meant by *youth work* and *Christian youth work* in particular. The debate is given further spice when the idea of *Christian youth ministry* is introduced into the mix. In one sense these debates don't really add to what work is actually undertaken with young people. Furthermore, it might be argued such contentions are unhelpful and somewhat artificial, and constructed demarcations have little relevance to those young people such work seeks to serve. However, there are subtle differences in approaches to work that have bearing on the subject matter of this book.

For example, work done by Christian workers with Christian young people in a church setting might encompass different political parameters than work undertaken by Christians with young people of different faiths or of none. I contend that the call on a Christian young person to live a life that is politically active, where Jesus is the role model, cannot be placed upon a young person who has no declared faith or who comes from a different faith. Consequently, how a worker engages, reflects and works with a young person from a Christian faith background will be different from how a young person from another background is approached.

Definitions of youth work are important because they reveal the intended focus of such work. For example, a definition might point towards an individual empowerment rationale that helps young people flourish, make educational progress and/or become good citizens. Equally, a definition might point towards a collective notion that supports ideas of community and/or developing, for example, societal cohesion, good behaviour or collective responsibility. Furthermore, definitions might indicate at whose behest work is undertaken. For example, a definition might suggest an agenda that supports state-orchestrated policies, a societal aspiration and/or a faith imperative.

In order to bring clarity to the terms used throughout this book, I set out below what I mean by differing natures of youth work practice. I am not arguing these are universally agreed definitions, merely my interpretations as used in this book.

While work with young people has probably always taken place, focused work with the teenage age range is now educationally cemented in a manner that can be clearly named – if not fully defined. Historically, Christians started such work and have continued to help develop it ever since. When I refer to *Christian youth work*, I imply that young people voluntarily participate in it. If they do not wish to join in, then they are free not to. Such work is rooted in the principles of informal education, namely, a spontaneous process of helping young people learn outside of a formal setting (such as a school). This is achieved through conversation and dialogue, experiences that value the here-and-now nature of young people's lives, where the activities and interests of the young people are centre-stage in order to help them flourish. For the purposes of this book, I would argue the main goal of Christian youth *work* is to see young people through *unconditional positive regard*[3] eyes and help them realize their full potential in order to build a better world. I refer to those who do such work as *Christian youth workers*.

Christian youth *work* might be undertaken with young people who are Christians, those who come from other faiths or those who have no declared faith. The *Christian* dynamic relates to the motivation of

---

3 A term popularly believed to have been coined by psychologist Carl Rogers.

the worker, how they work and who they work for, rather than who they work with. Such work might take place in the community, on the street, in an open youth club or at a specific location such as a skate park, community centre or church hall.

The content of the work undertaken may have many, limited or even no references to the Christian faith. There is often a social justice and/or a young people's development agenda associated with such work as it seeks better outcomes for young people, communities and society. Motivationally, this type of Christian youth work often draws on biblical narratives associated with developing shalom (Gen. 43.27; Exod. 4.18; Isa. 9.6; Jer. 29.7), meeting need (Luke 19.1–10; John 5.1–15; John 8.1–11), loving neighbours (Lev. 19.18; Mark 12.31; Rom. 15.2), being salt and light in a community (Matt. 5.13–16; Eph. 5.8; Col. 4.6) and healing and restoration (Exod. 15.26; Isa. 53.4–5; Jer. 30.17; Ps. 147.3). Findings from my PhD studies indicate this type of work is about caring for young people, being role models for them, nurturing them, being hopeful for them and seeking to build community with them.

The word *ministry* carries a different implication from just youth *work*. My use of the term assumes an agenda focused upon discipling young people in the Christian faith. This usually involves building intentional relationships with young people, teaching them about the Christian faith and providing opportunities for them to worship, pray, do Bible study, attend small groups and participate in churches. For the purposes of this book, I would argue the principal goal of Christian youth *ministry* is the transmission of the Christian faith: enabling young people to grow and develop in their faith. I refer to those who do such work as *Christian youth ministers*.

I am not suggesting the meaning I have applied to Christian *youth work* has no relevance to *youth ministry*. Youth *ministry* embraces many attributes of youth *work* – such as informal education principles, being about loving, caring and nurturing young people and helping them flourish. As Danny Brierley (2003, p. 10) argues, 'If youth work is the broad discipline involving all informal educators . . . then youth ministry is a "specialism" within it.' However, youth ministry has an overriding and very explicit Christian content. This is usually centred upon clear biblical narratives, Christian and denominational traditions and orthodox Christian teachings. The curriculum offered might be in the form of pre-prepared materials written by other Christians and be available in books, magazines or online. Work is mainly undertaken with Christian young people, or at least those who show an interest in the Christian faith, or who are evangelistically perceived. This type of youth *ministry* work is more often than not located in a church or other explicitly Christian environment.

It might appear a little pedantic to differentiate between *youth work* and *work with young people*. However, not everybody who works with young people does youth work. Teachers, doctors, social workers and, increasingly, private contractors delivering government initiatives all work with young people. They do not do so using the principles of informal education. Often young people do not participate on a voluntary association basis and the intended outcomes for such work are stated or determined by government, bureaucrats and funders, not by young people. There are schemes, projects, initiatives and courses that young people are told about or made to go on: inclusion projects, clubs to help them get jobs, rehabilitation programmes and courses designed to deliver accredited outcomes, to name but a few. These are usually related to government policy objectives in some form or another and aim for behaviour modification rather than being focused upon young people's interests and sense of flourishing.

Churches, Christian organizations and Christian workers often help deliver this type of work with young people. Such work is different from *Christian youth work*, because it is not based upon what the young people decide, and it is different from *Christian youth ministry*, because it is not focused upon the transmission of the Christian faith. If delivered by Christians, and for the purposes of clarity in this book, I would argue the aim of such work is to support government views regarding what is considered best for young people.

There are times in the book when I wish to refer collectively to Christian youth work, youth ministry and work with young people undertaken by Christians. When I do this, I use the term *Christian-motivated work*.

While I have set out clear demarcations and simplistic definitions relating to the different types of work Christians engage in, the real world is more complex than I have described. There are, no doubt, other classifications of work and many practice examples where individuals simultaneously embrace more than one type of work. While it might be more helpful to think of a kaleidoscope, spectrum or mosaic of approaches and practices, I have deliberately restricted my demarcations and definitions in order to provide a clearer starting point from which a discussion about how politics relates to different contexts can be undertaken. In order to bring together the main themes of this book, I now suggest how the subject of politics might be considered.

What politics is

In 1936, American academic Harold Lasswell wrote a book about politics entitled *Who Gets What, When, How*. In so doing he provided one of the most simple yet most profound and complete definitions of what politics is. His definition has stood the test of time because it captures what politics is: it is about deciding who gets *what*, *when* they get it and *how* they get it.

Be it discussions in the family, church, company, council, nation or United Nations, answering the questions of who gets 'what', 'when', and 'how' determines and shapes how our world is. From discussions about a youth club in a village, to international crises and conflicts, people and politicians argue, fight, discuss, disagree and/or come to an agreement about who gets *what*, *when* and *how*. Politics should not be associated purely with people in suits – all too often middle-aged white men – talking on television or debating in Westminster. Politics is much more than this. Politics is about how we make decisions in all aspects of life and how we negotiate conflict and mutuality. This includes addressing matters such as equality, race, gender and class, as well as issues such as economics, welfare and justice. Politics textbook author Andrew Heywood says, 'politics, in its broadest sense, is the activity through which people make, preserve, and amend the general rules under which they live' (2000, p. 33). Politics is also about deciding how we allocate resources, how we plan, determine rules and organize ourselves. Václav Havel was the first post-communist democratically elected president of Czechoslovakia. He believed politics was about serving others:

> Genuine politics – politics worthy of the name and the only politics I am willing to devote myself to – is simply a matter of serving those around us: serving the community and serving those who will come after us. Its deepest roots are moral because it is a responsibility expressed through action. (1993, p. 6)

Academics talk about politics as a science and there are many political theories and ideologies in existence – some of which are referred to later in this book. Politicians themselves might refer to politics as an art, where the art is about determining how people are governed. Politics is also an activity or practice people undertake and it can be a method or series of tactics used by one set of people to influence others. For a few people, politics is a profession and a career. It is a career individuals can have whereby they enter into public life to serve others. Others study politics as a vocation, and yet others commentate upon it as their career.

Inevitably politics involves the use of power. It seeks to manoeuvre people and groups in society towards a particular set of objectives and goals, using methods and means considered appropriate. Political scientist Karl Deutsch called this an 'interplay of interests' (1980, p. 11). Politics embraces principles, opinions, attitudes and positions and sometimes these are organized into streams of partisan political belief, political parties or movements. This results in competing political ideas, as individuals and groups wrestle with each other for control and status. To help simplify terms I refer to what is called *macropolitics* and *micropolitics*. *Macropolitics* is the type of politics and decision-making done by local authorities, regional, national and international governments and bodies, where power (authorized and mandated by election, constitution or law) is used to shape and dominate behaviour. *Micropolitics* is more the politics of individuals, families, groups and possibly villages and towns, where power (largely based on personality and resources) is used – both formally and informally – to realize goals, fulfil aspirations and determine local resource allocation.

So politics is a broad subject having many aspects to it. However, the basic proposition put forward by Harold Lasswell still stands. Be it an act of service, art, science, theory, career, use of power, opinion or attitude, Lasswell's key questions remain the issues. For these reasons, my introductory definition about what politics is, and background for the rest of the book, focuses upon the three questions he poses: 'Who gets what?'; 'When do they get it?' and 'How do they get it?' Throughout the book I describe the process, art and science of answering these questions as 'politicking'.

The common good

The principle of the *common good* is one I refer to often. Expounded as a virtue over 2,000 years ago, the common good is a contested principle embracing many shared understandings and perspectives. For example, Catholic teachings have shed light on the idea, with the Vatican (nd, GS 26, § 1) declaring the common good to be, 'the sum total of social conditions which allow people, either as groups or as individuals, to reach their fulfilment more fully and more easily'. Throughout, I refer to the aspirational principle of the common good as a lens through which we can view the world. I perceive it as an ideal or guide and a measure by which we can gauge societal progress. In short, I consider something is politically virtuous if it helps realize the common good. Similarly, I perceive the common good principle as a basis for contemporary Christian-motivated work. I believe it aspires to embrace young people's individual advancement within a framework of developing collective well-being for all of society.

Understanding about the common good is further illuminated by Julia Unwin (2011) from the highly respected Joseph Rowntree Foundation. She describes it as:

> The profoundly important belief, shared by people of all faiths and none, that every individual is precious, that everyone has worth, and that the hunger, need and despair of any, should rightly pain us all. A belief that in a good society we share the risks of our own vulnerability, can identify that which makes us collectively strong, and can contribute to the flowering of everyone's capabilities, not just the achievement of the very few. A good society that recognizes that what we hold in common is both important and valuable, and that jeopardizing the common good for individual gain, diminishes us all.

This proposition provides my introductory understanding of the common good principle as used in the book. I refer to it as a way of living that encapsulates a theology for our age, a mandate for a politically sustainable society and a philosophical idea that needs to be fully considered as a potential solution for the challenges the world faces.

The chapters

Following this introductory chapter, Chapter 2 explores God and politics. I set out a theological rationale for political involvement and identify eight themes highlighting God's involvement in the world. I consider the overarching patterns, rhythms, processes and principles found in the Bible that reveal understanding about God and politics.

Chapter 3 examines in some detail how Jesus does politics. I consider Jesus as politician, prophet and preacher, irritant and dissenter, philosopher and pundit, and activist and liberator. I relate these descriptors to Christian youth work and ministry, illustrating their relevance with contemporary practice examples and my research findings.

Chapter 4 takes a look at what is currently going on regarding young people and their political involvement, youth work and how it engages with the political dynamic and the drivers behind contemporary approaches to policy. It also highlights worker responses to these factors.

In Chapter 5, I propose a set of principles for being a prophetic and political youth worker. I argue that we need a cohesive and deliberate framework that takes seriously our prophetic responsibilities as representatives of God in the public square.

Chapter 6 considers some of the current politicking barriers experienced in Christian youth work and ministry. It discusses in more detail theoretical and dominant narratives at work in modern politics and approaches to social policy, highlighting how these run counter to kingdom principles.

I set out in Chapter 7 a personal mandate for future Christian-motivated work. I bring together some of the ideas I think help embrace a passion for politicking. I look at how we read Scripture; how we might collectively do things better together for the benefit of all and what relevance Catholic social teaching has regarding my ideas. My analysis assumes young people will be at the heart of everything considered.

Chapter 8 begins to focus more on practical approaches to youth work and politicking. It explores opportunities to develop work and discusses what workers and ministers can do to support their own training and development.

I set out Chapter 9 somewhat differently to the other chapters. This chapter is packed full of ideas for workers to do politicking in their own context. I address a number of significant issues and propose ways of responding to these at practice level. The book ends with Chapter 10, my conclusion.

My own perch and position

My FYT work affords me the privilege of travelling all over the UK, meeting people from many different backgrounds. During my travels I have become very aware we are all different and often have different opinions about almost everything. This awareness highlights that a book about faith, politics and young people has enormous capacity for contention, misconception and misunderstanding. In order to reduce possible misunderstandings, I therefore provide a context and offer transparency regarding my own background, potential bias and motivations for this book. I briefly consider here my own youth work background, faith perspectives and political views.

I always seek to reflect upon my subject matters and practice. I do so believing this is best achieved by asking difficult questions that bring together theology, theory and practice. This promotes a sense of reflexivity – that process that circularly examines both myself as researcher of a subject and the relationship I have with my research – particularly regarding my assumptions, preconceptions and potential bias. Inevitably, I have chosen to make certain arguments and explanations in this book, and these have no doubt been influenced by my own sociological and theological perspectives. This is something Sara Lawrence-Lightfoot (1997, pp. 50–2) helpfully describes as a 'perch and position'.

I wish to affirm I am not seeking to abolish my own views and presence in this book. However, I hope to be as objective as possible while acknowledging my agenda is to develop politicking more in Christian-motivated work. I cannot hide my conviction that we need to be more passionate about the subject of politics. This is something I wish to fully embrace. I am motivated by a desire to: witness better outcomes for (especially marginalized) young people; support those working with such young people; elevate the space and place of Christian-motivated work; improve the standing of youth work in social policy considerations and increase social inclusion and justice, while developing cohesive associational communities and approaches. I also want fully to take account of changing cultural and policy contexts in developing future faith-based youth work to maximize young people's thriving within communal settings.

I have undertaken youth work and ministry in a number of church, community and organizational settings as a volunteer, employed worker and self-employed consultant. I consider this work what Paulo Freire (1972, p. 48) terms my 'ontological vocation'. In other words, Christian-motivated youth work is what I am called into, and it is how I achieve my goals in life and help others and myself become fully human: it is who I am meant to be. While I might not have always been consciously aware of it, the aspiration to see young people flourish and realize the common good has always been vocationally centre-stage. I am, at heart, a youth worker. That is why I often refer to 'we' in this book; I wish this book to communicate with other youth workers.

Having discovered faith in my teenage years, I became a junior leader in the youth group I was involved in. While untrained, I enthusiastically developed my skills and understanding through personal experiences, theological reflection and attending conferences. In 1990, I decided more formal training was required: I moved to Nottingham undertaking a training course facilitated by a large city-centre church. Here, my training focused on creative-arts-orientated work, visiting schools, prisons, churches and community groups and working with young people and adults. This work developed, and I helped establish a charity to oversee the work and provide a legal framework for it.

As a result of this work, I networked with FYT, by whom I subsequently became employed, initially as part-time co-ordinator of a spiritual development project before becoming Deputy Chief Executive Officer. In 1995, I moved to North Nottinghamshire and worked extensively in the community alongside a local church. The pinnacle of this work was taking a lead role in converting a disused factory into a vibrant community centre. Throughout, my faith values were the main driver in my work. The combined interest generated by undertaking faith-based work, desiring community transformation and seeking better outcomes for young people fused to form the background and motivation for a growing political activism.

As a youth work practitioner, trainer, writer and coach of other workers, understanding my field perch and position enables me to combine both theory and practice, helping develop praxis, a practical, action-based process shaping how I do things. This is informed by the learning and consequential critical pedagogy that results when face-to-face work with young people asks questions *of*, and enters into dialogue *with*, theoretical frameworks, research, cultural dynamics, policy considerations and reflective practice. This praxis embodies a political dynamic that endeavours to help young people achieve self-actualization, experience well-being and have a valued place as citizens in the world. To help develop this praxis, each chapter in the book ends with a series of possible actions, entitled 'What can I do?' Youth workers can undertake these tasks and exercises to help support *their* political, faith and practice journeys.

Faith matters

Religious labels and descriptors have the propensity to stereotype and limit rather than develop understanding that values nuance and subtlety. However, I recognize some outline parameters can be helpful in aiding perspective and, therefore, I consider my faith perch and position as: being orientated around following the teachings of Jesus; seeking the kingdom of God and pursuing 'shalom'; finding resonance with

Anabaptist teachings; suspicious and cautious regarding the canons and institution of the Church, fearing what was pure and beautiful has become bureaucratic and institutionalized; critical, rather than assuming; and recognizing that Christendom has undermined early Christian aspirations and authenticity. I see faith as a developmental journey that is both personal and communal and not a static inherited tradition and position. Theologically, I consider this very important, as it allows believers to reflect upon and work with God in new and responsive ways as political environments and cultural contexts constantly change. As one youth worker who took part in my survey research said, 'interesting doing the survey – showed me how my change in context has changed my political priorities'. It is for these reasons that at the end of each chapter are another series of questions, 'Things to think about'. These questions are designed to aid the reflection process and help contextualize the place of politics in contemporary practice.

The consequences of my personal journey enable me to engage in my analysis with greater self-awareness and consciousness. This might not have been possible when I was younger, as I perceived belief in very exclusive terms. Were my research to have taken place then, I consider my perch and position would have lacked critical awareness and failed to recognize the frailty of knowledge, potentially biasing my faith and political thinking more than it has today. My current aspirations can be summed up by the hope found in what has become known as the *Nazareth Manifesto* found in Luke 4.18–19:

'The Spirit of the Lord is on me, because he has anointed me to preach good news to the poor. He has sent me to proclaim freedom for the prisoners and recovery of sight for the blind, to release the oppressed, to proclaim the year of the Lord's favour.'

For me, these prophetic and political propositions are rooted in a desire for transformation, freedom and social justice for the oppressed, located within what FYT founder Bishop David Sheppard (1983) termed 'a bias to the poor' theology. While not particularly reflexively aware during my twenties and thirties, my ideological development took place alongside my faith development. I have always sought *what ought to be* rather than *what was* – critically evaluating beliefs and societal structures in order to bring about transformation – nearly always working with young people.

After I left school, I worked for a bank in the affluent football and stockbroker belt of South Manchester and Cheshire. I witnessed many displays of the wealth and excess associated with the 1980s. I observed selfishness and hyper-individualism at work and can confirm there really was, as Mrs Thatcher infamously said, 'no such thing as society'. These experiences began to engender great political unease in my own spirit, forging a left-of-centre political positioning.

This developed more strongly during my time in Nottingham, a period that witnessed the wholesale destruction of the mining industry and consequential catastrophic fallout from economic policies. For 12 years I lived and did most of my youth work in a former coal-mining town. The town is a five-minute drive from the former ancestral home of the poet Lord Byron. Byron declared, 'The days of our youth are the days of our glory' (in Moore 1832, p. 295). This statement took on somewhat ironic grandeur during my time in North Nottinghamshire as the days of youth were far from days of glory for the young people I worked with: unemployed, disillusioned, without aspiration, socially immobile, in poor health and prone to substance misuse. These were truly marginalized young people and far from flourishing. They had been dumped on the political and social scrapheap, victims of a macropolitical policy decided many miles away. The poverty, oppression and lack of hope I witnessed only served to fuel my political development, becoming more left-wing in the process.

My political allegiance is not to any one political party. I consider that societal change cannot be achieved by elected politicians alone as they always have an eye on being re-elected. It is the exercising of democratic rights that I consider has the greatest capacity to bring about change. As a youth worker involved in my consultations said, change takes place 'when local people get involved to make stuff happen'.

For those interested and academically orientated, I would say my political ideology is in sympathy with the work and theories proposed by Brazilian educator and philosopher Paulo Freire, Italian political theorist Antonio Gramsci, the liberation theology movement instigated by Peruvian priest Gustavo Gutiérrez, and more contemporarily the communitarian ideals of German-born sociologist Amitai Etzioni, and the type of struggle for greater democracy movements advocated by Noam Chomsky. While I have sympathy for post-Marxist ideals and agendas, I believe what takes place needs to be rooted in democratic participation that seeks to overcome what French philosopher Pierre Bourdieu has called 'symbolic violence': a process whereby marginalized and dominated individuals and groups in society are so conspired against by the rest of society that they eventually see their domination as natural. They come to see what happens to them as normal and behave in line with being dominated. In time, they participate in their own suppression. Such violence is perpetrated by both a dominant society and subconsciously by those dominated. As I will discuss in due course, I consider young people victims of this type of violence as society conspires to keep them as *problems* and *victims*.

My perch and position sees my work with young people as a lifelong learning process. The reflexive relationship between theory and practice has witnessed a reordering of the political space youth work, and specifically Christian youth work, occupies in society. Since it began, the space and place Christian youth work has occupied have ebbed and flowed. Over time, such work has witnessed the rise and demise of state-provided youth work, a growing, emergent and fluctuating reliance on the market and a subsequent re-emergence of the faith and voluntary civil society dynamic as a key player in the youth work sector. In the future, it may be that the only youth work that exists will be that undertaken by faith organizations – notably Christian-based ones. If this is the case, it is more important than ever that such work is emphatically considered and well delivered. Those charged with doing the work need to be politically aware and astute, well informed about policy and prepared to help young people develop their own political consciousnesses and levels of critical engagement.

Matters I am avoiding

Having set out my own political perspectives, I would not wish these to put you off reading the rest of this book should you have a different view or set of beliefs. I hope you will approach this subject with an enquiring and open mind, seeking out the spirit of God in humility and with purpose. This is something I seek to do, believing it important when considering matters of faith and politics. Perhaps one of the reasons both the institutionalized church and party politics and politicians are not well liked by members of the general public is because they both often come across as closed and over-dogmatic in their beliefs and approach. Strong convictions are one thing, but fervent partisanship just for the sake of it – especially when an individual is at odds with the official party or church view – makes a mockery of true democracy. I have known a number of politicians and church leaders who say one thing in private, but then something completely different in public. This is unfortunate. I have also met politicians who come across as very nice, rational and reasonable people when speaking 'off the record', but who then become polarizing party political animals when speaking in public or to the media. I consider this highly regrettable.

It is not my intention in this book to focus on party politics or support any particular party view. In reality, none of the UK political parties reflect my own views sufficiently for me to say I support them. I feel able to embrace policies and proposals from all the parties, if I believe they uphold the values of the kingdom of God and, in the context of this book, help young people flourish and realize the common good. My desire to avoid partisan and polarized debates does not mean that forthright views and opinions will not be expressed. Jesus said some strong things about life, money, justice and forgiveness, and his statements need disseminating. Therefore, I don't intend to shy away from difficult questions confronting us.

One of the other things putting the public off being engaged with party political politics is the way politicians on all sides speak to each other. Personal attacks, organized smear campaigns, the spinning of stories and negative campaigning have become the order of the day. Consequently, I will do my very best to avoid personally criticizing individual politicians. You will notice I have not offered a guarantee that I will not do this, but I will do my very best. A guarantee would be just too difficult a promise to keep. Where there is criticism, I hope my critique is set against the benchmarks, imperatives and principles of God's purposes and Jesus' approach rather than my own bias and perspectives.

I also wish to state that I have high political ambitions. I want to be a politician, because I believe that is what God asks of us all. I want to do my politics in a manner that impacts both locally and nationally. My agenda is to realize better outcomes for young people and the resourcing of youth work in order to facilitate change, develop human flourishing and realization of the common good. However, I have no desire, agenda or ambition to serve in public office as a politician – that is not my calling. I do not want to be a parish councillor, local authority councillor, MP or MEP. In saying this, I would not wish to dissuade anyone from such service if that is what they feel called to do.

So, having introduced the topics of politics and Christian-motivated work, established the meaning of the terms used throughout this book and portrayed my own political and faith perch and position, I end this introductory chapter with some questions to think about and things to consider doing. I then turn to the detail and begin, in the beginning, by exploring 'God and Politics'.

Things to think about

- Looking at the definitions suggested above, what sort of youth work are you engaged in and what is the extent of any political dynamic in that work?
- Should Christian young people be as encouraged to engage in politics as they are in worship, prayer, mission and loving their neighbour? What are the reasons for your answer?
- Reflect back on your youth work journey and identify some of the key moments and defining experiences that have shaped your faith and political perch and position. Consider how these impact your youth work and how you can help support young people's political development.

What can I do?

- Hold a discussion day or event with youth workers, young people, councillors, MPs, MEPs and/or church members to discuss what people think about politics.
- Set out your political and faith intentions and beliefs in a short 'manifesto' – try and keep it to under 75 words. Write it down and ask yourself the extent to which you manage to live it out, pledging to make any lifestyle and youth work practice changes as appropriate, so it becomes a fully lived reality.
- Before reading the next chapter, design a poster or mind map about what you think a theological rationale for involvement and engagement in politics is.

2

God and Politics

Christians are told to keep 'religion' and 'politics' separate . . . the point is everyone brings their 'faith' into the political sphere. People have all kinds of belief systems, agendas and even lobbyists behind them. So Christians must not retreat from the political scene in any and every way God calls them.

Youth worker

I do not feel obliged to believe that the same God who has endowed us with sense, reason, and intellect has intended us to forgo their use.

Galileo Galilei, physicist and astronomer

A theological rationale

Different schools of theology interpret the book of Genesis in different ways. For example, there are those who perceive the story as an accurate historical account and literal description of what happened at the beginning of time. There are creationists, who believe the world was created in six 24-hour solar days. There are those who see the biblical account as a poetic and metaphorical framework, figuratively presented. They contend this is not specifically related to a distinct time period, but more akin to overlapping stages of an extended evolutionary process. There are also those who interpret the creation story allegorically and symbolically, believing it describes humanity's relationship to creation and God. Here, the pattern, rhythms, processes and principles found in the story each have meaning and symbolism, giving understanding about God and his perspective.

I am going to be a bit of a chicken and avoid stating exactly which of these schools of thought I agree with; my wife and I disagree on this matter, and I need to avoid matrimonial conflict. What I will commit to is arguing that whichever theological perspective one ascribes to, they all have things in common and several broad areas of agreed understanding. A quick overview of the Old Testament story, beginning in Genesis, establishes this background and illustrates an emerging political dynamic portraying how people out-worked their responsibilities, desires, ambitions and relationship with God.

First, God is a creator God, and he engaged in a creative act to begin the beginning. God gave authority, rights and responsibilities to the people, with the intention they live in a manner worthy of the ideal of *shalom*. Shalom is that encompassing ordering principle and intention, comprising a sense of peace, well-being, welfare, goodness, tranquillity, wholeness, prosperity, justice and security – concepts at the heart of God's purposes. A conceptualization where nothing is broken, nothing is missing and everything is as it was intended to be. This idea of shalom is mentioned many times in the book of Genesis (e.g., Gen. 15.15; 26.29; 26.31; 28.21; 29.6; 37.4; 37.14 and 41.16) and is present throughout the Old Testament. For example, some often quoted passages contain the word *shalom*:

'The LORD bless you and keep you; the LORD make his face shine upon you and be gracious to you; the LORD turn his face towards you and give you peace [*shalom*].' (Num. 6.24–26)

For to us a child is born, to us a son is given, and the government will be on his shoulders. And he will be called Wonderful Counsellor, Mighty God, Everlasting Father, Prince of Peace [*shalom*]. (Isa. 9.6)

Having been creative, God mandated people to live out shalom in a manner that supported the common good. Unfortunately, humanity could not live up to this mandate and things went wrong and ended up broken. From then on God provided them with rules and boundaries designed to realize shalom. The people had to put their trust in intermediaries – such as Abraham, Moses and Joshua – because they could no longer walk with God directly due to their selfish ways.

The Bible then tells us the people got frustrated with this approach and turned to judges, kings and rulers for guidance, protection and instruction (e.g. see 1 Sam. 8). The more people sought ways of making the broken world work, the more politics came to the fore. Rights were debated, choices argued about, decisions contested, power used and abused, and justice fought over, implemented and at times denied. It got messy, complicated and very political as people tried to find a way forward.

As God partnered with people, matters such as stewardship, decision-making, governance, welfare, caring for the marginalized, territory disputes, advocacy and representation were at the fore. These matters and a study of the entire Bible reveal a diverse theological rationale for involvement and engagement in politics. The debate has always centred on 'Who gets what?', 'When?' and 'How?' and what role God has in the answers to these questions. For me, as for the research participant I am quoting, the role of God is central:

> I find it difficult to understand those who eschew engagement with politics in the name of their faith. Not for overtly political reasons but based on an understanding of the Trinity. With such a central doctrine of Christian faith expressing a quintessential sense of community in communion, how can anything rest outside of the interest of God and thereby those who espouse belief in God.

As a means of establishing a theoretical rationale for Christians being involved and engaged in politics, I have identified eight themes appearing highly significant to God. These are biblical themes found in God's dealings with people, each being essentially to do with politics. They are themes about power, justice, the poor, blessings, advocacy, transformation, trust and faithfulness. I discuss these themes, exploring biblical stories, theological and political imperatives, contemporary illustrations and how Jesus embodies them. I also consider how these themes impact youth work practice and, where appropriate, use findings from my research to further illustrate the themes.

Power to the (young) people

I have to admit, I like things done properly. If a project is not going to plan, not being effectively led or at risk of going awry or over-budget, I will step in and try to remedy the situation. I think this is good leadership and management – others might allege I am being a bit of a control freak. If I were God and had just created everything (however long it had actually taken me), I would want it to work out exactly as I had intended. Sure, I would have allowed Adam and Eve to have dominion (Gen. 1.27–30), but if they then screwed it up . . . well let's just say I would have exercised assertive leadership and strong management to make sure no one made the same mistake twice.

God did intervene and there were consequences – for both Adam and Eve and the rest of humanity – but this did not stop God constantly exercising the principle of giving *power to the people*. God empowered people, trusted them, equipped them and continually mandated them to manage creation. Amazingly, God let them do politicking over all of creation. God gave them dominion and responsibility. Even when God intervened and gave Moses the Ten Commandments and a host of other rules (Exod. 20—23) the people were entrusted with the responsibility of keeping them.

God repeated this pattern throughout the Old Testament, giving power away to priests, prophets, kings, tribes and elders. Negotiations, compromises, sacrifices, times of boom and bust, blessings, curses and challenges of every description were encountered. God let people do the politics with and for the people. There might not have been any political parties like we know today, but there were debates and conflicts across and within factions, family clans and tribes. There were national and international contentions as prophets, priests, kings and people politicked their way through life, outworking their covenant relationship with God. They did not separate their faith beliefs and the rest of their life; religion, life and politicking were all undertaken in the public sphere.

Jesus embodied this *power to the people* principle in his time on earth as he too gave power away. He sent the disciples out on their own (Matt. 10; Luke 10.1–23), entrusted the kingdom to children and people who are like children (Matt. 19.4), gave Peter the 'keys to the kingdom' (Matt. 16.19), commissioned the disciples to carry on his mission after he had died (Mark 16.15), and he even promised help that would empower people to undertake the tasks he left us to do (John 14.16). The instructions regarding how all these things were to be exercised were left a bit vague. The details then, and still today, needed to be politicked and decided.

I am not convinced by doctrines of Calvinism, arguing the future of a person is predestined. The imperative established by God and modelled by Jesus is not one of overbearing control. While I am in no doubt God has a general will, heaven does not appear to be a central command module dictating every single act of humanity and creation. We are trusted and empowered to get on with making decisions; the politicking that makes the world tick. We often get it wrong, but this does not preclude God from continuing the principle. God is committed to a manifesto that is ideologically based upon choice, decision-making and people taking responsibility for their choices. So if God gives power to people, why do many in the church find it a challenge to trust their own people? It seems to be a particular challenge when it comes to trusting young people.

I recently worked with a great bunch of people in a church undertaking some really good Christian youth ministry. They wanted to build upon this work and involve the young people as much as possible in the life of the church. It was proposed the young people be allowed to become church members (previously membership was for those aged over 18 only). This would have enabled the young people to vote at church meetings and make decisions about what affected them and everybody else. At the church meeting where this was discussed, a very heated debate ensued, and the motion to extend membership to young people did not gain sufficient support from the adults. I believe all but one of Jesus' disciples were teenagers. In the Jewish culture of the time, men were married at 18 – but only Peter appears married. Taxes were paid at the age of 20, and again, only Peter appears liable (Matt. 1.24–27). Furthermore, the structure of first-century rabbinic tradition – where boys aged 14 would have a rabbi – would point to the disciples being teenagers and Jesus their rabbi. From what we can glean, Jesus was prepared to give power to the young people he journeyed with. Those in this church felt their young people could not be trusted with the responsibility of power. They were not considered old enough or mature enough to take their place as members. Power was not given to the young people. It remains a mystery why those who claim they are *Bible-based* would exclude the very children Jesus said the kingdom belongs to, denying them a formal say in determining the *what*, *when* and *how* for their context.

As an aside, I vividly recall delivering a sermon in Liverpool some years ago. I casually happened to mention the disciples were probably teenagers, setting out the evidence why I thought this the case. As I sat down after the sermon, the vicar felt obliged publicly to admonish me for getting this wrong. Without citing any evidence to contradict my understanding, she simply said I was incorrect on this matter and then moved on to announce the next hymn. Clearly, the idea of the incarnate God deciding to work with young people as a deliberate choice was way outside her comfort zone and world-view.

If young people are to be active members of church and society then I believe they need to have a say in how things are politicked. In my research, 39 per cent of youth workers wanted the national voting age to remain at 18 years of age, while 54 per cent wanted it lowered to 16 years of age. Two people wanted it lowered to 14, and two people wanted it to equate to the age of criminal responsibility – currently 10 years of age in England and Wales. Given these findings and the 'votes at 16' campaign,[1] there appears to be momentum supporting more power for young people. Realizing this, in my view, would rest well with a God who is continually prepared to put his trust in people, irrespective of whether they 'get it right'.

---

1 See www.votesat16.org.

Dealing with people justly

God's commitment to entrust people with power and responsibility was not a mandate for them to be selfish and act unfairly. The prophet Isaiah (30.18) tells us the very nature of God is to be just: 'For the LORD is a God of justice' (in Hebrew *Elohay Mishpat*; literally meaning God of Justice). The people of God were, and are, expected to do what is good, reflecting the *just* attribute of the nature of God. As the prophet Micah proclaimed: 'Human being, you have already been told what is good, what ADONAI [God] demands of you – no more than to act justly, love grace and walk in purity with your God' (Micah 6.8, Complete Jewish Bible).

Contemporary politicians can often be heard talking about what is 'fair'. Children and teenagers can often be heard saying, 'That's not fair'! I suspect neither have uppermost in their minds the theological imperative of *Elohay Mishpat* when they say these things. The politician usually uses the phrase to justify a policy born out of their own particular ideology. Because of the bias often associated with this, what they say can be profoundly unfair to one section of society, while emphatically favouring another. The teenager is usually complaining, perhaps justifiably, about the personal inconvenience they are encountering because of a decision made about them by a parent or teacher. Pursuit of estranged agendas and selfish interests potentially inhibit rather than help the development of the common good.

It is because we are instructed to act justly that I feel a compulsion to get involved in politics. I cannot sit idly by, keeping my faith and my politics separate when injustice is present. When a local youth centre is being closed down because of funding cuts, but a millionaire business person is getting a tax cut, I have to speak out. Twelve-year-old Nicky Wishart was taken out of his school English lesson by police officers, because he was organizing a protest about cuts to his local youth service. His youth club, which was in the Prime Minister's constituency, was under the threat of closure. Nicky decided to protest against this outside the Prime Minister's local office. He was taken out of lessons and threatened with arrest by the police. Newspapers reported that Nicky was told the anti-terrorist squad were looking at his Facebook account. He had done nothing wrong; he merely took seriously his democratic rights and responsibilities. What happened was unjust, and I joined with many others who spoke out about this via social media outlets and online petitions. It appears our national politicians want young people engaged in society, but only on their terms. Having heard

Nicky speak, I would like to see him engaged in politics on his terms – he is a profoundly mature and considered young man.

As far as I know, Nicky is not a Christian. Irrespective of this, I think it encouraging that young people are speaking out on issues important to them. They are endeavouring to *act justly*. What is perhaps a challenge is how Christian youth ministers can help their young people speak out and act justly. For me, one starting point is to encourage workers themselves to speak out. They need to model approaches young people can emulate. This means increasing knowledge about politics and justice issues, getting involved in social and civic life, building confidence to speak out and supporting others who do. As one worker in my research said:

> I think we need an understanding of politics to be able to make informed decisions in the world. I think it is a bit ostrich-like to ignore politics as a Christian. How can we promote justice and not get involved with how things are run?

Jesus knew when to speak out and when to be quiet. I often speak out when I should be quiet, and stay quiet when I should speak out. If it helps determine when we should speak out, perhaps we would do well to recall the harshest words of Jesus were preserved for those with religious and political authority. In Luke 11.42 he proclaimed 'woe' to the Pharisees, because they had diligently tithed every minute matter, but had neglected common good justice and overlooked good judgement. Contrastingly, he treated ordinary people with kindness and compassion. Perhaps we might learn from this and be politically strident and vocal towards pious leaders, but less vehement towards our peers and compatriots.

Good news for the poor

God had a plan to prevent poverty among the people of Israel. Everyone was to give a tithe of their produce in certain years of the agricultural cycle so orphans and widows would be provided for (Deut. 14.28). At the end of every seven-year period all debts were to be cancelled (Deut. 15.1). Every 50 years there was to be a Jubilee, and all land that had been acquired by lease had to be returned to the person who originally was assigned it (Lev. 25). Hence, if someone had fallen on hard times and been forced to lease out their land, they knew they would get it back in the year of Jubilee, not as restored private owners of the land, but as God's stewards of it. Additionally, the people of Israel were explicitly told to look after the poor; they were to 'open their hand to them' (Deut. 15.8, 11) and generously give. Even if someone fell on such hard times that they had to sell themselves into slavery, after seven years they were to be set free and sent on their way with livestock, food and wine (Deut. 15.9–14). While these safety measures were not necessarily designed to ensure income equality, they were designed to ensure Israeli families never lost completely their ability to enjoy the Promised Land. If you were poor, this was good news.

I have wondered what the modern state of Israel would look like today if these measures were practised by everybody. In my utopian daydreaming moments, I have mused over what the world would look like if we all did this, even what it would look like if just the Christians did this – or at least a contemporary contextualized version of it. I have also imagined the furore that would ensue if someone proposed this afresh today. Capitalists would argue that wealth generation and trickle-down economic benefits would cease. Entrepreneurs would claim they were being prevented from realizing their aspirations and that a punitive culture was an investment disincentive. Socialists would fear that the state would become paralysed and unable to meet its obligations. Environmentalists might fear land set aside for nature would become agricultural or industrial. Elected politicians would freak and come up with a thousand reasons why it wouldn't work. Of course, the world we have created now is very different to the one God intended and there may be some truth in these arguments. It may well be true that if we implemented this now, the world order as we know it would collapse. We have to consider whether this would be a bad or a good thing.

What we can say with confidence is that what we have now isn't working for the majority of the world's population. It is especially not working for the poor and marginalized of the world. They are kept poor, with global inequality staggering. Isabel Ortiz and Matthew Cummins (2011, p. vii), working on behalf of UNICEF, report that the top 20 per cent of the world's population enjoys more than 70 per cent of total income: the bottom 20 per cent enjoys only 2 per cent. These figures have been adjusted to reflect the relative purchasing powers of a currency in different countries. If actual market exchange rates are used, the richest 20 per cent gets 83 per cent of income, the poorest 20 per cent just 1 per cent. This calamity needs to be addressed and I have a suspicion the current world order does need to be turned upside down if the poor are to have a fairer share of the *what*. Richard

Wilkinson and Kate Pickett's (2010) ground-breaking study on equality highlights how wealth inequality is bad for everyone, rich and poor alike. In Britain, Oxfam's *A Tale of Two Britains* (2014) report says that the five richest families now own more wealth than the poorest 20 per cent of the population. This is a matter of national shame.

Even if we set aside any theological imperative requiring the Christian to exercise obedience to God regarding money, wealth and asset ownership, the issue of poverty and global inequality is a slur on all humanity. If there was to be just one single reason to be involved in politics, it would be to ensure the poor and marginalized get a fairer share of the *what* in the world. Politicians on the right of the political spectrum accuse people like me (who argue for a fairer wealth distribution) of being engaged in the 'politics of envy'. They suggest our arguments are based on the fact we are jealous of those with wealth and want some of it. This is not my contention. In 1977, Brian Wren – a writer way ahead of his time – asserted, 'For the Christian, a passion for justice cannot . . . be dismissed as the "politics of envy" if it is seeking to establish what is right, fair and good' (1977, p. 52). This is my motivation and quest. I believe it is the general social conditions in the world which politics needs to help change so the poor get a fairer deal. This politicking work needs to start with young people, both rich and poor, so they grow up seeing beyond themselves and their own needs. If this can't be achieved, then we risk continuing, as a youth worker in my research has eloquently stated, to 'shaft the poor':

> Working with young people has shown me in more depth what it means to work with those who are marginalized. Working with those that are vulnerable in so many ways has made me incredibly against the government as their priorities have been to augment the wealth of the rich and shaft the poor in all sorts of ways . . . I personally would like to become more proactive at fighting against the injustices I see within my context, but also enable young people to do the same.

There are those who say poverty is an everyday matter of fact and we just have to live with it. I have heard Christians, usually rich ones, use the passage in Matthew – 'The poor you will always have with you, but you will not always have me' (Matt. 26.11) – to justify this response. But what if Jesus meant something entirely different when he said this? What if he wasn't talking about the daily reality of people being poor, but assuming that the ministry of the disciples would always include poor and destitute people? In other words, people who were poor would always be with the disciples, they would have a place among the followers of Jesus; it would be a place they would gravitate to because their needs would be met. Truly, this would be good news for the poor if it happened today.

In my own Christian youth work and youth ministry across a variety of contexts, there have always been marginalized young people involved. Be it in affluent Cheshire, or deprived North Nottinghamshire, there have always been young people present who were poor, and I mean materially poor. The same has been true of the many projects I have visited over the years, and I witnessed the same in my PhD research among Christian-motivated youth projects – the poor have always been there. I believe this is one measure of what effective work looks like. If such work is truly worthy of being called 'Christian' and 'Christ-like', then the poor should always be present. They should be valued, involved, discipled, supported and empowered to flourish as part of the common good.

Be a blessing

I remember like it was yesterday the first time I heard someone explain the significance of the blessing given to Abram (Abraham) in the book of Genesis (12.2–3):

'I will make you into a great nation, and I will bless you; I will make your name great, and you will be a blessing. I will bless those who bless you, and whoever curses you I will curse; and all peoples on earth will be blessed through you.'

If you have not come across this before, God gave this promise to Abraham for the people of Israel, and it was repeated to Isaac and Jacob (see Gen. 26.4 and 28.3–4). This promise, as Paul reminds us, is passed down and received by all believers:

Understand, then, that those who have faith are children of Abraham. Scripture foresaw that God would justify the Gentiles by faith, and announced the gospel in advance to Abraham: 'All nations will be blessed through you.' So those who rely on faith are blessed along with Abraham, the man of faith. (Gal. 3.7–9)

The promise pointed to, and was inherited and embodied by, Jesus as the fulfilment of God's promise through Abraham:

The promises were spoken to Abraham and to his seed. Scripture does not say, 'and to seeds', meaning many people, but 'and to your seed', meaning one person, who is Christ. (Gal. 3.16)

As Paul goes on to say, we are, therefore, co-inheritors of the promise: 'If you belong to Christ, then you are Abraham's seed, and heirs according to the promise' (Gal. 3.29). Consequently, we too are blessed and can be a blessing to the world. This revelation changed my life. So what has this got to do with Christianity and politics? Well, the key questions are: how do we honour the blessing God gives to us and how do we bless others? In terms of the *what, when* and *how*, what do people receive and how should this be administered?

The word *blessing* conveys the idea of conferring, invoking or drawing upon the favour of God: conceptually, this is a problematic matter. Naturally speaking, what is a blessing to one person might not be to another; a blessing for one might be attained by taking from another; and how a blessing is realized might involve the use of might, force and coercion. We see all of these dynamics outworked in the Old Testament stories. Personally, I struggle with some of these stories and God's instructions about how to politically go about things. For example, I am disturbed with the way God told Moses to execute all the leaders of the people who worshipped another god (Num. 24.4); I am troubled by the waste of life involved in the mass slaughter of Israel's Canaanite enemies (Deut. 7.1–2); and I am appalled by the idea a person who smashes babies' heads on rocks will be blessed (Ps. 137.9). I can explain these passages with theological ideas about a holy and jealous sovereign God who wants to preserve his majesty and stand up for his people, but this approach does not sit easily with me. Furthermore, I can't simply ignore these stories hoping they will go away. In the space allowed here, the best I can offer by way of rationale is *that was then, Jesus is now* and if Jesus is the fulfilment of the promise *to be a blessing*, then how he goes about this (healing, restoring, forgiving, redeeming) is the model to emulate. While this might be an oversimplistic approach it makes possible a pragmatic response to how we should bless people. We cannot control God and respond with certainty to what happened historically. We can control how *we* respond *now*. My response is to try and bless others, because I am an heir of God's promise. I want to ensure young people receive a blessed *what, when* and *how*.

Whenever I work with young people or youth workers, I pray I will be a blessing to them. I want to bless people by facilitating political solutions and helping them resolve challenges. This means using political

29

skills – asking tricky questions, telling parables, being a provocateur, jester, dissenter, revealer of paradox, and an antagonist – in order to help people discover what truth is for them on the next stage of their journey. Recently, there have been lots of cuts in youth work provision, including cuts in provision churches have offered. I have intervened to try and protect these services, because the cuts deny a potential blessing to young people. This has meant being political and campaigning, arguing, petitioning and visiting people and projects to try and protect services under threat.

The sad thing about modern politics, including politics practised by Christians, is that there has been a tendency to reverse the ideal of blessing others. All too often, politicians simply curse one another. I hope youth workers will model something different in their political activism and bless others in line with the call of the prophet Jeremiah:

'Seek the shalom of the city where I have caused you to be carried away captive, and pray to the LORD for it; for in the shalom of it shall you have shalom.' (Jeremiah 29.7, Hebrew Names Version)

Advocating and acting

In Jeremiah 29, the prophet writes to the people of God who are in exile. He brings together the idea of shalom previously discussed, invites God's people to get involved in the place they find themselves in and work for the mutual benefit of everybody. God wanted the people to be linked in enough (Jer. 29.5–6) to be able to advocate for others and invested enough to want to. He didn't want them 'set apart' people, isolated from and not invested in community concerns. This must have been a tough challenge for the people of God. They were waking up to the fact that this was going to be a long exile (70 years), and now they were being instructed to help make things better for the very people who were holding them. The Message translation of verse seven puts this starkly, 'Pray for Babylon's well-being. If things go well for Babylon, things will go well for you.'

In a world that is broken and often appears to be conspiring against the people of God, this seems an amazing offer: if we seek the well-being of others and pursue the common good, then we win too. Of course, we have to ask how we get hold of this shalom for others to make things better for us all. The answer to this question would probably take up a whole book on its own. What is clear, however, is the answer will not be found in doing nothing. If we can politically serve others in the manner Václav Havel describes (see the quotation from him on p. 8), then we can collectively progress. If things are to be improved, then we need to be advocating for and acting out a way of living (for both individuals and communities) that supports the common good, so everyone benefits. A worker in my research captures this eloquently:

> To be human is to take action, to think about it critically and to take further action – this happened in Genesis, where we see God in an iterative cycle taking action in creating the world and reflecting on it and then taking more action (and I believe we humans are created in the image of God) and in Freire (amongst other theorists), who argues to be human is to take action to transform the world (rather than to adapt to it, like animals) . . . I think to be human is to take action and to think critically about that action and then take further action based on this reflection, so my stance is we should always take some thoughtful, committed action . . . To believe we can make no difference is to deny our humanity.

There is an African proverb that says, 'When spider webs unite they can tie up a lion.' If people come together to do something, they can achieve great things. If humanity weaves together for the benefit of all, then a lifestyle of action centred on others not ourselves can result. When combined with the reflective cycle process described by the youth worker above, societal transformation can take place.

Advocacy and action is a principle common throughout the Bible. Abraham bargains with God on behalf of Sodom (Gen. 18.23–33), Moses entreated God on behalf of the Israelites (Exod. 32.11–14), and Samuel was asked by the people to plead with God so they might be saved (1 Sam. 7.8–9). Nehemiah acted as an advocate as he rallied the people to rebuild the walls of Jerusalem (Neh. 2.17–18), and Esther advocated before the king to save her life and spare her people (Esth. 7.3). Bringing together the themes of shalom and care for the poor, King Lemuel encourages advocacy and action saying, 'Speak up for those who cannot speak for themselves, for the rights of all who are destitute . . . defend the rights of the poor and needy' (Prov. 31.8–9).

My survey results indicate workers have mixed levels of activism regarding politics. In the past six months 74 per cent of them have signed an online petition about a social or political concern; 53 per cent of them have contacted an elected official about these types of concerns; and 50 per cent of them have attended some form of seminar or lecture about such a concern. However, only 9 per cent have attended a political rally, protest or lobbying meeting. While 73 per cent of workers have 'sometimes' or 'often' focused on politics in their Christian youth work and ministry, 69 per cent 'agree' or 'agree strongly' that Christian youth work and ministry should be more politically engaged. These findings suggest workers are active and seeking the welfare of others, but they want to and could do more.

If there is a requirement for further understanding about the need for advocacy, then we can look to Jesus. Incarnationally, he advocated for others (in the story of the woman caught in adultery, for example, John 8.1–11). He is also the ultimate advocate. We are encouraged in the first letter of John: 'But if anybody does sin, we have an advocate with the Father – Jesus Christ, the Righteous One' (1 John 2.1). Jesus is our legal helper and patron in defending us. He is on our side, pleading our case. We need to be Christ-like, advocating on behalf of others to ensure *their* well-being. We need to be on *their* side, pleading *their* case. Politically this means we have to advocate so others can get their just *what*, and we need to be active to ensure there is a *when* and a mechanism for the *how*.

Long before I moved into the village where I now live, the young people of the area wanted a skate park. In fact, there have been discussions about it for over 14 years! It is not beyond the bounds of possibility that those with the original idea are now married and have their own children. The good news is funding for the park was secured, nearby residents consulted and planning consent for the project was granted. A few residents objected on the grounds of possible noise pollution and there were the usual anti-young people and NIMBY (not in my back yard) sentiments that have tended to proliferate in British society of late. The Parish Council decided to hold an open consultation meeting to consider further representations before making a final decision about the park. I felt compelled to go along.

During the meeting I was able to speak in support of the skate park idea. FYT facilitates the StreetSpace network of youth work projects, many of which have a connection with skating and the like. I outlined my knowledge about such projects and argued for the park. The degree of expertise gained through StreetSpace allowed me to advocate in a way that was based upon real practice experience and insight. The atmosphere was quite intimidating and a wide range of opinions was offered in the meeting. It was all getting a bit heated, and this inhibited some of the young people from voicing their opinions. Then, to my surprise, the Chair of the Council asked me to speak again. He invited me to address some of the issues raised by those opposed to the skate park and share my experiences. I willingly did so. The public meeting then closed, and the Council voted on the proposal. I am pleased to say it was passed, and the village now has a new skate park. It would be scandalous to claim this was down to my input as many people have worked very hard over a number of years to make the park a reality. I do know, however (because Council members subsequently told me), that speaking up for the idea helped in its own way to secure the approval. Politicking, advocacy and a bit of local activism helped support the young people in the village secure something they had waited 14 years to get.

Making a difference

God is in the business of transformation and making a difference. As noted, God does this by giving power to people. God doesn't need people to achieve his purposes, but he wants them and chooses to work through them. God calls, invites, positions and enables people. A glance at the much quoted faith 'hall of fame' passage in Hebrews 11 highlights how people acted in response to God's call and mission. By faith, they made a difference.

However, God does not just employ believers to fulfil his purposes and make a difference. In the book of Exodus we see how God uses Pharaoh (Exod. 9.16). Ruth was originally a Gentile and an outsider (Ruth 1.4). In Jeremiah we read about how Nebuchadnezzar, perhaps unwittingly, served God's purpose (Jer. 25.9), and we even see in the book of Numbers how God spoke through a donkey (Num. 22.28). I often pray – frequently with entirely selfish motives – for doctors, dentists, football players and airline pilots in the belief God has domain over them. I intercede for governments, rulers and politicians to be agents of God, in the belief God can make things better.

In recent times, there has been a growing interest in the ideas behind the Latin phrase *missio Dei* – the belief that it is God's mission, rather than ours, and that God's people are instruments in that mission. Over time, two basic understandings about *missio Dei* have emerged and evolved. First, there is the *Christocentric* view that perceives the mission of God through the lens of the Church, with missional work being centred upon the Church. Second, there is the *cosmocentric* view that embraces the idea God is on mission throughout the world and church is just a small part of helping realize that mission. I do not propose to engage in an argument about which view is most correct, but instead highlight how both views have significance in biblical narratives and politics.

The Christocentric view is focused on the development, influence and enlargement of the Church as the means by which the *missio Dei* is realized. Politics here is about what the Church does to usher in God's kingdom. For example, a church might run a youth group in response to their belief that the current *missio Dei* is about engaging a local group of marginalized young people and supporting them to flourish so the common good develops. This view gravitates towards the belief work only has value if the Church does it. The main weakness in terms of good youth work and ministry practice is that too often such work ends up being judged by the number of young people's 'bums on seats' in Sunday services.

For supporters of the cosmocentric view, the work of God – and the building of God's kingdom – is orientated around involvement in the social, political, environmental and economic challenges facing the world. Advocates of this position are not working with God primarily to build the Church, either in numerical, influence, need-meeting or quality terms. As Graham Ward notes, 'the Church has no control or monopoly over the kingdom of God; God will act where God wishes to act' (2009, p. 288). The politics dynamic embraced is about working with God to make a difference to the wider world. For example, local people might help out at a local authority youth centre. If they are Christians, they might be responding to the same sense of *missio Dei* described in the Christocentric example above. However, they might not be Christians, simply unwitting agents, entirely ignorant of the *missio Dei*, yet delivering the work on behalf of God. This doesn't matter to proponents of this view. The cosmocentric view contends what is important is that God's work gets done and the cosmos is improved in support of his purposes and mission for humanity; who does it is less relevant. The main weakness with this approach is that any association of the work with the Christian faith and identity is often absent. For pure cosmoscentrics this doesn't matter as long as God's mission is realized.

My take is that both these positions have value. God works through the Church, but is not bound by it as a means of building his kingdom. In political terms, the Church can accomplish many things in furtherance of the *missio Dei*. Equally, God is able to use anyone or anything to bring about political change and make a difference. If this is the case, Christians need to open themselves up to the possibilities that God is in their midst and at work in the political domains of life.

By way of illustration, I believe God was at work in my village regarding the skate park Council meeting. It is not a *Christian* project, but I think it is something God wanted to happen – part of the *missio Dei* for my village.

These matters are important. Opportunities to work with, and for, God might be missed if levels of awareness are inadequate and critical consciousness skills absent. I first became aware that these skills might be lacking in workers in my lectures with Christian youth work and youth ministry undergraduate students. For several years I have delivered lectures about social policy, and almost without exception there is at least one student in every year group, and normally several, who says something like, 'Oh, I have never thought about politics or any of these things. I guess they are important in my work and I should think about them more.' If the workers are unaware and not thinking about such matters, then it is unclear how they can equip young people to be critically engaged.

Trusting God – even in adversity

If we want to use the power we have, act justly, *be* good news to the poor, advocate and make a difference we need to trust God and stick to kingdom principles, even when times are difficult and circumstances overwhelming. This can be a challenge. A very experienced youth worker who took part in the research consultation at the Palace of Westminster said, 'I am committed to all of this [politics, youth work, God], but I am exhausted – I am passionate and angry, but absolutely knackered!' This is a perspective I have much sympathy with. Life, families, relationships, work, health and finances can all be very challenging. Throw in church, young people and the community, and things can get even more stressful. Add a dash of the Holy Spirit, a smattering of *missio Dei*, some political convictions, and the heat can really be on. Rather like Elijah, we can just want to run away and hide under a tree (1 Kings 19.5); or in my case, curl up on the sofa and watch a DVD box set for hours on end. God sent an angel to feed Elijah baked cake and then sent him on a 200-mile, forty-day journey to recharge his batteries and recover: I would prefer gooey chocolate cake, forty days on the sofa and 200 box sets.

My own personal experience resonates strongly with my 'knackered' youth work colleague and Elijah. It can be tough and exhausting trying to make a difference in the world. Even without any direct opposition, travelling, debating, writing, speaking, arguing and trying to win people over is very tiring work. Sadly, direct opposition can come as well; just as Elijah experienced. I have had bruising encounters with secular colleagues, academics, councillors, fellow service providers and even close colleagues over matters relating to politics and activism. It is only a personal reflection, but it does seem some people consider it fair game to attack Christians simply because they are Christians. They don't just debate the matter in question, but introduce a whole host of other topics, agendas, vendettas, accusations about the Church and personal attacks, which I do not observe taking place when a non-Christian is involved. I say this with some experience: in some more academic work settings where people have not known I am a Christian, I have not felt attacked in the same way as when my faith beliefs have been known. I am not espousing a claim of persecution – my trials have been light compared to many – but there is definitely some political opposition to the Christian perspective. I have also encountered others who are not anti-Christian, but supportive and complimentary. More often than not such people are secure, well-rounded atheists. They often feel no sense of competition from faith, and are also helping young people thrive, while seeking the common good.

During these tough times we need to trust God. Elijah lost his trust for a while, but the figures of Abraham, Noah, Moses, David, Gideon, Nehemiah, Esther, Jesus, Peter, Stephen and Paul – to name but a few biblical characters – all had to trust in God as they went about their politicking. Even when things didn't go to plan for them, they had to keep trusting and believing in what they thought was right, even if it was the hard thing to do.

It is probably a little known fact on this side of the Atlantic, but the United States has an official government motto: 'In God we trust.' The phrase first appeared on a coin in 1864, but in 1956 an Act of Congress made 'In God we trust' the official motto. It still appears today on all US currency notes and coins as a reminder. We could debate the extent to which the USA does trust in God, but nevertheless it is a helpful prompt from the founding fathers of the USA as to who should be trusted. I can think of no better motto for Christians seeking to get involved in politics than this.

Jesus expressed ultimate trust, saying 'not my will but yours' (Luke 22.42). My aspiration is also to trust God, but I am aware of my significant shortcomings. I learnt some valuable lessons when I was in my thirties, living (or perhaps more accurately, struggling, resisting and dying!) by faith, as I endeavoured to work with young people and young

offenders without any regular or formal salary. Relying on God to provide pushed me to my limits. However, it was a part of my journey I
will always cherish; great times, but tough times.

A man with a prophetic gift once said to me that I was to push all the
doors before me and see which ones opened. This is what I have tried
to do in my ministry, particularly regarding my politicking. This necessitates trusting God to open the right doors. It is often tempting to push
some doors quite hard, when God doesn't seem to open them. Be it
local activism, trying to influence national youth work policy, negotiat-
ing partnerships, or engaging local politicians, I have had to trust God
and ultimately accept *not my will but his* as I endeavour to use the
power given to me in a way aligned with the *missio Dei*. Inevitably, disappointments occur, because my will and desires are not, as yet, lined up
in symmetry with God's. I have been disappointed when my representations have been ignored by national politicians; grieved when my arguments have been dismissed by government officials; frustrated when
denied a place on local committees and been downright indignant when
my petitions are ignored. In all these disappointments, I have to believe
and trust God. We can get side-tracked and put our trust in people and
elected politicians, who may well let us down. Elected politicians are
not flavour of the month at present and trust in them appears low. As
youth work participants in my research commented:

> All people see are a bunch of suits that say politically correct things
> in the hope of getting people to like them, not because they actually
> believe what they are saying.

> It often seems that very little changes as different governments take
> up their seats.

Putting our trust in people rather than God is just one of a number of
possible distractions, but there are many others.

Avoiding distractions

There is a strong sense of paradox at work in politics. In order to change
something, a certain degree of power is required to bring influence. To
change everything demands total power. However, one person, body,
faith group or political party having total power inevitably negates
other people's power, views and perspectives. How much influence we

have and how we go about getting power are key issues in determining society's *what*, *when* and *how*. These are the challenges of politics.

A worker in my research describes how, in order to bring about change, they needed to get involved:

> I did not engage with politics before becoming a youth worker and was ignorant to many of the issues that affected me. When I started getting to know young people and witnessed their struggles . . . it made me want to do something about it. I realized it was no longer acceptable to think that someone else would do something about the problems of the world and so I had to be more active when it comes to politics.

This worker could achieve a lot if they had the power, but it is so easy to stop being faithful and get distracted by having too much power or using what power we have inappropriately. Lord Acton's famous quotation from 1887[2] – 'power tends to corrupt, and absolute power corrupts absolutely' – encompasses great truth. It is not just the abuse of power that distracts and corrupts. Sexual impropriety, financial corruption, manipulation, over-competiveness, greed and a host of other misdemeanours can compromise our intentions. Even those close to Jesus got corrupted. Judas sold out his master (Luke 22.1–6). James, John and their mother grasped who Jesus was and understood the power he had. Unfortunately, they let this go to their heads and started vying for top positions in the kingdom (Matt. 20.20–28).

It is not just putting trust in people rather than God and seeking and abusing power that distract. Moses (Num. 20.1–12), David (2 Sam. 11), Peter (Matt. 26.69–75), Ananias and Sapphira (Acts 5.1–11) all got distracted. Samson was seduced, enticed and totally distracted by Delilah (Judg. 16.4–16). Be it by sex, personal security, revenge, personal gain, envy and/or jealousy, the people of God have often been distracted from the calling they have been given. We need to ensure we stay on track, loyal to our values, honourable to God, faithful in how we use the power we have been given and consistent in our dealings.

Position, fame and having a high public profile can distract us from our mission. Regrettably, some people find the distractions of having their name in lights, a seat at the top table and people kowtowing to them all too much. They might have entered the political sphere with

---

2 Quotation from a letter Lord Acton sent to Bishop Mandell Creighton.

impeccable motives, but sadly history is littered with stories of people who have become distracted by the trappings of influence. We need to be equally at home in the presence of both princes and paupers, young people and old, the illiterate and the academic.

The paradox here is that many of us want to have access to government ministers, MPs, royalty, the honoured, the titled, the wealthy, celebrities, bishops and superintendents because they are the people who can often bring influence in our politicking. A photo with a government minister, letter of support from a bishop and/or quiet word from a wealthy local business person to the council can all help us achieve our political objectives. I know this to be true, because I have done all of these things and seen the results. Knowing and being among the elites brings influence. However, we need to be careful this pursuit of influence doesn't stop us losing sight of who we represent, who we are, and what we are trying to achieve. About 18 months ago I went, along with about 35 other youth workers, to the home of a multi-millionaire businessman. He was interested in young people and wanted to hear stories about what was happening in the world of Christian-motivated work. His home – it was actually his estate, complete with electronic gates, CCTV, security guards and car park attendants – was very grand, and he was a wonderful and generous host, supplying us all with a hearty supper. After the meal the youth workers began to tell their stories. I don't know if it was the setting, the hope this man might fund us or the abundance of wine on offer, but soon the stories took on a somewhat self-centred tone. Everybody was bigging-up their work and fighting for their slice of the cake: egos emerged, embellishments ran amok, and a rampant competitiveness swamped the proceedings. I was embarrassed. We had succumbed to the distractions of being coerced and corrupted by the hope of what might be to come. I fear we might have pursued personal gain rather than any higher calling pointing to God and the kingdom.

We have to balance working with the elites of the world with kingdom objectives. Yes, we need to be political, but we need to avoid manipulation. Persuade, not manipulate. Persuasion aims to get someone to do, believe or accept something and serves them as part of the process. Manipulation seeks to control others by abusing power, fooling people and making them believe something that might harm them or rob them. Manipulation is based on domination and social inequality. Persuasion should hopefully support the common good while manipulation favours only the manipulator. Biblically, those who have been schemers and manipulators have always opposed God. Characters like the serpent, Jezebel, the young Jacob and the devil himself have always opposed advancement of the kingdom. We need to ensure we, and our politicking, don't fall into these distracting traps.

In this chapter I have focused on some general theological themes that my experience, research and academic considerations indicate are important when considering Christian youth work, ministry and politics. I have made passing reference to Jesus as the model for our politicking. In the next chapter, I seek to drill down into how Jesus went about his political ministry. I offer a number of reflections, youth work stories and additional research findings to further illuminate debates about Jesus' approach. Before doing so, I offer further matters to think about and some pointers for action and response.

Things to think about

- If God were to send you a tweet (of 140 characters or less) about politics, what do you think it would say? You might want to write it down.
- Who are the 'poor' in your youth work context? How can you be 'good news' more effectively for them? Do you need to give them something or change something to help alleviate their poverty? If so, *what, when* and *how* will you do this?
- What power do you have and how do you use it? In what ways would you like to have more power and in what ways could you give some power away to those you serve?

What can I do?

- A contextualized translation of Jeremiah 29.7 might read something like:

  'Pray and work for the peace and prosperity of [*insert name of place/city/town/village you work in*], the young people of [*insert name of place*]. If things go well for them, you will be better off!'

  Reflect on this verse for a moment. Then draw up a list of actions you can take to increase the peace, prosperity (and this is not just about financial gain) and shalom of the location you work in and the young people you serve. Make a schedule of when you will undertake these actions.
- Is there someone or something you need to advocate on behalf of? An issue or matter you need to speak up about? Do it now. Write it down, email it, text it, make a call about it or arrange to meet someone to talk about it. Just do it . . .
- Visit the website www.loesje.org. This is a creative poster-tool website that helps people design posters about everything that happens in society. Work with your young people to design a poster about 'God and Politics'. Make copies of it, and then display them everywhere you can in your local community: church noticeboards, websites, social media pages, magazines, local newspapers, street corners – everywhere. Stand back and see what reaction you get.

3

Jesus and Politics

When I have tried to be political, I get badly criticized by the Church for being political!

Youth worker

I regard the teachings of Jesus as having very radical political importance.

Tony Benn, politician[1]

A Christ-like balance?

During the formative years of my teens and twenties, I was taught Jesus was the role model for how to live out the Christian faith. I gladly embraced my disciplers exhortations that Jesus set the example of how to love, forgive, behave morally, win people to the faith, heal the sick, disciple others, be humble and lead a sinless life. No one ever told me he might also be a political role model. That side of his life was completely ignored by the people who influenced my early discipleship years, but I am not sure why; they were godly people whom I greatly respected.

Jesus trashed the Temple when he saw it being misused (Matt. 21.12), but there were no encouragements from my mentors to smash up the local worship centre if churches were using their money, power and buildings inappropriately. I was invited to turn upside down my own life and turn away from a sinful and destructive path, repent and then head in a different direction. However, I was never told I could try and turn upside down the dominant and sinful governmental and authority structures of the day, so they could go in a different direction. I was certainly never advised that if I followed Jesus as a role model, I would be arrested on political charges, be held a political prisoner and then executed as an enemy of the state. As biblical scholar, Warren Carter, states: 'Crucifixion is a very political act. Folks got crucified because they were a political problem for the Roman Empire' (2006). So, in this chapter I want to highlight the political aspect

---

1 Quotation from Tony Benn on Jesus for 4Thought, Channel 4. Available from www.youtube.com/watch?v=d8qC8KKdkeU&app=desktop.

of Jesus' ministry and suggest a more balanced approach to discipleship, more accurately reflecting who Jesus was and what he modelled.

Jesus as politician

In my survey research, less than 4 per cent of participants felt Jesus was not a political figure. This finding offers strong evidence that youth workers at least see Jesus as political. In Chapter 1, I quoted the Nazareth Manifesto as an aspirational objective from which my overarching convictions emerge. This manifesto declaration from Jesus comes right at the start of Luke's Gospel. Jesus arrives on the scene having been tempted in the wilderness for 40 days. He comes full of the Spirit and begins his public ministry. This was it: the launch of the campaign to heal the world. From a PR point of view, it didn't go too well. In fact, so incendiary were his opening statements that he filled the authorities with rage, got thrown out of the city and only just managed to escape an attempt on his life. No doubt the Jewish people were expecting a military leader, or regal-figure-coming-in-splendour type of messiah to bring them freedom and overthrow the Romans, not some carpenter upstart, with messianic aspirations endeavouring to reappropriate historic promises.

As Jesus begins to read his manifesto we can imagine there being many nods of agreement and shouts of 'Hear, hear' (if it were in a modern parliamentary setting) and 'Alleluia' (if it were in a Pentecostal church setting), for the passage (from Isa. 61.1–2) would be familiar to those present. It would have gone down well with those anticipating the coming of a messiah. However, it soon starts to go downhill from the audience's perspective. We get our first clue from Jesus that this was going to be an upside-down kingdom. In reading from Isaiah, he misses out the verse about 'the day of vengeance of our God'. This would have caused great alarm in the synagogue because this was the key political part of the prophecy for the Jews – the vengeance of God against those who ruled the Jewish people. Jesus omits saying he will deliver vengeance. He sets this aside, leaving it for a later date. I believe the Nazareth Manifesto has plain meaning, spiritual meaning, metaphorical meaning and deep political consequences for the people who heard it then and for those who hear it now. Jesus sets out his focus, agenda, philosophy, pedagogy and, as Dave Andrews declares, 'the mandate for his own mission in life' (2012, p. 9). It is via this manifesto mission statement – enveloped, immersed and bookended by a love of God and for our neighbour – that we must interpret everything that Jesus says and does, and does not say and do. It is the manifesto of the kingdom fundamentally turning upside-down the existing and anticipated *what, when* and *how*. Unlike the outworking of many contemporary political manifestos, Jesus goes on to fulfil his completely.

Whatever our theological view of anything and everything is (and I use descriptive language in this paragraph consistent with the original meaning of the Greek words found in the manifesto text), this passage is good news for destitute, cowering beggars – those devoid of wealth, influence, position and honour in the world. It offers to bring freedom, forgiveness and deliverance for those imprisoned; recovery of sight for those who have stopped seeing, and release from oppression for those who have been crushed, bruised and oppressed. If the lens through which we perceive our mission and theology does not resonate with these sentiments, then I would like to suggest it is fundamentally flawed. Furthermore, this was, and still is, political dynamite. The kingdom was (and still is) not going to be realized by might, military conquest and mandating an elite to lead us forth in victory, but by a life-changing impact on the most needy in society – revolutionary! This was really power to the people: the most lowly and sinful of people. Good news now, judgement later. Furthermore, the subsequent inclusion of those who had thus far been marginalized in society (the poor, women, prostitutes, tax collectors, children and young people) was a political red rag to the bulls of Jewish authority and Roman occupation.

If the mandate in this manifesto is the lens through which we should view, act and assess the authenticity of our walk with and love of God, then it should form the basis of measuring our effectiveness. If we want to measure our politics against kingdom values, this is the standard: how we treat the poor; bring freedom to people; help the oppressed; enable the blind to see; and reflect a jubilee mentality. If we want to measure governments and how 'Christian' they are, this manifesto is the benchmark; not how popular they are or how well the economy is doing. If we want to measure churches and how successful they are, this is the yardstick; not how big they are, or how dynamic their sung worship is. If we want to measure ourselves and how obedient we are being to God, these are the criteria and the point to start from. If we want to measure our work with young people, the Nazareth Manifesto is the template and mandate for contemporary ministry. It should be against the intentions set out here that we assess how effective we are being. If you want to measure how effective this book is in helping us be Christ's ambassadors, then use this manifesto as the gauge.

The problem with many so-called *contemporary* Christian political and theological ideas is that, while they may contain lots of biblical references, they present individual verses in isolation. Consequently they distort what Jesus was all about and end up advocating for political policies and conditions that betray the overarching purposes of Jesus and the kingdom. It might be argued that I have similarly taken these verses in isolation, but this was Jesus' inaugural sermon, his scene-setter, the intentions of his mission, and, as Richard Burridge says in his classic best-selling *Four Gospels, One Jesus?*, Jesus was 'true to his opening manifesto' (2014, p. 120) as set out in Luke 4.

Ideas about a prosperity gospel, obsessions with legislation about sexuality, abortion, unfettered capitalism and narrow views of the family are some of the policy foci that plague contemporary political expressions of Christianity and poorly reflect the heart and nature of God as set out in this Nazareth Manifesto. Furthermore, over-reliance on some aspects of Pauline theological thinking risks disassociating theological messages about individual salvation from broader contextual messages about social, economic and political imperatives. The result is that those who are not Christians all too often end up stumbling over things Christians do and say, rather than the challenge and good news of Jesus. This is lamentable.

Prophet and preacher

Throughout the earthly ministry of Jesus, we can see that he perceives everything through the lens of the Nazareth Manifesto. This is continually illustrated in Jesus' prophetic words and actions and in his teaching and preaching. It is embedded in the political messages that turned societal norms on their heads as he spoke to *power* and *situations*.

There was strong support in my research findings for the idea that being an effective Christian meant understanding that politics *and* religion went hand-in-hand. Over 65 per cent of respondents 'agreed' or 'strongly agreed' with this sentiment, suggesting a desire to embed faith *words* and *actions* into the political domain. I think my question focuses on the extent to which we allow the prophetic teaching and preaching of Jesus to, first, shape our faith and, second, allow any shaping to impact our actions in a way worthy of calling them Christ-like.

In exploring the political dynamic of the Beatitudes (Matt. 5.3–12; Luke 6.20–23) we hear Jesus proclaiming heavenly politics, the nature of the new messianic order and instructions for holistic living. Again, he sets out how the values of the kingdom are different to the societal norms of the day. He illustrates how they conflict with the religious, military and social expectations present. Poverty, hunger, humility, weeping, peace-making and persecution are the blessings and new attributes – I suspect this was not very popular among the gathered people then (except the poor, broken, grieving and desperate) and I cannot see these aspirations being prominent today in any politician's election rhetoric. As with the Nazareth Manifesto, there are many who seek to argue these Beatitudes are spiritual metaphors, not to be taken literally. This argument may have some merit, but I strongly believe we need to take Jesus at face value here. There is nothing in these sayings that was contradicted by who Jesus was and what he subsequently said and did. His politics gravitated towards including the poor, broken, grieving and desperate. In contemporary language, and at the risk of reducing Jesus to a mere election candidate, he wanted the votes of the poor and marginalized.

For example, in his encounter with the woman at the well (John 4.1–42), he not only met her needs, but prophetically challenged the rules and structures of the day. Jesus does something sure to stir up trouble. He starts talking to a person at the other end of the social spectrum; someone of a different gender, different race and someone marginalized by her circumstances. She even identifies him as a prophet. Because of this encounter with Jesus the woman's *what, when* and *how* are completely transformed. We read later that she consequently guided many others towards Jesus. We need more youth workers who will do this type of prophetic work, bringing about transformation. Of note here is the Greek word *metanoia* (μετάνοια). This is the word often translated into English as 'repentance', but this word means much more than this. It refers to a transformative change of heart, mind, way of life and inner being brought about by a compunction (a deep sense of unease and regret) about what is and has been. It is this transformation Jesus beseeches. When we do, and live out, *metanoia*, we should see the *what, when* and *how* of the world very differently and speak out in the light of this revelation.

When asked in my survey, 84 per cent of respondents felt church leaders should speak out about social and political issues. While some said they were 'unsure' about speaking out, no one thought leaders should be silent. In the recent past I don't think we have spoken out enough, and we seem to have domesticated Jesus to make him more palatable and acceptable. As one worker in my research put it, 'for too long the Church has been a clanging gong' lacking love (1 Cor. 13.1).

Over the centuries we have *bred* a Jesus markedly different to the one found in the Gospels. He is tame, politely spoken and well behaved.

Our understanding of him has been influenced by *us*, to meet *our* needs, fit *our* expectations and resonate with *our* world-views. This domesticated Jesus plays it safe. He has his place in society, but is not allowed to step outside of that place. I reflect that the Jesus we have now is a little like the two pet rabbits my wife and I have. Bob and Bubbles (the rabbits) are tame, take food out of our hands, respond to our words and are dependent upon us for their place in our house. We let them run around the living room most evenings, but not when visitors are around. Occasionally we show them to close friends and family. They remain a little frisky and are sometimes hard to catch, but largely we are in control and they do what we want them to do, when we demand it. I fear this is what we have done to the political Jesus: tamed him, caged him, only bringing him out now and again when it suits. We certainly don't want him to upset the neighbours or say anything out of place in mixed company.

I do not think Christian youth work and ministry can effectively and authentically exist with a domesticated Jesus. It needs a radical and political Jesus who helps such work rediscover its prophetic voice. It is this Jesus that should 'preach' to the world and speak into the public and political sphere, not the 'gentle Jesus, meek and mild' many children are socialized into believing exists.

As I mentioned, a few years back I helped turn a disused factory into a youth and community centre. It was a great project to be involved in and I learnt a great deal during the process. When the initial renovation work was completed we had a big opening ceremony. The local MP was the then Minister of Defence. He had been a big supporter of what we were doing and I got to know him a little. He was invited to open the new building. We also invited our funders, local councillors, police representatives, church leaders, headteachers, architects, the boss of the building contractors and other local dignitaries. The list was full of those we thought politically significant in our development journey. This is what you did, or at least what it was expected of you. Looking back, I have often wondered who Jesus would have invited in similar circumstances. Would he have gone for the political great and good? Perhaps he would have invited the local leader of the British National Party (they had a strong presence in the area, but were often despised by many); maybe the father of the notorious family whose children continually caused mayhem in the town; the local drug dealer; the mentally ill people who used the community centre; or perhaps the young people we knew who lived in chaotic circumstances? We will never know who Jesus would have invited, but I have a sneaking suspicion his invitation list might have been different from ours. I suspect he would have wanted to make some sort of prophetic statement about *who* and *what* was important. Youth workers need to think about these things and ask how they are being politically prophetic, Jesus-style, honouring the Nazareth Manifesto and the sentiments implicit in the Beatitudes.

Political irritant and dissenter

I am sufficiently self-aware, I think, to realize that from time to time people find me a bit irritating. Those close to me have even suggested I occasionally come across as pompous and arrogant. I don't mean to be like this, but I do think about things a lot, have strong opinions and high expectations. I want things to be right, whole and complete, justice is very important to me, and people misrepresenting God drives me to despair.

I am comforted to some extent by the fact Jesus was also an irritant. He was clearly a much better irritant than I am and his motives were always beyond question. However, he must really have hacked people off. I don't know if he set out to irritate people or, like me, it just sort of happened because of what he said and did. Politics needs irritants. If things are to change, then people and things are needed to engage in politicking to bring about transformation. If one puts light in darkness (John 1.5), salt in food (Matt. 5.13), seeds in soil (Matt. 13) and yeast in bread (Mark 8.14–21), then things alter. These components all irritate the status quo and bring about change. While I suspect Jesus irritated the disciples, this is because they were often simply confused, by what he said rather than any particular political discourse. So who were the people Jesus really irritated? I believe they were the people with political power, the religious leaders of the day who denied ordinary people life in all its fullness (John 10.10). Ched Myers says – in his classic book, *Binding the Strong Man: A Political Reading of Mark's Story of Jesus* – we see how 'virtually every identifiable ruling faction in Jewish society' (2008, p. 117) opposes Jesus. Based on what we can glean from history, these rulers operated under Roman occupation laws (this was no modern western democracy) creating a political crisis for the people of Galilee and Judaea. The Jewish leaders didn't want to be ruled by anyone other than their own and they ultimately wanted rid of the Romans. However, the Jews had religious freedom under the Romans and so their leaders wanted to retain this while under Roman dominion.

The priests of the day lived lavish lifestyles and sought to minimize political dissent in order to avoid conflict with the Roman authorities. Some were probably under the control of the Romans while others endeavoured to make the best of a bad job and get out of the system what they could – particularly by collecting taxes (see Matt. 17.24–27). The Sadducees thought it best to try to get along with the Romans in order to keep their power and status. They were materially well off and appear content to have co-existed with their occupiers. The Pharisees were big on piously keeping all the oral laws of the Jewish tradition and appear to have been responsible for day-to-day religious matters and giving the meaning of God's law to the people. They really were pompous and arrogant. I suspect the Romans simply wanted to keep a lid on things and be able to rule one of their colonies with minimum effort and maximum return. So when Jesus comes along, ushering in a superabundant kingdom alternative and starts criticizing the status quo, trouble looms.

There are numerous illustrations (Matt. 5.20; 15.3–6; 16.11–12; 23.2–9; 23.13) of the way Jesus irritated and criticized these authority groups. For example, in Matthew's Gospel he says, 'Woe to you, teachers of the law and Pharisees, you hypocrites! You shut the door of the kingdom of heaven in people's faces. You yourselves do not enter, nor will you let those enter who are trying to' (Matt. 23.13). Not only did Jesus keep breaking the oral laws about mixing with the wrong people, eating and drinking the wrong things (especially with unclean hands), the Sabbath and forgiveness of sins, but he had the audacity to challenge the political authority of the Pharisees. To the Pharisees this was outrageous (see Luke 6.11); no one ever criticized them. It appears that whenever the religious leaders hindered people from the kingdom of God, contradicted the teachings of the Nazareth Manifesto or the Beatitudes, they were in for a verbal rocket. Jesus seriously rocked the metaphorical boats of power and politics.

This is a contemporary challenge to us: are we prepared to rock the boats of power and politics when these core kingdom teachings are diminished? As one research participant said, 'We do lots of back-rubbing, but not addressing the issues . . . there is no rocking the boat. It's dull!' Another commented, 'Churches want an easy life and well-behaved youth! We are not really engaged in real youth work, it is tokenistic and unsupportive to workers – workers are exhausted arguing for young people to have a place in church life.' If workers can't even find a political place for young people in their churches, then the challenge of how they might help them be politickers in the wider world appears a big one.

In *Here Be Dragons*, my FYT colleague Richard Passmore talks about the value of dissent in contemporary missional youth work: 'Dissent helps suggest new, innovative ways of doing things to give longevity and new life. It offers movement to a static and shrinking institution.' He adds that this 'disturbs the equilibrium' and 'can cause confusion, anger, and a "pulling of ranks" as old ways are jealously protected' (Passmore and Passmore 2013, p. 23). This appears to be Jesus' experience when he dissented from the norms and challenged the dominant narratives of the day. In New Testament times there were dominant narratives about the social and political status people had in society. There were narratives about expected norms regarding, as already mentioned, the law, the Sabbath, the role of women in society, foreigners, Roman occupiers and Jewish elders. Jesus tore these apart whenever they prevented access to the kingdom and implementation of the Nazareth Manifesto. He took these narratives on and established new ones. He moved the emphasis, empowered the weak and marginalized and lambasted the political elite of the day. In order to illustrate how shocking and dissenting Jesus was, I offer a couple of contemporary parallels to engage our imagination and challenge our paradigms. Can you imagine the political reaction if the Prime Minister or President of the USA spoke at a conference alongside a prostitute and suggested her insight about poverty was a model to be copied? What about the Queen doing a walkabout with a convicted tax fraudster and then buying him a cheeseburger (with extra-large fries and a milkshake) in McDonalds? Or imagine the media response if a priest from a religious cult declared a convicted sex offender 'not guilty' and let the offender go free? What could possibly go wrong?!

Jesus ministered to people who did not conform to the norms of the polite and socially regimented Jewish society. It required courage and perseverance to keep challenging the status quo and go against expected societal patterns. Jesus did not hesitate to dissent from popularism and political and religious protocols if it would advance the kingdom. We need look no further than what happened in the stories of the widow's mite (Luke 21.1–4) and Roman centurion (Luke 7.1–10), or in the parables of the good Samaritan (10.25–37) and great banquet (Luke 14.15–24) to discover what Jesus was about.

One of the great things about the internet is that it has given a bigger and wider voice to the irritants and dissenters of the world. Such people have often been excluded from sharing their opinions about religion, Church, politics and the general state of society, but they now have a platform. Certainly there are extreme views and opinions shared that might be better kept private, but I would rather have some wild fire than no fire at all. I suspect how we share our views and the tone of them is what gives them credence. My hope is that we don't tone down what we think, but we share it respectfully, motivated by a love for humanity and in the hope of a better world. One research participant captured this sentiment well, saying:

> Submission is a big theme in the Bible but Jesus was our role model in that he challenged tradition and rules that were detrimental to people . . . We can challenge the status quo without appearing anarchist. Passion is the key, expressed in a non-judgemental way.

In recent times I have felt compelled to speak out about several issues negatively impacting work with young people. When an Anglican diocese informed some of its staff by letter that their jobs had been 'deleted', I burned with rage – godly rage, of course. I felt that no organization claiming to be 'Christian' should ever use the word 'deleted' when talking about people's livelihoods and vocations – simply appalling. Furthermore, for a church seeking to grow its work with young people the action was a backward step and a disgrace. I joined the campaign of dissent. I have also lent my support to secular bodies seeking to fight closures of youth centres, projects and services for young people. These closures threaten young people's development and undermine the common good of the community. I have therefore attended rallies, signed petitions, written letters, campaigned on social media and encouraged others to do the same. I want to be an irritant to those who have made these retrograde decisions.

Sometimes dissenting and being an irritant is successful and sometimes not. However, we need to note that in our heart of hearts, we are either on the side of the one who needs liberating or the one who is oppressing. If we believe oppression is wrong, we need to dissent and act irrespective of what the outcome might be. While achieving success is encouraging, the outcome is a secondary issue. It is more important we obey God and act rightly and justly. I leave the last word of this section to another research participant: 'For me politics is about justice and equality . . . [and] continuing to agitate in whichever way means not being complicit in oppression.'

Philosopher and pundit

I had a great deal of discussion with colleagues, friends and my publisher about the title for this book. I wanted something that said what it was about, something provocative and something exciting. I didn't want a title that was unduly negative, or one implying politics was something separate to other issues, life events and aspects of ministry. As one research participant aptly said, 'Politics is only one strand of a many-stranded rope.' This is something Jesus seemed to understand and journey with. His approach was holistic, transformative and illuminating with multifaceted philosophical musings and insights. He talked about economics, politics, government, power, social priorities, welfare, justice and children's rights. As two research participants noted: 'Politics affects every aspect of life from the food we buy to housing, roads, education etc., and I think our young people need to know that'; 'Youth work is political. Young people need to know this as it's their future at stake.'

Jesus was a radical economist. He had much to say about wealth (Luke 16), money (Matt. 6.24) and giving (Matt. 19.21). He was an anthropologist, bringing insight and perspective to humanity (John 8.12) and reflecting on human motivation (Matt. 6.21). He was a sociologist offering insights about birth (John 3.3), death (John 11.23–26), marriage (Matt. 19.3–12), disability (Luke 14.12–13) and power within the political structures of the world (Matt. 28.18). Fans of programmes like *Match of the Day* will be aware that each match is disseminated by pundits, usually former players or managers who bring experience, expertise and analysis about each set of tactics, display of skill or controversy. Jesus was also a pundit. Not about football, but about life. He brought his heavenly experience and perspective, his rabbinic expertise and his divine analysis to individual, societal and political life. In addition to the punditry seen in the passages and stories already mentioned, he answered one question on taxes that has prompted many philosophical and political reflections over the years.

In Matthew's Gospel (22.15–22), we are told some rather cowardly and manipulative Pharisees sent some disciples (these disciples were probably teenagers, as already discussed) along to Jesus with a question. They asked, 'Is it right to pay the poll-tax to Caesar or not?' Jesus was aware of their schemes and asked for a coin so he could turn the question around. He enquired whose picture and name were on it. He then uttered what have become some of the most famous political words in history: 'So give back to Caesar what is Caesar's, and to God what is God's.' Over the ages, pundits have suggested this passage means various things. For example: that Church and state should always be separate; that we should always fully submit to secular authorities when asked; that there is a choice to be made over what is the state's and what is God's; that we should stay out of secular affairs; and that we should only pay taxes if they are for a cause not opposed to God's purposes as the believer's primary loyalty is to God and no one else. One of my research participants asked if Jesus was implying that we can engage in politics and government, but 'there are more important things to worry about' in life. Another suggested, 'We should pay the national governors, ignore them and get on with the local issues impacting us.' We cannot know for sure what Jesus really meant, but we do know from this passage that Jesus did not exhibit or plead ignorance about this vital political consideration. He gave a stunning answer, or, as Paul Rowntree Clifford (1984, p. 8) puts it, he gave 'a trick answer to a trick question'. He was a very shrewd operator (Matt. 10.16) and a great philosopher.

We could do with a bit more shrewdness and philosophical reflection about how we go about *what*, *when* and *how*. During a recent visit to the United States, I heard a challenging reflection about life. I met a lovely man who was a surgeon in New York. We got chatting about the political and cultural differences between the UK and New York. He proceeded to tell me that in his opinion someone could be dying on the streets of New York, and thousands of people would step over the body without helping, simply continuing to rush about their busy lives without a care for anyone else. However, he said if the person was to cry out and ask for help, then hundreds would come running! I can't speak for the accuracy of this reflective parable, as I don't know New York well enough. However, I suspect it might be true not only of New York but of many cities in the world. Those who *have* and those who *have not* live side by side without ever the two really meeting and sharing their lives. I think Christians need to do better than this and be proactively looking for needs to meet. Furthermore, we need to help our young people be better than this. As L. R. Knost (2012) has wonderfully commented, 'It's not our job to toughen our children up to face a cruel and heartless world. It's our job to raise children who will make the world a little less cruel and heartless.' In order to do this, I think we need to equip them to be prophets and pundits: Jesus style.

The Feast youth work project in Birmingham is one such project doing exemplary work of this nature. They think philosophically about what they do, passing cultural comment in the process and changing the world as they go. They work with a Christian motivation to bring together Christian young people and young people of other faiths, so they can go about, as their strapline says, 'exploring faith, creating friendships and changing lives'. A few months back I joined with them on one of their political ventures. The English Defence League (EDL) political party had announced they were going to be marching through Birmingham in protest at high levels of immigration, promoting what can be seen as their particular racist and Islamophobic view of the world. The folks at The Feast wanted to pass comment about this and do something positive, bringing communities together rather than driving wedges based on colour, race and religion between them. So they organized a counter-demonstration – a demonstration based on love, not hate. Fearing violence, they did not wish to be directly confrontational with the EDL, so they organized something the day before the EDL march was due to take place. Christian and Muslim young people, along with some adults (myself included), met outside Birmingham Cathedral and spent the lunchtime period giving out Asian sweets to passers-by, demonstrating a commitment to joint and reconciled ways of co-existing. This action led to many fantastic conversations with business people, shoppers, old-age pensioners and young people alike. The atmosphere in the cathedral square took on a life-bringing carnival ambience – an atmosphere sharply contrasting to the one the following day generated by the words of hate and abuse shouted by those from the EDL.

Activist and liberator

Jesus practised what he preached. As already noted, he preached about defending the weak, marginalized and poor, and he ministered to them in practical ways that changed lives. He talked about loving neighbours and told stories about them. For example, he told the story of the good Samaritan (Matt. 14.13–21) and used the metaphor of the sheep and the goats to establish who our neighbours are (Matt. 25.31–46). He also blessed and practically met the needs of his neighbours in, for example, the feeding of the five thousand (Matt. 14.13–21) and the meeting with the Canaanite women (Matt. 15.21–28). Here Jesus moves from coming across as almost racist to healing the woman's daughter. He valued women and shattered societal conventions to embrace them, turning political power structures upside down in the process and lambasting the self-righteous elite. There was the woman caught in adultery, whom Jesus saved (John 8.1–11); the woman haemorrhaging, whom Jesus healed (Mark 5.25–34); and Joanna, who was set free by Jesus and then helped pay for his ministry (Luke 8.1–3).

He fundamentally altered the *what*, *when* and *how* for the people he encountered. Activism and liberation went hand in hand. It was, and still is, about saying and doing, doing and saying. There is a need to vocalize, advocate and endeavour to change the macropolitical circumstances of people, but this needs to be accompanied by practical actions that impact the real life (micro) circumstances of people. If these two considerations do not function together, a lesser outcome might be expected. Words without transformative actions risk the Church and Christians becoming the clanging gong referred to earlier. Actions without impacting words risk perpetuating the very political frameworks that caused the injustice and inequality in the first place. If we are not careful we can get swamped by the need to be active; there are many needs in our world we could respond to, so we need to be discerning. Jesus only did what he saw his Father doing (John 5.19). We need to develop the same spiritual awareness, intimacy and union so we work with God and do what we see him calling us to be, do and say – that *missio Dei* discussed previously.

In Mark 7.31–37, Jesus heals a deaf and mute man by using spit to liberate his speech. In John 9, Jesus spits into the ground and makes some mud which he then uses to heal a blind man. Sometimes we need, metaphorically, spiritually and politically, to spit in the face of that which confronts us and prevents liberation. We need to take radical action to bring about healing and redemption. Just as in the case of Jesus and the blind man, this is likely to get us into trouble with the law-makers. Our old friends the Pharisees were not best pleased by what Jesus had done and our modern-day Pharisaical compatriots are just as likely to be unhappy when we help the blind see and the mute talk – even if we only do this metaphorically.

Back in 2007, FYT helped run a campaign entitled 'Labels R4 Jars Not Young People'. This was a piece of advocacy designed to combat the very negative press young people were getting in the media and from politicians. We thought it would be an excellent idea to go and interview and film some of the media people who were poisoning public perceptions with their negative stereotyping of young people. We turned up at various London media outlets with a professional TV camera, seeking interviews and comments. If you like, we were seeking to spit in the faces of those who were spitting venom at young people. They really didn't like it. For some reason, those who used microphones and cameras to impinge on the lives of others didn't like it when the tables were turned and the same was done to them. We were denied access to several newspaper buildings and escorted off the premises by some beefy security guards at the offices of ITV.

As I reflect back on some of the youth work I have done, I note how activism and liberation have worked together. In north Nottinghamshire, political campaigning for better resources for work with young people and working with those young people went together; there was praxis between the two. In the youth projects I visited for my PhD research, political work for liberation was supported by being practically active. These projects were all practically active, creating a space and place for young people to be free from the perils of poverty, inequality, lack of power and restricted opportunities. I suspect this praxis between activism, causes believed in and liberation is much more achievable at a micro and local level than a macro and national level. Jesus worked very locally, until after his resurrection – then he went global. As a vicar working alongside one of the projects I studied remarked, the problem with national government's approach to local needs is that 'they just don't get it!'

In my research there were mixed responses regarding what actions Christian youth workers and ministers would take to support the causes they were passionate about. The table below summarizes these. Participants were asked what they would be prepared to do in support of a social/political issue they felt very strongly about (see Table 1).

Action	Yes	% No	Not sure
Protest about it on the streets	58	12	30
Give money to support the cause	84	4	12
Lobby policymakers (writing letters, signing petitions, attending meetings)	98	1	1
Join a political party or movement that supported the cause	30	18	51
Go on strike in protest	29	32	39
Engage in acts of civil disobedience (i.e. refusal to obey certain laws, demands and commands of government)	29	31	39
Get arrested for the cause	26	24	50
Go to prison for the cause	18	26	55

Answers are in per cent and rounded to the nearest whole number (this may mean the numbers don't add up to 100 per cent).

Table 1.

It is understandable that people don't want to get arrested or go to prison, but this does indicate we are perhaps not as radical as we might like to think we are and certainly not as radical as Jesus. We are somewhat reluctant even to undertake acts of civil disobedience. We must ask if the likes of Emmeline Pankhurst, Anne Frank, Martin Luther King, Mahatma Gandhi and Nelson Mandela had been as conservative as we appear to be, what would have been achieved? We like to see these people as heroes and I often hear youth workers and ministers tell young people stories about them, but we appear to be reluctant to do what they did. Somehow, embedded in our spirituality, is a *soft option* gospel. Back in 1978, Tissa Balasuriya (1978, p. 112) observed how young people have a latent radical capacity within them, but this is tempered by the Church:

> Social justice is one of the principal concerns of the more generous youth of our time. When they discover the radical call of Christ, they are happy and motivated . . . Often they have to contest the existing values, practices and regulations of the church to experience an authentic relationship of justice and love in their action.

Reflecting upon my practice experience, I don't think much has changed since 1978 regarding this. Perhaps the level of liberation we achieve is directly related to the amount of activism risk we are prepared to take? This in turn is shaped – as Balasuriya goes on to say – by the physical, psychological and social suffering we are prepared to endure. In Jesus, we find someone prepared to endure the ultimate suffering, who acted in profound ways that rebooted the *what*, *when* and *how* of humanity and realized the possibility of complete liberation.

Things to think about

- Think about the word *metanoia* and reflect upon what it means to you. What do you want to change, transform and repent of regarding your heart, mind and way of life that has direct bearing on the political aspect of your work?
- What traditions and rules, conventions and norms have you kept that have hindered advancement of the kingdom? How might you go about dismantling these to ensure a more enlightened political future?

- The nineteenth-century philosopher and social reformer Jeremy Bentham wrote a series of papers entitled *Not Paul, but Jesus* (1823). He sought to emphasize that Jesus was the primary reference point, theologian and model for Church and ministry, not the apostle Paul. Spend a while reflecting upon any aspects of your life, theology and ministry with young people that have overemphasized Paul's teachings (or, for that matter, Old Testament teachings, Rob Bell's, Rick Warren's or Mike Pilavachi's teachings). Evaluate the impact of this and, assuming this is not the best way to exist, analyse what this might mean for your future work if allowed to go unchecked, particularly regarding your politicking.

What can I do?

- Print out on a small piece of card (something small enough to fit into your purse or wallet) the Nazareth Manifesto from Luke 4.18–19. Carry this around with you for a week, a month or even a whole year. Every day, or at least regularly, read through it and ask yourself how your youth work matches up to the words on the card. See this as both an encouragement regarding what you are currently doing and a challenge to what you might do better in the future.
- When you are next planning the work you do with young people, specifically aim to do something politically risky, something that will push the boundaries and challenge the status quo of your group, church, the local council or national government.
- This exercise involves going for a walk. It needs to be at least a 20-minute walk, and you will need something to record your thoughts on – paper, phone or pad. For the first five minutes just, *relax and unwind*. For the next five minutes, *look out*. Look around you at the context and environment you are walking in. Imagine you were looking at this through a window. What do you see that could do with some Jesus-style politicking? Record what you see. For the next five minutes, *look in*. Hold an imaginary mirror up to yourself and consider

how you might do some politicking in the style of Jesus. As before, make sure you record what this is. Finally, for the last five minutes, *look ahead.* Imagine an open door before you and ask yourself what your Jesus-style politicking goals are. Record them. When you get back from the walk, devise an action plan to implement all you have thought about and recorded on your walk.

4

The Current State of Affairs

As a young person myself, it upsets me that I am growing up in a democracy that fails young people and that does not represent our wider society. In the UK we have a parliament that does not speak to the interests of young people and that fails to make worthwhile attempts to include all young people in politics. Young people and youth policy is not on the Government's agenda. I feel very strongly that too many politicians remain uninterested in the issues or aspirations of young people, often due to the fact that young people seem uninterested in politics and the fact that fewer than half of us (18–24 years old) vote.

Kenny Imafidon, youth policy advisor

If you don't do politics, politics will do you.

Sue Atkins, youth worker

Contemporary factors and paradoxes

Recently, I went to meet the new local MP. He was on the campaign trail and came to do a 'meet and greet' session in my village hall. I do not share his political views, but wanted to meet him, say 'hello' and begin to build a relationship with him. I arrived at the village hall to find about 20 people awaiting his arrival. Soon the number grew to around 30. I was shocked to find that, apart from a local parish councillor and his wife, I was the youngest person there – by a long way. Most people appeared to be retired and were presented in their Sunday best. They all came with their issues and worries about very specific local matters rather than the macropolitical issues I was interested in. I really, really, really felt like the proverbial fish out of water. Fortunately, I knew the parish councillor, and he introduced me to the MP, and we had a bit of a chat.

As I walked home, I was kicking myself for not taking someone else with me to the meeting: a younger person who might have been able to talk about *their* different issues and how they impacted young people. While I did talk to the MP about the skate park mentioned in Chapter 2, it would have been nice if a young person had done that. I so wish I had taken the opportunity to mentor, walk alongside or stimulate the interest of someone younger by involving them to try to counter the emphasis on older people's issues. There is nothing wrong with their issues, but the fact that everyone there was older meant their concerns were the only ones discussed. This quite small local meeting highlighted what is happening across the country: young people tend not to be involved in electoral politics, so politicians focus on the issues of those who are involved. Different generations of people experience, engage with and perceive politics in different ways.

In this chapter I consider a number of contemporary factors relating to young people, youth work, faith and politics impacting this generation. I examine the paradoxical lack of engagement young adults have with national political elections, while noting they usually have strong views about specific issues. I then proceed to question if churches and Christians have de-politicized Jesus, youth work and ministry – especially in the discipleship of young people – and assess the impact of this. I also consider what it means for young people and youth workers to be both British 'citizens' and 'Christian', highlighting the potential conflict between these two identities. I explore how the modern world is full of paradox, particularly relating to how governments go about engaging and orchestrating their citizens. Finally, I discuss the engagement, participation and empowerment of young people in political and policy discourses, considering a statement made by a youth work colleague: 'If you don't do politics, politics will do you.'

Young people and politics

Last year, I visited a church in Suffolk to facilitate some training for youth workers in the area. I always like to get a feel of the place I am working in and often look at the church and community noticeboards in order to help me do this. I was doing this here and noticed a local health body was doing a public consultation about what services it should provide. Their poster said, 'Every Voice Counts'. I am sure this is true for the health body, and I hope it is true as a general principle, but it doesn't currently seem to be a reality in macropolitics when it comes to young adults exercising their right to vote. Their voice may count in theory, but even when they have a voice, the 18–25 age range is choosing not to use it in local, national and European elections. The number of young adults choosing to vote is plummeting.

There are some people who say there is no point in voting in elections. They argue all politicians and political parties are the same and that they do not represent ordinary people. In short, they do not believe voting can change the *what*, *when* and *how*. Most notably of late, the comedian Russell Brand gave an interview to BBC journalist Jeremy Paxman that attracted widespread scrutiny and coverage. He eloquently encouraged people not to vote as he considered it pointless. Others, like Kenny Imafidon – whom I quoted at the beginning of this chapter – are passionate about getting young people participating in politics and campaign for more active involvement.

The Hansard Society is an independent, non-partisan political research and education organization. Each year they produce an audit report high-lighting people's opinions about politics and voting patterns in the UK. In their 2012 report they found the public were disengaged and disillusioned with politics and were turning away from it. In 2013, they found just 41 per cent of people would be certain to vote in a general election – 10 per cent lower than a decade ago. For 18–24-year-olds, just 12 per cent of people would be certain to vote – down 30 per cent in just two years! Just 32 per cent of voters believe that if people 'like me' get involved, they can change the way the country is run. Only 22 per cent of the public can correctly name their own local MP.[1] These findings do not make encouraging reading for those who believe our current political system is important. The facts are particularly dismal regarding young adults.

Furthermore, the Electoral Reform Society report that up to 800,000 young adults are not even registered to vote in elections.[2] This means they couldn't vote even if they turned up at a voting station. However, I do not believe we can automatically conclude from these facts and figures that young people are apathetic about politics. Indeed, research commissioned by Vinspired, the young people's volunteering charity, found that 80 per cent of young people care about key issues but don't feel represented in politics. They also found that 57 per cent have cam-paigned on at least two issues in the last three years and that 69 per cent of them disagree with Russell Brand's idea of not voting. However, 78 per cent of them agree with him that the current political system doesn't represent their generation's needs.[3] The Institute for Public Policy Research reports a dramatic reduction of late in poorer people voting. They say that in the 1998 General Election there was just a

---

1 See Audit of Political Engagement 10. www.hansardsociety.org.uk/wp-content/uploads/2013/05/Audit-of-Political-Engagement-10-2013.pdf.

2 See Electoral Reform Youth Voter Survey (2014): www.comres.co.uk/polls/Electoral_Reform_Society_Youth_Voter_Data_Tables_January_2014.pdf.

3 See www.vinspired.org/blog/swing-the-vote-vinspired-calls-on-young-people-to-make-their-voices-heard-in-election-year.

4 per cent gap in turnout between the highest income groups and the lowest. By 2010, they report this had grown to 23 per cent.[4]

There was also little support for Russell Brand's view in my survey: youth workers almost unanimously rejected his call to stop voting. Many rejected his perspective outright, the following quotation typifying this: 'Ridiculous. It is our responsibility to vote. Even if we don't have a clear favourite we need to vote as recognition of our privilege to do so.' However, many participants shared his anger at the current situation, with the following exemplifying such views: 'I agree with the frustration behind the comments, but also feel strongly that by not voting you lose your right to complain.'

Still others went further, sharing the view of the young people who feel the current system didn't serve their generation. One participant summed this up, saying:

I struggle. I know we should choose our leaders by democracy, but I'm unconvinced that a) parties differ as much as they say they do, b) the party system works/represents the people and c) the pre-election campaigns are anything more than that – a campaign to win. I will probably vote but only because doing nothing doesn't seem productive on my own.

Overall, my research reflects the findings of the Hansard Society and identifies a widespread belief that the current system is broken. People believe it needs significant reform if it is to re-engage people (especially young people) to participate in elections. While it would no doubt help in some way, I am not convinced simply lowering the voting age, as discussed in Chapter 2, would substantially increase voting among younger people. Using technology to aid the voting process may increase levels of participation. Enabling people to vote by text or online may increase involvement simply because this is the type of voting younger generations are more familiar with. Making voting compulsory and encouraging dissenters to spoil their ballot papers might also help highlight the failings of the current system and provide clear statistical data about the levels of dissatisfaction with the current system.

However, I think there is a more fundamental macropolitical problem to hand. In re-quoting Kenny Imafidon, 'we have a parliament that does not speak to the interests of young people and that fails to make

---

4 See Birch, Gottfried and Lodge 2013.

worthwhile attempts to include all young people in politics' (2014, p. 1), it appears apparent that unless politicians begin genuinely to include young people in the actual process of politics, they will not return to the voting booths in numbers large enough to restore the integrity of the process. According to a survey undertaken by the think tank British Future,[5] only 4 per cent of 17–21-year-olds feel that politicians pay most attention to them. This is a view shared by 12-year-old Florence Coleman. Florence came to talk to FYT at an event we participated in. She is remarkably passionate about politics and said:

> If I wanted to make a change [to society], one of my only options (especially as a young person) is to write to my local MP. It's likely they won't listen to me, and even if they do they won't do anything about it. Politicians don't care about what young people think because we can't vote. We can't decide if they'll stay in Parliament. We can't do much at all when our libraries, youth clubs and out of education care is slashed.

Politicians have to start serving young people not because they want their votes but because they want to serve them. I recognize some politicians do this already, but unless they do it en masse, I foresee no substantial change in voting patterns.

While voting in elections among 18–24-year-olds might be in decline, participation in new and other forms of political activity is increasing. A study of young adults across Europe (Horvath and Paolini, 2013) indicates they are less likely to use voting as a means of influencing decision-makers, but are more likely than their elders to use social media, attend a demonstration and go on strike to assert influence. This shift in political activity was roundly evidenced by participants in my research who frequently talked about 'new forms of engagement', 'real change being achieved by hard-working campaigners in key places', where the role of the youth worker is to 'facilitate young people's participation in civil society' as a whole.

In the Vinspire research, 71 per cent of young people said they wanted basic politics to be taught at school to help them make informed choices at the polling booths. I think this would be a positive move. If done appropriately, it would not only increase young people's knowledge about politics, but it would also encourage them to care more about

---

5 See 'Voice of a Generation: What do 2015's first-time voters think?' at www.british future.org/wp-content/uploads/2014/05/Voice-of-a-Generation-report.FINAL_.Embargo-6.5.14.pdf.

politics. It would need to be done in a way that considered and advocated for all forms of political activity, not just voting. The motivation would need to be about empowerment, increasing passion and activism, rather than simply adding to knowledge banks and encouraging any sense of public duty. Some schools already teach some aspects of politics in lessons. However, as the following story illustrates, the outcome of these is not always successful.

Ellie is a 16-year-old A-level student with a keen interest in politics. She attended the Westminster consultation day, as she wanted to visit the Palace of Westminster, find out more about politics and contribute to the debate. She made a great contribution. At one point during the consultation she remarked that at her school she had attended 90 hours of classes about citizenship – which included input about politics – but all she could remember being taught was how to put a condom on a cucumber (although she asked me to point out that she didn't actually get to try this as there weren't enough condoms and cucumbers for everybody in the class to have a go). I am not too sure what condoms and cucumbers have to do with citizenship – although I guess a very broad interpretation of the subject matter would include reproduction and sexual health – but if Ellie's experience is anything to go by, it is very sad that in our education system even those young people who are interested in discussing politics are not suitably engaged and effectively taught about it. While the latest school curricula endeavour to improve approaches to teaching politics, it is clear they have some way to go, especially as many schools no longer follow a national curriculum. As Andy Thornton, Chief Executive of Citizenship Foundation, notes:

> Instead of introducing the coming generation to the necessary knowledge of their democracy; instead of introducing critical thinking around public life; instead of helping students prepare for the responsibility of running this country in the face of the most uncertain future we might possibly imagine, we have near-silence. (Thornton 2014)

Depoliticized youth work

In the current climate, it is perhaps too easy to be critical of our contemporary party-political and voting system. There have been ongoing scandals about MP's expenses, sexual impropriety, allegations of Etonian nepotism, payment for political favours and disregarding pre-election promises once elected. Perhaps Christians shouldn't be so quick to point the finger when our own actions often fall well short of what might be expected. Even if we set aside our numerous own vices, scandals and shortcomings, we have often not done too well at engaging young people in the decision-making processes of our churches and organizations. Even where we have successfully done this, we have still tended to look to government to solve society's big problems. As one research participant noted, we need to look at:

> The disastrous state of what life is like for children and young people in society today and actually be prepared to say, 'You know what, it is not just the job of government to try and fix that, it is the job of all of us to try and fix that.'

Sometimes it feels like there is an unspoken pecking order regarding what is important in contemporary Christian faith. Prayer, reading the Bible and worship seem to be top of the list. Then there are things like listening to God, evangelism, healing, the gifts of the Spirit. Then matters concerning the Church, giving, relationships, parenting, families and marriage. Then, if you are lucky, focus on the workplace, school, education and health issues. Finally, some get introduced to social action, societal justice issues and politics. It feels as though there is an expected progression disciples go on as they mature. This is not how Jesus operated. As already noted, God and Jesus trusted and empowered people. They thrust people into the most demanding of situations as soon as they called them, introduced them to faith or invited them to discipleship. The biblical narrative suggests people became fully active often even before they were fully aware of the faith and discipleship implications of what they were doing: we see this in the stories of the call and subsequent sending out of the disciples and of the woman at the well referred to in Chapter 2.

The problem with the progressive, stepped, linear approach to matters of faith – and it is very starkly evident in things like the Alpha Course – is it suggests a hierarchy of importance regarding the Christian life. It is as though we have become subconsciously benign regarding any political imperative in discipleship work.

Jonathan Oliverio works for the Youth Genesis Trust in Torbay. He notes how approaches to faith can be similar to the way those of us who can't do it very well seek to solve a Rubik's cube. We might, for example, get all the yellow panels neatly in place, but when we turn it over we find the other colours have been neglected and are in complete disarray. People concentrate on one aspect of faith or ministry and completely forget about others. Politics too easily ends up being like one of the colours in disarray and too often becomes an optional extra. For young people, this might mean they are only introduced to politics and social justice matters much later in life when their walk with God is well established. This depoliticizes Christian youth work and ministry. If we want young people to be fully immersed in the purposes of God, we need to change the approach so Christian young people get used to politicking at an early age. They will then carry this through and out into the wider world as they grow older and there won't need to be books like this arguing for a more holistic and complete presentation of the gospel. We need to normalize matters of justice and politics within the context of the teachings of the Nazareth Manifesto and Beatitudes in Week 1 of any course about faith, not Week 756.

A recent Hollywood film came in for some sharp criticism. The film didn't accurately portray the content of the book it was based on, nor the period in history the story related to. In response to the criticism, the production company behind the film issued a defensive statement saying the film was 'inspired by' rather than 'based upon' the original story. I suspect this is what Christians in the UK have done regarding the political Jesus. Faith is loosely 'inspired by' but not 'based upon' his life, actions and ministry. Perhaps being *based upon* would simply be too controversial for many middle-class and conservative church congregations. In essence, I believe we have depoliticized Jesus.

Many churches won't even risk reordering their Sunday services, trying out a different type of worship, allowing women and young people to lead others or even laying out the church chairs in a different way. Consequently, the task of developing more holistic and impacting approaches to faith development is a big one. Empowering young people to make decisions and equipping them to be involved in micropolitical initiatives requires a concerted effort and planned implementation. Youth participation in decision-making in churches has improved in the last few decades. However, there is a long way to go and what we do now is simply not good enough if we want to see young people rise to the challenge of taking on micropolitical powers and principalities, let alone macropolitical ones.

If we have depoliticized Christian youth work and ministry, we have robbed young people of a full experience of who God is and what he is about. There is nothing like a big challenge, an adrenalin-filled protest, a way too ambitious project, or a journey into the unknown to excite the mind, body and spirit. It is in these circumstances faith most completely comes to the fore and flourishes. Current practice risks removing the passion, sense of adventure and transformative life experiences that come with engaging in political and social matters. This short-changes young people and creates a false impression about what being a disciple is. It is no wonder so many subsequently give up on their faith and church because it is boring. If we do seek to convert young people and make disciples of them, then we need to help them convert their faith, relationships, finances, aspirations, politics and how they live. Everything needs converting to be consistent with principles of shalom and the Nazareth Manifesto; then young people will genuinely live differently from the dominant culture around them. I realize this might take time, but we could do more to help than we currently do.

In the Bible we see God speaking through prophets into situations, nations and justice matters. In contrast, many contemporary churches seem to focus on speaking about God blessing individuals, churches and engendering church growth. This hardly encourages people to do politicking and adds to a sense of depoliticization. There have been some encouraging developments of late. We have seen campaigns about poverty and modern-day slavery, people setting up foodbanks and providing debt advice for people. For example, one youth worker taking part in my research talked about what they and their young people had done:

> After a session about slavery in cocoa farms, some of the young people wrote a letter to the MP asking him to raise the issue. He replied saying he'd send it to the appropriate people in government, and that he agreed the UK government should stand against slavery. Not quite 'world changing', but receiving a reply was a great boost to the young people who recognized that they could have some influence in political processes.

There have also been initiatives aimed at relieving debt for those in the developing world. The London Citizens[6] community organizing movement has now spread to other cities and these movements often have large numbers of churches and Christian groups as members. This is welcomed, but not always easily accessible for local young people. What about the day-to-day teaching of young people? What is in the Christian youth work and ministry curriculum that is political?

In my survey research, 40 per cent of youth workers 'agreed' or 'agreed strongly' with the statement that their work had 'failed to disciple

---

6 For a discussion about London Citizens, see Ivereigh 2010.

young people to be active political participants'. Seventy-one per cent 'agreed' or 'agreed strongly' with the statement, 'Young people should be encouraged to engage in politics as much as they are encouraged to engage in worship, prayer, mission and loving their neighbour.' It is my hope that we can change this first research finding, disciple young people more effectively and ensure the second finding becomes a reality in our day-to-day work. The last word in this section goes to another research participant, who encourages us, saying, 'When young people show an interest in anything political, you shouldn't stifle that but encourage them to be involved, setting up ways of engaging with it.' If embraced and acted upon, the spirit behind this call would go some way to ensuring Christian-motivated work is not depoliticized.

Citizenship and politics

Citizenship is a complex subject and for the Christian it can be an even more complex subject. Christians have (at least) two overarching identities: one afforded by their national status and the other provided by their faith. Believers are primarily citizens of the 'City of God', as St Augustine described way back in the fifth century. Their primary loyalty and responsibility is to the kingdom of God. However, they are also citizens of the country they identify with or live in. As such, they have a responsibility, as described in Chapter 2, to help that country flourish, develop its common good and work for shalom within it.

In Romans 13, the apostle Paul talks about the authority of earthly rulers and our relationship to them. Throughout history people have used this passage to demand subjection to the rulers of nation states in order to develop compliant citizens. Given Paul's passion for God, and his constant trials, tribulations and conflicts with authorities (2 Cor. 11.24–28), it would be somewhat contrary if this is what Paul intended by this passage. The Christian cannot obey a civil government if it means denying Christ. Equally, the Christian cannot obey laws if they are incompatible with living as a Christian. My take on this passage is that Paul is recognizing the dominion and authority of the Roman rulers and telling the Christians to keep their heads down so as not to get into trouble for trivial and wrong reasons, like not paying taxes or behaving inappropriately. The subsequent verses give credence to this understanding. Paul immediately follows these initial verses in Chapter 13 with a plea to keep the commandments (Rom. 13.8–10) and behave morally (13–14) before going on to say that how the Christian judges and behaves should not become a stumbling block to anyone

(Rom. 14). Irrespective of our interpretation of this contentious passage (some scholars[7] even argue it was inserted a long time after Paul originally wrote Romans) we need to be extremely careful that we do not confuse our Christian faith identity and citizenship with our national or ethnic one: we are citizens of the kingdom first and last.

It is important not to confuse the two senses of citizenship in order to ensure that our patriotism – particularly regarding political matters – is to God and not our homeland, nation state or ethnic origins. We are new creations and citizens of a new kingdom; our old self and primary identity is dead (2 Cor. 5.17). We should strive to avoid assimilating Christian young people just into Britishness, or a British version of Christianity. We need to invoke a primary allegiance to the banner God flies over us (S. of Sol. 2.4), not the Union Jack (or English, Welsh or any other national flag). If we can do this, arguments about whether we are a Christian country or not become irrelevant. In Christian youth ministry, what is important is that young people are discipled so they 'seek first the kingdom' (Matt. 6.33). This does not mean they should not honour their homeland, but it gives a context to such honouring.

In 1535, the philosopher and politician Thomas More (who was Lord Chancellor at the time) was executed for treason. Even though he was a close confidante and personal adviser to Henry VIII he opposed the King's separation from the Catholic Church. More refused to take an oath acknowledging Henry as head of the church and he was consequently beheaded. His final words were, 'The King's good servant, but God's first.' It is in this spirit that we should disciple young people: God first, everything else second. In more modern times, British Muslims seem to have a stronger sense of prioritizing God than do British Christians. In my experience of talking to and working with Muslims, it is very clear it is *Islam first, nation second*. This upsets some people who see such a perspective as unpatriotic and divisive. I do not believe it is. We must not confuse a radical passion for Islam or politics informed by Islam with Islamist radicalization. Furthermore, I consider that if Christians adopted a similar approach to their faith, they would be stronger and better off for it. Perhaps we need to learn from the loyalty Muslims have to Islam in order to have a better understanding of the relationships between Christianity, politics and citizenship.

Some attempts have been made by policymakers to develop a sense of citizenship in young people. The nature and precise detail of these

7 For example, Kallas 1965.

has varied over time but, irrespective of which political party has been in power, there has been a desire to encourage young people's citizenship as part of a strong society. Nearly always policymakers describe this in terms of what young people need to become and what (mainly economic) role they will play in the future, not what they can offer in the present. Similarly, the emphasis has been on duty and responsibility, not on helping young people (as Andy Thornton noted in the quotation above) become democratically critical. The Christian youth worker has a responsibility to help young people develop a critical consciousness regarding their citizenship, asking questions of them about their identity and the values underpinning it. For example, I recall working with a group of young boys in north Nottinghamshire and challenging them about their view of being English. Their views were very racist and misogynistic. I presented a broader understanding to them and invited them to reflect upon this. I believe this approach is essential if societal and individual development is to take place. As one research participant commented, 'It is important for young people to understand the world they live in and factors that contribute to this.'

The National Citizen Service (NCS)[8] is the most recent example of an attempt by government to establish a coherent approach to promoting citizenship with and for young people. The NCS seeks to help young people become active and responsible citizens, but it fails to set out what this means and the form and shape it might take. I cannot imagine the Government intends it to mean the type of irritant, prophetic voice, social activist and dissenter Jesus was. The last thing any government wants is people taking to the streets to protest against its policies. The NCS is not a programme designed to challenge the status quo; it is an initiative developed to produce good citizens and ensure compliance and conformity with British values – values policymakers perceive are under threat. The problem here for the Christian-motivated worker is that God helps us define what a 'good citizen' should be, not the nation state. If the nation decides what it means to be 'good', then the political *what*, *when* and *how* risks becoming an extension of nationalistic hegemony, not kingdom principles. We would do well to remember that God is not British.

I consider citizenship is a relationship of associational identity between an individual and membership of a political community where all citizens have equal rights to participate in that community and equal responsibilities to promote and sustain it. However, young people often

---

8 See www.ncsyes.co.uk.

struggle to be heard and participate in elections, so this presents a number of challenges for them and for those who work with them. For the Christian-motivated worker, creating alternative ways for young people to voice their opinions and needs is required if they are to be active citizens. Workers need to help young people discover what kind of community best promotes citizenship, both in wider society and in the Church. In Matthew's Gospel, Peter denies Jesus. A servant girl catches Peter out with a difficult question (Matt. 26.69), and Peter goes on the defensive. If we are to give young people a voice in society, we must allow them to ask difficult and accusing questions. Workers have to risk being *caught out* and being put on the defensive. In the same way, workers should not shirk from challenging young people with difficult questions. Difficult questions should not be the reserve of theologians and academics. If youth work and ministry is to be Christ-like, it must develop models that include and demand of everybody, not just those perceived as being knowledgeable. Simultaneously, workers need to help build communities so that the *what*, *when* and *how* enables individual flourishing and realizes the common good. If this *questioning* and *building* is done Jesus-style then it may well bring workers into conflict with authorities, parents, churches and governments.

Neoliberalism and the paradox of governmentality

Conflict is inevitable in politics. One of the challenges for the Christian is determining how to respond when conflict arises: how to react when governments, for example, do something contradicting core Christian values. Not only do Christians experience conflicts, but governments do too. They have choices about what policies they implement, which sections of society they prefer in the design of such policies and how much power they exercise in order to achieve what they want to.

In recent times, the globalized world has embraced what is known as neoliberalism. I discuss more fully in Chapter 6 how this ideology impacts the modern context and politics, but here I explain what neoliberalism is, how this makes governing paradoxical and why it presents a number of challenges for Christians politicking. Neoliberalism[9] is an idea that revolves around the belief that if people can be skilled, empowered and liberated to be entrepreneurial then their well-being can be improved. This happens, neoliberalists argue, when governments create

---

9 For a further discussion about neoliberalism and youth work, see Nicholls 2012.

conditions that free up markets, promote free trade, decrease barriers to enterprise and enable increased property rights and ownership. By increasing the role of the free market, opening up to the market things previously done by government, allowing flexibility of labour markets, reconfiguring state welfare activities and reducing regulations, neoliberals argue that wealth will be created. Fans of neoliberalism argue that the state has got in the way of people doing things and generating wealth, and that by freeing up society we can all flourish and benefit. The market has thus become the organizing paradigm for all social, economic and political decisions in most of the contemporary western world.

Critics of neoliberalism say it threatens democracy and puts economics before empowerment, and profits before people. It makes a few people rich and casts adrift the poor and needy. It uses the language of enterprise, clients and maximizing returns rather than people, relationships and community. Because the focus of neoliberalism is on money, everything tends to be seen through economic eyes and focused upon individual choice and gain, rather than, for example, equality, justice, the community or the environment. Consequently, critics argue this obscures bigger discourses about any sense of shared well-being and the common good. All of this neoliberal ideology impacts how we are governed.

The big paradox of neoliberalism is that while it advocates freedom, government has to be very prescriptive in order to instigate, promote and protect that freedom. It has to pass laws to create the conditions for neoliberalism to prosper. It has to control what we think and how we act – often very subtly – so that the conditions underpinning the rationale are supported. The French philosopher Michel Foucault has talked about these approaches, using the term 'governmentality'.[10] In its simplest guise, governmentality is about the *art of government*. It is the way governments try to shape and mould their citizens so they are best suited to fulfil government policies. Public relations and political spin have sold a variety of ideas to the public in ways that have changed perceptions and created a new paradigm about what is perceived to be right and wrong. Close examination of views about matters such as war, terrorism, immigration, benefits cheats, young people being problems and industrial strikes being bad reveal a clear narrative that government has told in order to change public perceptions about these matters. For example, in order to support policies restricting immigration

---

10 See Gordon 1991, p. 1.

to the UK, we are told immigration is bad, despite it having clear and well-evidenced benefits.[11] To justify welfare spending policy cuts, we are *nudged* – as Richard Thaler and Cass Sunstein (2009) term it – into thinking everyone who claims welfare benefits is a scrounger. This is despite the fact that the majority of the welfare budget is being spent on old-age pensioners or those in poorly paid work. To support a particular economic view of the world, we are told we are in a global economic race and that young people in schools must start education earlier, have more tests, do harder exams and be rigorously inspected, despite other countries (like Finland) doing exactly the opposite and educationally out-performing us.

Neoliberal governments try to get people to think about things in certain ways. It is not in their interests to encourage people to critique the dominant neoliberal narrative because this would undermine its effectiveness. Christian-motivated workers need to challenge these approaches and invite young people to think about the world afresh – without all the spin, prejudice and distortions present in our broken world. We need to see things through God's eyes, not neoliberal economic spectacles. If we don't, money, greed and the continued and tolerated sin of UK and global inequality will continue to grab us by the throat and throttle the life out of our very beings. The Beatitudes passage in Luke's Gospel starts by listing some potential blessings, but it has a second part to it. Having talked about how to be blessed, Jesus talks about those who are cursed:

> 'But woe to you who are rich, for you have already received your comfort. Woe to you who are well fed now, for you will go hungry. Woe to you who laugh now, for you will mourn and weep. Woe to you when everyone speaks well of you, for that is how their ancestors treated the false prophets.' (Luke 6.24–26)

For the neoliberals who have told us – as Bill Clinton's 1992 presidential election campaign infamously advocated – that it 'is about the economy stupid', this is a stark warning. Life in the kingdom is not simply about wealth and popularity. Modern politicians and Christians entering the politicking field would do well to remember this and remind young people that there is more to life than money, individual happiness and street cred.

---

11 For example, Dustmann and Farttini 2013.

There is a dichotomy at the heart of neoliberal governmentality: what is presented policy-wise as non-intervention actually requires strong intervention in order to construct and maintain it. In the same way that government has to construct and maintain markets by implementing policies to avoid monopolies, combat cartels and protect the environment, government strongly intervenes to ensure individuals and civil society conform to neoliberal ideas. Ironically and paradoxically, government attempts to give freedom to markets and protect its citizens from external threats (mainly alleged terrorists) have resulted in unprecedented levels of managing our conduct and behaviour, leading to oppression. We are now spied upon, subjected to surveillance and have data collected (and sold) about us in unparalleled fashion.[12] Charities are told not to get involved in party politics and campaigning. Dissent is increasingly not tolerated and peaceful protesters are routinely arrested, aptly illustrated by the cases of the five Christians who were charged and subsequently acquitted of aggravated trespass because they peacefully protested at the London Arms Fair. Similarly, Green Party MP Caroline Lucas was charged with obstructing a public highway and a public order offence, and then acquitted, for linking arms with other anti-fracking protesters. It seems those who protest against neoliberal interests must be prepared to face the wrath of the powerful forces supporting those interests. The poor are punished disproportionately (we only have to compare the benefits sanctions handed out to people with the lack of legal sanction taken against those who caused the financial crash of 2008), and a culture of fear is perpetuated by policymakers. In youth work (and for that matter social work, teaching, the police and health service professions) everything is micro-managed with data collected to justify existence, expenditure and activity. Those who do not rise to these neoliberal challenges and comply are branded 'failures'. Governments seek to control what we eat, what we drink, how we drive, and even define who the deserving poor are (as if there is another type of poverty), as they seek to orchestrate what they think is in our best interests. A friend of mine recently went to India and told the people she was staying with about the 'five a day' fruit and vegetable initiative. Her Indian host burst out in hysterical laughter when he heard this, mocking, 'Your government even tells you what to eat!'

All these approaches seem a long way from 'life in all its fullness' (John 10.10) and 'freedom in Christ' (Gal. 5.1). As one research participant

---

12 See Clark's (2007) account and struggle against the surveillance society.

commented, 'I don't feel fully part of what society is doing or what the Government is doing. You just feel like people are deciding. Stuff is there and that's it.' I consider this very sad: these neoliberal ideas and values need challenging. Christians need to help young people be critics of what is going on if we are to avoid sleepwalking into an increasingly unequal and controlled global nightmare that simply puts more and more wealth and power into the hands of an elite few.

Personally, I find politicking in this neoliberal context very difficult and dispiriting. All the main UK political parties broadly agree and ascribe to the neoliberal position. Making people more wealthy – and promising to do so continually, however unrealistic this notion might be – is what gets modern-day politicians elected. It is the be all and end all of modern electoral politics. The market-driven process, however, is very unforgiving, lacks compassion, neglects the centrality of relationships and can be very harsh. I struggle with the notion that crime policies and welfare reforms have targeted the poorest and most disadvantaged in society, rather than the rich and powerful. Young people have their benefits cut for missing a Job Centre appointment and the sick and disabled are instructed they are fit to work, despite in some cases them dying within a few weeks of being so ordained. Yet footballers earn scandalous amounts of money, celebrities establish elaborate tax-avoidance schemes to avoid paying their share of tax and bankers escape with intact lifestyles despite overseeing the most spectacular of neoliberal failures where free markets and unfettered capitalism brought the world to its knees in the 2008/09 economic crash. I am emotionally crushed by stories of gagging orders being put on some local authority youth workers by their employers in order to prevent them telling others how the council is cutting youth services. I am mentally drained by constantly having to prove my youth work worth in funding applications, endlessly setting out the economic benefits and outcomes achieved. The inducement to lie, distort and exaggerate my effectiveness, because I know this will help my case, is an ever-present temptation.

Nobility, empathy, virtue and kindness are not words that feature in neoliberal approaches to youth work. Nor do words like spirituality, creativity and having fun: it is all about value for money, returns on investment and getting young people into work. Despite the promise of freedom, empowerment, opportunity and being given responsibility, I am overwhelmed by restrictions, controls and competitiveness. I observe larger and more powerful bodies entering into the youth work 'market', running services for profit, not because it is the right thing to do for young people. Yet despite all of this, I know *not* politicking and seeking change will achieve nothing. I feel we are compelled to do something about this and get involved. I don't want to be in the same position as Dietrich Bonhoeffer and conclude we 'learned a bit too late in the day that action springs not from thought but from a readiness for responsibility' (1977, p. 298). I want to be responsible and act because I fear if we don't do politics in the neoliberal age, both the market and politics will *do us*.

Doing politics

The TV presenter posed the question to the audience, 'Should religions meddle in politics?' I thought this a curious question to ask. The word *meddle* was a very loaded verb to use; it implied unwarranted interference and a tampering with something that is not one's concern. No doubt it was chosen to provoke a reaction, but the heart of the matter is that religions are intrinsically compelled to be involved in politics. They are not compelled because of statute, privilege, tradition and/or any consequences of a marriage between Church and state. They are compelled, because the heart of matters of faith – specifically in this context the Christian faith – is to be political in order to advance everything faith stands for. This cannot be done if politics is declared off limits. We all need to 'meddle in politics' because politics is for everyone, religious or otherwise.

I am both an idealist and a realist. I am idealistic in that I want Christians to be involved in politics at every level of society, including Christians standing for public offices. However, I am also a realist. This means I am not dreaming of some utopian Christian republic where everyone who governs us is a perfect Christian. I don't think this is possible given the propensity for Christians in power to say and do ridiculous things. What's more, I find it embarrassing when some politicians say they are Christians, but their actions seemingly bear little resemblance to even the most basic of Christian teachings of love, grace and forgiveness, let alone some of the more radical narratives explored in this book. I am not even sure I think it desirable that every elected politician be a Christian. In a plural society I think we need a diversity of politicians representing that plurality. I think it would be advantageous for the Church of England to disestablish itself from the state. It would then be free to appoint who it wanted to lead it (currently the Government approves who the Archbishop of Canterbury is), be liberated to speak out more forthrightly when the state corporately sins against society and the kingdom, and be more counter-culturally provocative in the public square. What I really dream of are more Christian people politicking: people, especially young people, who are passionate, act with integrity and who work together for our common good in ways that embrace the values set out in Chapters 2 and 3. Christian-motivated youth work needs to help people do this more. I believe Christians need to be more succinctly tuned in to what is happening in society and respond accordingly and more effectively.

My cousin has a dog – a whippet called Geanie. It often goes out into the back garden, to do what dogs do. Over time, my cousin's neighbour befriended the dog and started to give it treats over the garden fence adjoining the two houses. Geanie, being a clever dog, worked out that if she barked loud enough and long enough, the neighbour would come out and give her a treat each time she barked. Pretty soon, this got really annoying for my cousin and, indeed, for the neighbour. So they set about trying to train her out of this and had a reasonable amount of success in stopping her barking. For several weeks she did not bark. However, one day Geanie was heard once again barking at the fence. My cousin angrily went out into the garden to try and stop her. When she got to where Geanie was barking she began remonstrating with her. Suddenly, my cousin stopped the telling-off. She noticed that over the fence, the neighbour was lying on the floor collapsed. The man had cancer and he had fallen over and couldn't get up. Geanie, somehow, was aware of this and was barking – not for treats but to raise the alarm. If only we were as aware as Geanie was. If only we had the awareness to spot when something was wrong, to notice when someone had fallen over, and the courage to shout about it so they could get some help. We should be barking (rather than barking mad) on behalf of others about injustice, inequality and the needs of the poor and needy. We need to do politics if only for the sake of others.

It was youth worker Sue Atkins who first told me about the 'If you don't do politics, politics will do you' rationale. She told me she often used this idea in her conversations with young people. I was so taken with the concept that I used it as a question in my research with Christian-motivated workers. I simply asked them what they thought about it as an idea. One or two respondents thought the emphasis of the phrase was a bit negative: it might imply young people are excluded because they can't vote in elections until they are 18 years of age. However, I felt this said more about youth workers' understandings about what counts as politics than it did about Sue's reflection. To associate politics purely with voting in elections is, as already argued, a mistake. Politics is much more than that. A reflection from another youth worker stated: 'It's a fair statement; encouraging young people's understanding in how politics impacts on their lives is an important part of the youth worker's role.' A further worker highlighted the point made earlier about young people's capacity to vote and the relationship this has with the power they appear to hold:

> I think lack of engagement allows the government to do what they like. The government tend to focus on doing things that benefit those that they know will vote. This means that young people get a raw deal due to not voting or speaking out about issues. I happen to think that the young people of today will suffer loads in the future because the government are so focused on keeping today's adults happy. They are stealing from the young people's future in order to do this.

For me, this sentiment is why we need to do politics. It is why we need to equip youth workers to be involved. It is why we need to help young people engage with politicking, so they can exercise what power they do have about the *what*, *when* and *how* of society, the society they have a legitimate interest in. We need to help them, to use the words of the TV presenter, *meddle* and take every opportunity they can.

One worker offered a very sobering and honest assessment of their politicking success:

> I know that I have failed as a youth worker to encourage my young people to engage in politics, mainly because I don't know where to start, and I am not sure I would have the backing of the church that I work for.

If this worker's assessment is an accurate one, then this is very sad. We need to start with where people are at and, to borrow a concept from God, begin with what we have got in our hands (Exod. 4.2). Doing something is better than nothing. I think any starting points need to distinguish between making critical statements about personal morality issues and speaking out on justice and equality issues impacting all of society. If we are to comment about personal morality issues, we can only do this (if at all) when we have earned the right to do so through our relationships and witness rather than because of any assumed positions arising through power and arrogance. I would suggest that concentrating on the latter justice issues is a better approach, leaving the morality matters to the likes of the *Daily Mail* and Fox News.

I end this chapter with three brief lists of things Christian-motivated workers told me they have done as they have set about 'meddling in' and 'doing politics'. I offer these as an encouragement as to what is possible when people decide to act to make the world a better place. I have used their words and offer the lists without further comment or critique:

- Christian-motivated workers did politics and campaigned about housing homeless young people; regulating pay-day loans; child poverty; youth services and provision; disability issues; education policies; national and international development matters; G8 Summits; Robin Hood tax; surveillance and monitoring stuff; living wages; welfare cuts; green issues; young people in prison; politics being taught in schools; young people and mental health; gender equality issues; youth unemployment; gagging laws; marriage laws; modern-day slavery; recruitment of young people as soldiers and human trafficking.
- They did politics and facilitated meetings with local councillors, MPs; a 'Christians and Politics' presentation; lectures in social policy; a conference about democracy; internet debates; social media postings; research into local needs; work with a group of young people who presented their concerns to local councillors about mental health issues; a debate about Scottish independence for young people and meetings with the local police to stop them harassing young people.
- They politicked and set up a foodbank; local residents meetings; a rally about world hunger; protest about climate change; social enterprise; debt advice process; Fairtrade scheme in church; local expression of a national scheme to increase young people's involvement in politics and started an initiative to collect toiletries and clothing for the homeless.

Things to think about

- Have you depoliticized your Christian youth work or ministry? If so, what steps can you take to make sure politicking *Jesus-style* gets back on the agenda?
- How would you define 'citizenship'? Does a moral obligation to vote in elections form part of your definition? How do you balance your citizenship responsibilities to God, your family,

your church or organization, your nation, your ethnic identity and your favourite sports team or other body/institution/
interest you have loyalty to and affiliation with?

- What do you think about the statement, 'If you don't do politics, politics will do you'? You could ask your young people,
church or community what they think about it too.

What can I do?

- Whenever there is a local, national or European election,
organize a shadow polling event for your young people. Find
out who is standing in the relevant election, summarize who
and what they are standing for (the candidates' websites will
help you prepare this), prepare ballot papers and invite the
young people to vote for their chosen candidates. Do this in
secret just as in an 'adult' election. Count the results and see
which candidate won. Review the process with the young people as a means of preparing them for the future when they
are old enough to vote.
- Think about some of the bigger social issues in your community that need addressing. Now imagine that you are in
charge. Pick three of these issues and consider what policies
you would introduce to help improve them in your community. Act upon your considerations by campaigning for, lobbying and being the change you want to see.
- Make a list of the things you think the current government
does well. Make a second list of the things you think they do
less well. Timetable a series of actions based on these lists. For
example, you might want to encourage, protest, write about,
support, pray and/or propose improvements. You could do one
thing each month and encourage others to do the same.

5

The Prophetic Youth Worker

It is understandable that Christians seek social influence. Responsibility to 'mend the world' and serve the common good is inscribed into the very character of Christianity as a prophetic religion.

Miroslav Volf (2011, p. 78)

It may have been love that held Jesus on the cross, but it was the politics of resistance that got him there.

Richard Passmore

Frameworks and perspectives

Artists have long used a 'perspective frame' to help them in their work. Most famously, Van Gogh used one to help him accurately paint his subjects and give him a precise depth of field in his paintings. The frame consists of a rectangular structure and a series of perpendicular, horizontal and diagonal strings or lines that divide up the frame into a grid. This type of frame enabled Van Gogh to capture the principal features of his subject, thereby enabling him to make a more accurate drawing. The frame helped him transfer what he saw in the field on to the flat surface of his canvas. In a letter to his brother Theo he said the result of using the framework was that 'on the beach or in a meadow or a field you have a view as if through a window'.[1] In the same way, Christian-motivated workers need perspective in order to help them see the world as it is. Workers need a framework to help glean an accurate understanding of what is happening in the world they exist and operate in. Such a framework gives perspective about what is going on in society, what God thinks about it and what prophetic actions and messages need consequently to emerge.

In this chapter, I seek to use the framework of the Nazareth Manifesto and the imperatives identified in Chapters 2 and 3 to consider the philosophy and values of Christian-motivated work and the political nature of these. I also consider the pedagogy of such work and what the political

---

1 See http://vangoghletters.org/vg/letters/let254/letter.html.

component in a curriculum might be. I examine community organizing possibilities for workers, the young people they work with, and those they represent. This enables a rationale to be developed for ways that workers, churches and Christian organizations engage with policymakers. Finally in this section, I reflect upon the prophetic responsibilities of being a representative of God in the public square, the costs of being a prophetic dissenting voice and how to handle those challenges.

Philosophy and values

I scanned the conference programme looking for something I might find interesting, something that might go beyond the usual 'how to make the worship more dynamic', something that might look further than an overview of youth culture, something more than another reminder of the perils of sex, pornography, drugs and young people's challenging behaviour. Nothing. Yes, there was the now traditional session about some aspect of global poverty and a passing note to justice issues, but nothing explicitly, unashamedly, controversially and radically political.

There is nothing wrong with any of these usual subject matters and I don't mean to criticize any specific youth work conferences – my critique could be applied to most if not all conferences. Youth workers and ministers need to discuss populist matters and fully consider them. Indeed, I have often delivered sessions on them myself; but I want, I need and have to have more. I also believe God wants, has to be and demands more: that prophetic dynamic that stops the soul in its tracks; that spiritual jolt reminding us of our own vulnerability and failings as humanity; and those momentary releases of heaven into earthly realms. What we do has to be prophetic if it is to shape and help mend the world. If it is not, I am left questioning what it is we are doing and why.

Being politically prophetic enables us to act and speak about the nature of God, impregnating our broken world with hope, encouragement and improvements so the *what*, *when* and *how* is more justly apportioned. I do, however, consider there is a difference between prophesying and being prophetic. I believe being prophetic is not exclusively talking in 'thus saith the Lord' proclamations (although they have their place and are also welcome). It is more the redemptive acts, healing words and saving graces that emerge when the distinctive philosophy and values of Christian-motivated work impact political domains and unjust structures. These dynamics challenge inequality, build shalom and develop the common good.

Prophesying about the specific direction an individual, group, organization or nation should take is a weighty responsibility. It needs to
be undertaken with great care and accountability and is a specific gift
of the Spirit (1 Cor. 14.1). Acting *prophetically* in a counter-cultural
way that upholds God's values also requires a careful and considered
approach. However, I believe *being prophetic* can be done more sys-
temically as part of a lifestyle choice and considered personal quest, as
well as a specific manifestation of God's Spirit.

I have already discussed how Jesus was counter-cultural in his
approach to women, the poor, the religious, people from other faith
backgrounds and children and young people. We too can be prophetic
in our choices and quests. For example, people might choose to buy
Fairtrade goods as a prophetic statement about justice and economics.
Others might choose to give up particular foods or meals (or even not
to eat at all) during Lent to stand with those on the margins of society
who have no food. Vicar Keith Hebden did this as part of the End
Hunger Fast campaign. He prophetically fasted and also wrote an open
letter signed by forty-two Anglican bishops and more than six hundred
clerics, calling on the three main party political leaders to work to end
food poverty. When he and the Bishop of Oxford tried to present this
to the Prime Minister's constituency office (by appointment), the office
bizarrely called the police. Fortunately, Keith and the Bishop did subsequently meet the Prime Minister to discuss the issue.

In my youth work, I have opted to be prophetic and counter-cultural
by espousing an ultra-positive philosophy and value base towards
young people. This has meant valuing them, communicating positive
stories about them and what they do, saying 'hello' to them in the
street, welcoming their opinions and endeavouring to involve them
in everything impacting them. My doctorate research into Christian
youth work projects identified a number of clear philosophical drivers and evident values underpinning the work undertaken. These
include:

- a firm belief in human dignity where young people are treated with
  unconditional positive regard;
- going the extra mile to serve and empower them;
- a commitment to, and a declared vested interest in, working at a
  clearly defined local community level;
- embracing approaches that are salugenic – in other words, doing
  things that are life-bringing, coherent and help human flourishing;
- developing the ideal of the common good;

- making a difference, not only to the young people but to the communities and contexts within which they exist;
- creating opportunities for them to be heard;
- maintaining symbiotic and synergistic relationships where workers, young people, the community and other stakeholders really are 'in this together';
- maintaining sustainable work that values good stewardship both in times of possibility and uncertainty; and
- being values-driven and reciprocal in everything undertaken.

These philosophies and values both manifested themselves within the projects studied and became externally evident in political and counter-cultural actions, attitudes and frameworks enabling work to be developed and young people to be served. Consequently, the work I researched was not only effective in terms of meeting young people's needs and helping fulfil their aspirations, but it also conveyed prophetic messages to society about what was perceived to be important. Excitingly for me, these drivers (some of which I discuss further shortly) are entirely consistent with the theological imperatives of shalom. I can think of no better prophetic rationale and stance upon which Christian-motivated work should be based.

Improvising and rehearsing what we do: our pedagogy

If Christian-motivated work is to embrace the passion of politics more effectively, then it will not only have to start doing more politicking, but it will need to start talking and thinking about it more. The survey results already discussed strongly suggest this is what youth workers want to do, providing they have the tools and resources to do so. The challenge is making this politicking happen in a way workers find empowering and releasing rather than alienating and restricting. One way of achieving this is to design a Christian youth work and ministry curriculum specifically and deliberately containing politicking elements, right at the fore. If this is to occur, workers need to understand what pedagogy it is they are using in their work.

Pedagogy is the method and practice of what is taught. It is the art and science of education. It is how we lead and guide someone educationally, the approach we take to convey knowledge and manage learning, and the methods we use to help young people grow and develop. It is the process we create for learners so that they learn effectively.

The original Greek meaning of the word *pedagogue* was 'a leader of children'. It would seem entirely appropriate then to consider how this educational leading might best be done to teach prophetic politicking in youth work and ministry.

One of the great strengths of the Christian-motivated youth work field is that a large number of volunteers deliver the work with young people. These volunteers represent a committed and vast resource of people and experience. Often, these volunteers are busy people with other jobs, family and church responsibilities. This usually means that what they teach or seek to impart to young people and the resources they use to do this need to be readily available and easy to use. 'Off the shelf' Christian youth work ministry resources have become the staple diet for many church-based youth work volunteers. Many of these resources are excellent, but usually they do not encourage the volunteer, or employed worker for that matter, to think about their pedagogy. The process is usually: look at the resource; prepare the youth work session; and then deliver it. If the resource is not pedagogically robust, does not contain political elements and use the theological lenses of shalom, the Nazareth Manifesto and the Beatitudes then we risk selling young people short. We will be offering a slimmed-down version of the good news and a potentially diminished experience of God. In my experience, not all resources are as pedagogically designed and robustly considered as they deserve to be.

Christian youth workers have an added challenge as they try to uphold the values of informal education as well as their faith convictions. Tony Taylor from the In Defence of Youth Work organization has used a very apt phrase to describe an approach embracing the idea that youth work starts with the needs and concerns of young people, while maintaining a commitment to undertake values-based work informally and educationally. He describes this as being 'improvisatory yet rehearsed', where the ability

> to be able to think on your feet, react 'spontaneously' to twists and turns in conversations with young people demands that you spend significant time keeping abreast of political and current affairs; that you rehearse in your head how you might respond on an issue if it comes up or indeed how you might introduce an issue in a 'natural' rather than forced way.[2]

---

2 Quotation from correspondence between Tony Taylor and myself. Also see www. indefenceofyouthwork.com.

The British film maker and playwright Mike Leigh uses this improvised but rehearsed approach in his work. Rather than present actors with a tightly written script, he comes with stories, ideas and possibilities. He then creates a rehearsal space, gathers actors together and begins to improvise the script. Characters develop, plot lines emerge and a narrative begins to take shape. What he does in this rehearsal and improvising space is then put before the camera and turned into an actual film. Perhaps we can learn from this approach. If we *practised and rehearsed* our politicking before we did it for real with young people we might develop better skills and a richer narrative. This would enable the worker to respond to where the young people are at, having previously considered their faith and political tools, processes, methods and responses: improvised, but rehearsed. I think this is what Jesus did. He had an overarching motivation and agenda (building the kingdom of God and implementing the Nazareth Manifesto), and an array of creative pedagogical approaches. He met people where they were at, practised and rehearsed with his disciples before he sent them out into the world.

Some European youth workers appear a bit more enlightened in these approaches than those of us in the UK. They talk about workers being 'social pedagogues'[3] – carers and educators of young people working holistically and participatorily, concerned with individuals and wider society, seeking to reduce inequalities in society, showing solidarity with the marginalized and focusing on relationships and challenging social problems. This social pedagogue approach liberates the worker and aptly reflects how Jesus worked. The Christian youth work projects I have studied also seemingly embrace this ideal. While they might not be aware they do, they manage to bring together care and education, resulting in change, and do so via political, social action and justice-orientated approaches. Specifically, I found their work is about nurturing young people, caring for them, building community with them, advocating on their behalf, being socially structured and educational, while transmitting the Christian values they believe in. I think these elements form a challenging basis upon which an *improvised yet rehearsed* curriculum might be shaped, thereby enabling a more just *what, when* and *how*. However, as one research participant noted, 'There has to be a relationship and a long process which is supported by youth workers and other professionals to enable and equip young people to become more politically engaged.' Taking the time and developing a robust pedagogy will significantly help such engagement.

---

3 See Cameron and Moss 2011.

This process needs to consider when and how young people will be exposed to ideas that stem from the important theological imperatives I set out in Chapter 2: empowering people, justice, good news for the poor, blessing people, advocating, making a difference and trusting God. For the Christian youth minister, there might have to be specific sessions about these things: exercises, workshops, practical activities, prayers and Bible studies. Consideration will have to be given to the pedagogical methods and processes employed, and there will need to be a commitment to being intentionally political.

For the Christian youth worker, there will be a need to *rehearse* thoughts about these ideas, constantly ensuring that the value base worked from reflects them. I am an advocate of *prophetically rehearsing* what it is I do. That is, praying, reflecting and asking God what it is he is doing and what it is he wants me to do before a session or season of work. Young people will also need to be engaged and equipped to determine what they think about these matters and be encouraged to become active. Workers might additionally opt to invite the young people they work with to think about the most effective pedagogical approaches to take in the work. Simply asking young people what they think about different ways of doing things (that is, establishing their preferred learning style), or what issues interest them (that is, a needs analysis) or what they would like to see in their community (that is, basic profiling) would be a good starting point.

Community organizing as local activism

I have already discussed that if we want to have a Jesus-like approach to what we do, then we need to be an activist and do everything we can to ensure we act politically to liberate people. However, I want to explore this idea a little further here as something significant has happened in the last few decades regarding a political practice begun long ago. There seems to be a renewed interest and focus on *community organizing*: a process where people are brought together to be political activists by exercising their collective power to bring about change pursuant to an agreed common agenda.

It was American Saul Alinsky who helped bring the idea of community organizing to the fore. His work with poor African American neighbourhoods in Chicago in the 1950s elevated the idea of organizing to new levels. Unorthodox and confrontational, Alinsky developed a set of rules and tactics formulated around what local people wanted.

He addressed one specific issue at a time and was highly agitating towards those who had the power that impinged on what local people said they needed or wanted. His goal was always to realize change.[4] Alinsky was not a Christian. In fact he had an agnostic Jewish background with a penchant for the dark side of spirituality: many right-wing American Christians believed he was an agent of the devil. However, he was prophetic, very pragmatic and got results. His work has taken on added significance of late since Barak Obama became President of the United States. The President studied and was influenced by Alinsky, undertook some community organizing work when he was younger and has been an advocate of it ever since. The thing youth workers and ministers can learn from Alinsky and community organizing is that activism, realizing power and politicking are not things that should be left to chance – they should be planned for. It needs to be an orchestrated process that calls people out of their private worlds, into the political public sphere. At the beginning of this book, I made reference to the origins of the word 'idiot' and how it referred to those who withdrew from Greek political life. For Alinksy, apathy and non-participation was a bad thing. People, therefore, need to be trained, educated and organized to prevent this occurring.[5]

The Citizens movement, mentioned in Chapter 4, is an example of community organizing on a city-wide scale. In the UK, the initiative started in London as an alliance of local groups (churches, mosques, synagogues, trade unions, charities and academic bodies) coming together to politick. The movement is now spreading across cities in the UK and seeks to develop the capacity of its members to build power locally in order to hold politicians and other decision-makers to account. My local Citizens groups has recently won 'living wages' (where people are paid an amount based on the cost of living, rather than the minimum wage) for several thousand people, and realized substantial changes to health care and policing provisions.

Whether it is through formal bodies like the Citizens movement, practitioner networks like the ones FYT facilitates, or more informal associations, youth workers can come together to realize power and organize themselves to campaign for the things important to them and the young people they work with. Christian workers cannot divorce what is going on around them from what God wants and what they are called to be and do. They need to build and maintain alliances and

---

4 See Alinsky 1971, pp. 126–30, for a list of his 'rules'.
5 For a further discussion, see Shannahan 2014.

draw upon their prophetic callings to ensure their ongoing spiritual credibility and relevance.

An exciting example of local community organizing comes from a group living on a housing estate near to where I was born in Macclesfield, Cheshire. A youth work colleague, Rob Wardle, helped set up Moss Rose Community Limited. The Trust has the aim of trying 'to be a voice for people about what is important to them and what they want to see happen' on the estate. Membership of the Trust is open to any person who lives in the area and who completes an application for membership: this includes young people in either School Year 7, or who are 12 years of age or older. The Trust is very much focused on improving the lives of those who live on the estate and this means listening to people, running events they want and campaigning about issues they are concerned with.

While I was writing this section, news broke of a community organizing, local activism campaign following an incident in a Nottingham sportswear store. The shop apparently asked a woman who was breast feeding to leave the store, because they considered it inappropriate. In response, a large group of women organized a sit-in protest. They turned up at the shop with their babies and started to breastfeed them as a way of highlighting how the store had behaved. The store apologized for what it had done.

Community organizing opens up many possibilities for both workers and young people. If we believe God is working in our midst, it can be a truly prophetic response to the *missio Dei*. It might even be a very tangible alternative to voting, because it seems to get things done in a way elected politicians often fail to. It might, as one research participant said, 'stir up passion and therefore potential action from youth'.

Engagement with policymakers

Community organizing is just one way of engaging with the powers that be in order to bring about change. It seems to be very effective at addressing certain issues, but it is not always possible to approach policymakers in such an organized and collective way. Indeed, it might not necessarily be the best way to tackle every issue. Different issues, involving different people, looking for different outcomes require different politicking approaches. If we want to impact the *what*, *when* and *how* determined by policymakers, we need to consider carefully which is the best approach to take in each and every circumstance. As our consciousness about politics increases and develops, it is likely we will want to influence what policymakers do, both at a local and at a national level. If we are to fulfil prophetic promptings and callings, we need to take God's just ideals to policymakers and apply them to social policy narratives. This will take time, energy and courage as we endeavour to engage those with the power and seek change.

It is not always easy to build strategic alliances to campaign about an issue. As we have seen from exploring how Jesus ministered, confrontation and provocation have their place, but the personal touch and 'critical friend' approach also works. I recall sitting in a government minister's office with a group of young people and my good friend Bishop Roger Sainsbury, talking about youth unemployment. We had a constructive conversation and developed an ongoing relationship with the MP, which continues to this day. The young people involved also greatly benefited from the opportunity to talk in a non-threatening and non-confrontational environment.

I also recall a time when I was quite critical of a local youth policy and service – it just didn't resonate with what the young people I was working with were saying and experiencing. I attended lots of meetings. I got involved in the management of the service, the strategic direction it was taking, and also some of the direct delivery of the service. I was quite vocal (OK, very vocal) about what was happening and probably a real pain for the people on the other side of the table. However, we worked together for several years to try and make things better for everybody. Sometime after these events, one of the people with whom I was arguing a lot of the time publicly commended me for being a *critical friend* of the local service and stated how important it was to have partners and stakeholders who would bring challenge and perspective. I really appreciated this and was humbled by the man's deference and sentiment.

What I particularly like about community organizing is that it brings together those who might think they have little power and challenges those who take their power for granted. If we are to engage policymakers effectively, then we have to get to the people that have power. In the context I am talking about, there seems little point being prophetic to the wrong people. My research suggests those doing Christian youth work and work with young people are more likely to be interested in engaging with policymakers than those doing Christian youth ministry. I understand why this is the case: the former types of work are probably more impacted by policy – particularly policy directly relating to youth work and services for young people. However, I think it regrettable that those doing Christian youth ministry are not more motivated to embrace those wider dynamics of their ministry relating to the common good of society. For example, I met a Christian youth minister recently who worked in an isolated rural area. She worked in a church, discipling the Christian young people, and had little contact with anyone or anything outside of her context. Other service providers had no contact with her and she none with them. She said the world just carried on, and she let it go by. She acknowledged this was not ideal, but said it was how it was. I fully understood where she was coming from and we had a very fruitful conversation, but I left feeling somewhat dissatisfied with where she was at and the lack of impact her work was having on the wider community. As I have indicated before, I think we can and should do better than this – for all our sakes.

Even if we try to do better, success is not guaranteed. The policymakers that many Christian youth ministers tend to engage with and influence are officers of church institutions: these institutions need prophetic challenge too. However, as one research participant said, this is not always easy. They told the following story:

> Being 'political' is not simply about government or being interested in parliament. 'Politics' is everywhere, office politics, church politics etc. A few years ago I initiated a petition to try and save one of the national posts in the Church of England . . . over 1,000 signatures and a load of questions asked in General Synod . . . ultimately it was not successful. However, the 'powers that be' were made uncomfortable and made to think about their decision making . . . sometimes that is the best we can do.

Irrespective of whether it is secular or religious policymakers we are seeking to influence, the challenges of prophetic engagement are the same. For example, we may have to play the long game and invest many years of work in a particular domain or relationship. I have spent much of the last 15 years endeavouring to get policymakers to recognize the spiritual side of life as a component of well-being. I have done this not just because of my Christian faith beliefs, but because I consider spirituality a human development imperative. Some policymakers give the brush-off and I have received many standard letters of reply from some, had my questions left unanswered by others and had my emails ignored by yet others. When presented with a challenge, some power-holders say, 'Prove it'. Parliament did this recently when it examined the value of youth work; workers were effectively told to go away, do some research and prove their worth to society.[6] Other policymakers might seek to stall and delay on a particular issue even though they know that the argument made or evidence presented is not on their side. A case could be made that the 14-year delay about the skate park in my village I talked about in Chapter 2 fell into this domain. Others seek to engage you, but on their terms and for their purposes. This happened to me recently when I took part in a process to frame how youth work outcomes were shaped and positioned. I was very critical of the shortcomings encompassed within the proposals. When the final framework publication was launched, I noticed my name appeared in the document. It thanked me, along with several others, for giving my time to help shape the framework. *Prima facie*, this was a nice gesture. The only issue was that they had ignored all my input. It looked as if I'd endorsed what they had written, when I hadn't.

I have also experienced other policymakers who have endeavoured to marginalize those who make representations to them. Because of the faith aspect of my youth work this is a particularly common experience. The macropolitical culture is better than it was, but there is still suspicion of faith-based work. More than once, it has been implied to me that Christian youth work is not proper youth work and, therefore, the opinions of those doing Christian work are not important. Some policymakers seem incapable of accepting that someone with a strong faith can do excellent work with people of all faiths and of none, without needing to ram their faith down everybody else's throats. Yet other policymakers, I am sorry to say, act deplorably. They lie, manipulate, rip you off and do everything to protect their position and diminish yours (for legal reasons I had best not give examples about this or name names). Of even more regret is that some of these policymakers work for church institutions.

Despite all these challenges, I remain convinced that we have to engage with policymakers. The many disappointments that come with this engaging are compensated for by the joys that result when a policy or decision is changed and a difference is made in people's lives.

Prophetic responsibilities

Whether it is relating to policymakers or addressing the many wider issues and narratives Christian-motivated workers encounter, there is

---

6 See House of Commons Education Committee 2011.

a need to be prophetic, persistent and stay courageous. If we want a better world, we have to engage those with power and prophetically speak into matters impacting our work. We need prophetically to pave the way, creating space for workers and young people so they can flourish. As Miroslav Volf reminds us, Christianity is a 'prophetic religion' (2011, p. 78). I wish to underline again that I am not exclusively talking here about the prophetic utterances favoured by those from a charismatic or Pentecostal Christian tradition. I am talking about a way of being that emerges as we get close to, and serve, a living God: a life that is counter-cultural and akin to the one Jesus lived, one that fully represents that ambassadorial role Paul talks about in the second book of Corinthians (5.20); one that is salty, full of light and delivering hope. This approach carries responsibilities.

There is a responsibility to be an effective witness for God. Christian-motivated work needs to model what shalom looks like. It should be good news for those young people who are poor and it has to speak out for those who have no voices. It needs to embody all that God is, and faithfully represent the gospel in all its dealings. Workers cannot stand idly by and passively hope things will miraculously change or get better for the young people they work with. While appreciating there are not enough hours in the day to fight every battle, there is a responsibility to at least fight some. We need prayerfully to choose which battles to fight and how and when to fight these. Prompted by God's Spirit, we need to remember 'our struggle is not against flesh and blood, but against the rulers, against the authorities, against the powers of this dark world and against the spiritual forces of evil in the heavenly realms' (Eph. 6.12). This sentiment might explain why Jesus chose not to avoid paying the temple tax (Matt. 17.24–27). As the son of God he was exempt from paying tax on his Father's house, but in order not to cause offence he opted to pay it – miraculously with a coin from a fish's mouth. Of late, I have chosen not to join campaigns about modern-day slavery. I have opted not to fight for the rights of the homeless, or lobby about the extortionate rates of interest charged by pay-day loan companies. This is not because I don't think these issues are important. It is because I have chosen to prioritize and campaign about other things: the youth service, education matters, unfair cuts in welfare, young people's rights, and church cuts in youth work advisors, to name but a few.

When we take our prophetic responsibilities seriously we risk getting into trouble. Being a representative of God in the public square means taking on those principalities and powers. A worker in my research described what this was like for them and the young people they worked with:

> It is very difficult to bring up many issues in youth work, as assumptions are easily made about the sort of person you are – even if you are simply discussing the issue. I can imagine sharing your considered opinion on some topics, however considerately one might do so, could potentially jeopardize your employment or liberty. So how young people themselves are meant to have the confidence to do such things without severe repercussions is beyond me.

This is a difficult one. Many workers in my research said they felt constrained by the attitude of their employers and often these were said to be churches. It is unfortunate the very powers that should be backing Christian-motivated workers often become the powers against which they end up fighting. We spend far too much time in FYT supporting youth workers who are damaged (usually avoidably) by their churches. My only advice regarding this is to follow the leading of another research participant who said they would 'invite involvement from a foundation that . . . starts in love of people, love of God and love of the created order'. If we are to speak out, act prophetically and choose when and how to do this, then we need to be motivated by this sense of love. We might be angry and full of righteous rage, but we must not forget that it is the love of God and our neighbour that bookends all we should be and do. Being prophetic is about pointing people towards something that does not currently exist in their world-view, lens or framework. It highlights injustice, ushers in alternative ways of being and doing, reorders the micro and macro stage and creates places and spaces for the marginalized to prosper. Most importantly, it points to God as the pioneer, author, perfecter and finisher of faith (Heb. 12.2) and life. Christian-motivated work should aspire to do the same, taking its prophetic responsibilities extremely seriously.

Criticism and how to handle it

There is no doubt that politics can be a bruising business. When faith and politics are bought together, in the name of righteousness, then the bruising can be painful. Jesus said, 'Blessed are those who are persecuted because of righteousness, for theirs is the kingdom of heaven' (Matt. 5.10). Taking on micro and macropolitical powers and principalities is rarely done without a price being paid, but, as Ann Morisy argues, 'community ministry cannot claim to be rooted in the gospel if it does not engage with the principalities and powers . . . associated with earthly oppression' (2009, p. 68). The price impacts our personal relationships, our health, our finances and our standing in the community. I am not sure it necessarily amounts to the type of persecution Jesus had in mind when he delivered the Sermon on the Mount, but the cost should not be under-estimated. I don't think we are really persecuted in the UK. We might be mocked a little and at times restricted, but not persecuted in the manner I believe Jesus foresaw. Clearly people in lands further afield are persecuted. In some countries, doing politicking gets you arrested, tortured and sometimes killed. Thankfully, we do not have to endure this in the UK. However, we need to be mindful that at a practice level there will be conflict and we need to develop strategies to handle it.

I have been hurt by some of the criticism I have received. Sticking my head out and voicing my opinion has not always gone down well. Challenging the vestiges of Christendom's approaches to politicking – by rejecting appeasement, politeness, endorsement of the status quo and fighting for rights, seeking radical reform and combatting the abuses of institutional power – risks upsetting not only elected politicians, but also those embroiled in benign churchmanship practices. At times, being a dissenter is lonely. It has often left me feeling vulnerable and sometimes there have been despondent feelings as I have questioned – 'I am the only one?' 'Why does no one else care?' 'Why isn't everybody protesting about this issue?' A personal pity party all too easily ensues – rather like that one described in Chapter 2 involving Elijah and the solitary tree. Workers in my research talked about feeling 'hopeless', 'tired', 'angry', 'stuck' and 'drained'. When we are feeling like this we have to do what I talked about in Chapter 2; first and foremost we have to trust God. Experience suggests there are some other things we can do too.

- We need to remember any criticism directed at us is probably not a personal attack – it is more likely an attack on and conflict with our ideas, not us as individuals. See past the person criticizing you; it's probably not a conflict with flesh and blood, even if it seems like it.
- Try to avoid being oversensitive. The idiom 'water off a duck's back' can teach us much. Meekness is an underrated quality that Jesus highlights (Matt. 5.5). Meekness is not about being weak and

pathetic, but about developing an inward grace of the soul that is focused on God. When this is fully developed, it puts worldly things in perspective and literally enables us to 'inherit the earth' (Matt. 5.5) without being crushed in the process.

- Find people who support your politicking. They don't have to be people who always agree with you, but they do need to be people who believe in you and believe in what you are called to be.
- I mentioned earlier the role of critical friends. Make sure you have some of these who can challenge your perspective and keep it rooted in godly reality. I find a partner or spouse does this quite effectively.
- We need continually to recognize that the cost of making things better is often a price worth paying. Several people in my research mentioned Emmeline Pankhurst, the suffragette who paid a very heavy price in order to ensure that women got the right to vote. The cost for her was high, but the result changed the place of women in society.
- In a similar vein, we need to keep our ultimate goal at the forefront of our minds and spirits. If being a prophetic dissenting voice, advocate for others or local activist builds shalom, develops the common good and creates a better world, then I can be encouraged to put up with a bit of personal criticism from time to time.
- We can draw further encouragement that Paul talked about his 'light and momentary' troubles being inconsequential compared to the glory of what awaited him (2 Cor. 4.17). He was imprisoned, beaten up (so many times he can't remember and nearly to death), half-drowned (three times), whipped (five times), sleep-deprived, in constant danger of being robbed and often cold, hungry and thirsty (2 Cor. 11.23–27): perhaps a little criticism is not that bad in comparison.

It might sound a bit arrogant, but I think some people are critical simply because they don't know any better. They criticize out of ignorance, fear and their own limitations. For example, I have encountered churches who don't think anything exists outside of the box of their Sunday meetings. I have met people in schools who think the type of education they offer is the only form of learning with real value, and I have met many, many statutory youth workers who consider voluntary sector and faith-based work second class compared to that delivered by local authorities. When faced with this type of criticism we can but hope to be gracious, if not even a little smug and grateful for the greater knowledge, understanding and experience we quietly entertain.

Criticism is just one personal barrier that hinders effective politicking work and needs to be overcome. In the next chapter I explore some contextual and cultural barriers that also exist and consider how we might best address them.

Things to think about

- Think about Van Gogh's perspective frame. What do you see when you look at the world through whatever framework you use to gain perspective? How does this make you feel, and do you need to realign any perspectives you may have?
- What are the key values (be as specific as you can) underpinning your work? Can you see evidence of those values all the way through your work and approach? Think about what you do, how you do it, how you treat people, what results emerge from your work and how others perceive you – are your values ever present?
- To what extent do you agree that Christianity is a 'prophetic religion'? What stories, examples and evidence can you think of where you have been prophetic in your work? Is there an area of work/life that you would like to be more prophetic in? How might you go about achieving this?

What can I do?

- Write out on a series of cards some of the things to do with politics, social policy and/or Christian youth work and ministry you would like to know more about – one thing/issue per card. Don't make these too abstract: try to connect them to the world the young people you work with exist in. Put these cards in a diary and bring one out each month. Each month, commit to exploring the 'thing' or issue as part of your 'rehearsal' time so that you are better equipped to improvise about the matter in hand next time you talk to a young person about that thing or issue.

- If you work with a regular group of young people, why not do some community organizing-based activities. Identify with the young people what issues are important to them that need changing. Find out who has the power to change them and go about seeking to realize that change. Input into an internet search engine 'Alinsky's rules for radicals' and use the rules he came up with (there are 13) to inform your organizing and actions.
- Some personal criticism is unjust or unwarranted and the negative effects of it can be long-lasting. Spend a moment or two in silence thinking if any criticism of your politicking from the past is holding you back from doing more (or more significant) politicking in the future. If you think it is, write down what the criticism is on a piece of paper or Post-it note. Put the paper or note in an envelope or small paper bag. Then shred it or burn it, praying – as you do it – that God will release you from anything unwarranted that is restricting you.

6

Barriers to Effective Work

For if I was really to take the teachings of Jesus seriously, would I not, sooner or later, find myself being dragged before the authorities? If I were to really live a life which reflected the subversive and radical message of love that gives a voice to the voiceless and a place to those who are displaced, if I were to really stand up against the systemic oppression perpetrated by those in power, then would I not find myself on the wrong side of the law makers?

Pete Rollins, writer, lecturer, storyteller and public speaker

If you are to be on the side of the voiceless, you must confront the vested interests of the rich and powerful who have constructed a justification for their wealth and power.

Tom Cullinan, Catholic priest

Papering over the cracks and other sins

During my lifetime, I have lived in two houses with subsidence. In one house the subsidence was caused because the property was not built very well; it had poor foundations. In the second house, it was caused by the deep underground mining works associated with the area. In both houses, my DIY skills were kept busy. I kept filling in the cracks that appeared in the walls as the subsidence took its toll. My intensive crack-filling didn't stop the subsidence; it merely temporarily made things look slightly better and 'papered over the cracks'. What was needed was something to stop the subsidence movement at source. The first house was subsequently underpinned, and this stopped the movement. Underpinning is where engineers dig beneath the foundations of a property and effectively put in new, reinforced foundations. This house was put on a different footing and the cracks stopped appearing. The movement in the second house wasn't fixed and couldn't be fixed. The cause was hundreds of metres underground as the old mining works of the area impacted the strata and geology and caused the ground to resettle and periodically move. The previous owners of the property had been compensated for this, but the cracking continued.

'Papering over the cracks' is a common metaphor for life and our world. Its popularity doesn't mean it lacks relevance regarding approaches to politicking. In this chapter I consider some of the barriers preventing Christians doing politicking as part of their youth work and ministry. I do this because I think our politicking needs to challenge current ideological barriers as well as respond practically to the needs before us. We need to influence current ideology in order to change the macro-political context – if we don't change it at its core then we risk just papering over the cracks of a broken and unjust system. We need to put what we do on different foundations so that we stop the cracks appearing.

Some of the barriers I consider are particularly relevant to those doing Christian youth work, some youth ministry and some to those doing work with young people. Others are universally relevant. Different barriers exist in different contexts. I explore some theoretical concepts and examine the impact these have upon work and ministry. These barriers have embedded approaches that conspire against young people, the kingdom of God, and the common good, and contradict Nazareth Manifesto aspirations. They need to be seen for what they are – sins (personal and corporate) – and responded to accordingly.

Generally speaking, I am not in favour of using long, complicated academic words to explain something. Doing so can be a bit alienating and come across as unnecessarily pompous. However, some of the barriers I talk about in this chapter are heavyweight issues and I want specifically to name them in order to ensure we engage with them at the level required, helping us begin to address and overcome them. I will be exploring barriers associated with political socialization, symbolic violence, isomorphism, commodification, militarization and debates about secularism. If you are not sure what these words mean, don't worry as I will explain them all. My motivation is not to confuse, but to help us get to the real issues so we don't end up simply repairing cracks and continually filling holes.

Self-defeating socialization

Socialization is the way culture is transmitted from one generation to another and can take place in families, peer groups, religious bodies and communities. It can be imposed by laws, the media, education processes and race and gender stereotyping. Socialization is not about learning the facts or methods of how something is or is not done. It is more about how individuals develop a world-view that becomes habitual and culturally cemented, thus ensuring they become *good* citizens within their context. Political socialization is a process that introduces the norms, rules and behaviour by which individuals (particularly children and young people) participate in the political system of a nation or specific context.

What is important to note about political socialization is how young people learn political values, beliefs, attitudes and behaviours from what academics call *agents* – people and things that determine them. These *agents* influence and transmit what it is that is expected and create a set of perceptions impacting behaviour. Young people tend to imitate what agents convey to them; how a child or young person is politically socialized tends to impact how they do politicking in later life. The way a young person learns about *what*, *when* and *how* in their formative years influences how they behave in their adult years. I was socialized into believing certain types of shops and supermarkets were for rich people and others for those less well off. I was socialized into believing people wearing certain clothes were dangerous and should be avoided. I was socialized into thinking a good job would set me up for life and I would do that one job for all my working life: how things have changed!

I am not suggesting everybody will adopt all the partisan political beliefs of those socializing them, but the whole point of socialization is that it introduces people to a way of being that is meant to be imitated. Voting loyalties and views may ebb and flow over time, but the way we do politicking is a consequence of how we are socialized. There was an incident near to where I live illustrating this *way of being*. During an election campaign, one prospective MP was heckled by a disabled man with a megaphone. He went over to the man and a scuffle ensued. The police got involved, and each party blamed the other. The prospective MP, speaking via the media, demanded an apology because, he said, 'this is not the way we do politics in Britain'. I am not sure who appointed him the arbitrator of how we do our politics, but he clearly felt a *way of being* standard had been ignored.

As children grow older, they may rebel against what they have been told and change political allegiances,[1] but I strongly believe the pattern of socialization imposed upon them will win out and they will ultimately conform to societal norms and patterns. People might be anarchic punk or goth teenagers, but there are not many 30- or 40-year-old punks and goths. Elected politicians wear formal clothing. They have to be seen to be tough on crime and opposed to mass immigration, and

---

1 For a discussion about this, see Dinas 2013.

they always need to be politically correct. Socialization wins out. Politically, I was socialized during my childhood and adolescent years into believing British lives are more important than the lives of people from other countries. The death of a British citizen or British soldier, especially if they were white, was considered far more important than anything else. I have been politically socialized into believing the 'first past the post' democratic electoral system is the best (if not only) way of effectively governing a country. Other systems like proportional representation, tribal governance, demarchy (a form of government in which the state is governed by randomly selected decision-makers who have been chosen from a group of eligible citizens – a process it might be argued was used in Acts 1.21–26, when Matthias was chosen as a new apostle) and one-party states are frowned upon by most UK analysts. Even though we have had one recently, the UK does not appear to welcome governments built upon coalition and cross-party consensus (they have been very effective in lots of countries: Germany and Denmark, for example). Media commentators nearly always portray such governments as second best compared to governments elected with an outright electoral majority.

We see in history far more stark and frightening examples of political socialization and how it has worked. In Nazi Germany, Stalinist Russia, Communist Romania and more recently, despotic North Korea, we witness how children and young people are targeted by policymakers and indoctrinated into systems of belief, cultural norms and societal expectations. This approach perpetuates oppressive ways of government. The consequences for anyone daring to step outside of these norms and expectations are extremely severe.

American young people often swear 'allegiance to the flag' in their high schools. While this is significantly less draconian in nature than the examples above, it is, nonetheless, political socialization. While students can opt out of doing this (as long as they do so quietly and without showing dissent), the process is rooted in embedding conformity and patriotism. While it might not be too popular to say so in America, for the Christian, this socialization process is a significant barrier. Swearing allegiance to anything risks subordinating God (Matt. 5.34) and puts the believer in the unenviable position of trying to serve two masters (Matt. 6.24).

The British are socialized by cultural expectations into being polite, keeping our opinions to ourselves and keeping our heads down. This cultural landscape is not a very fertile field in which vibrant and healthy politicking can grow. Furthermore, it does not encourage challenging the status quo. Generally speaking, UK young people are explicitly socialized into believing that democracy is the only way to be governed, that the rule of law must be respected, and capitalism is the only economic mechanism appropriate for society. More subtly, we are socialized into believing that politics is done by those who are well educated, we must respect those who know better than us and we should participate in politics, but only so long as it doesn't contradict the explicit beliefs of democracy, respect for the law and capitalist hegemony. The problem with this is that the way culture introduces politics to young people results in a somewhat benign 'take it or leave it' dynamic. All too often this embeds powerlessness into the political learning of young people. In short, they are brought up believing things are done in a certain way, and they have to play by these rules, learn the ropes of compliance and endorsement or risk being marginalized. They learn that they can't really make a difference in the world, certainly not one that is contradictory to the all-prevailing dominant democratic, law-abiding and capitalist narratives. It is perhaps no surprise young people work out that something is very wrong with the world and how we do politics and that the mechanisms we have for correcting this currently don't appear to work. Consequently they give up on these types of models, don't vote and instead focus on social media approaches that do not demand conformity and socializing compliance.

One of my PhD research participants drew attention to the sense of powerlessness he had experienced. He highlighted and described how socialization barriers inhibit political involvement:

> I think there's always a fear . . . when something becomes driven by a government or a party because it gets drawn into the political machine of party politics. People are . . . thinking, 'You know what, it's just another government spiel and we'll just get on with what we're doing and maybe we can tap into some stuff and get some funding and some money and hopefully some people will listen but actually the machine will . . . keep doing what it's doing.' It's hard . . . to not have that level of scepticism . . . you know people's mistrust of politics, politicians.

I think these perspectives are very sad and sobering. I also think they need to be challenged and changed; not because my participant was incorrect in his analysis, but more because this scenario is politically unhealthy. There are lots of 'Keep Calm and . . .' posters and cards about in gift and art shops. The original 'Keep Calm' rhetoric was produced by the UK Government in 1939 as a pre-Second World War morale booster. I hate them! I don't think we need to keep calm, I think we need to get angry, bloody angry. We need to mandate our young people not to be calm and carry on, but to take issue with a broken world. We need to equip them to stop, look at what is happening and take action to put it right. We need to disciple Christian young people so they are empowered into challenging injustice and poverty, authentically responding to the call of the kingdom of God. In politicking terms, keeping calm and carrying on will achieve nothing. Continuing to politically socialize young people in the way we currently do simply perpetuates the current system of elitism, oppression, inequality, injustice and marginalization. Political socialization controls people. We need to ask what we are politically socializing people into and – when introducing a Christian perspective – question if this way of politicking is fully reflective of what God calls us to be and do.

Socialization can begin at an early age in the Church. Over many years, I have witnessed a particular pattern of approach that has sought to socialize young people into a predetermined way of being. In Christian youth groups, Sunday school type contexts, family services and events there is often a desire to involve children and young people. However, what ends up taking place simply socializes them into a particular way of behaving. Young people are often asked questions as part of the 'teaching'. Observation suggests the facilitator/teacher often only wants one specific answer in response to the question asked. For example, I recently observed one facilitator do a really interesting session about prayer. She had a series of letters from the alphabet that formed a mnemonic. The mnemonic was PASTA – she hadn't noticed it could have been TAPAS, but we will set that aside for now. The children were asked what the letters might stand for regarding prayer. The children involved came up with some great words and ideas and gave fantastic answers, but these were not what the facilitator wanted. She had specific answers in mind and only validated these answers. This type of approach is routinely common, and when embedded into a pedagogical approach, it all too easily becomes controlling, socializing and educationally self-defeating. It can reduce critical consciousness levels among young people and undermine confidence to be creative. It inhibits young people stepping into the unknown. It is an approach many churches carry on into adulthood. This is evidenced by the way those with priestly power rarely have biblical question-and-answer style sermons and teaching sessions in Sunday services that offer a more broadening socialization model. They prefer restrictive socializing monologues with no right of reply. I think this is spiritually and politically disabling.

There is one further socialization barrier I wish to highlight regarding the work of the Church and Christians. Some of the churches I have been part of and worked with over the years stress the importance of unity. Using Psalm 133 as a socializing tool, they enthusiastically and assertively encourage people to be of one mind because then God will be pleased and deliver blessings. I am in no doubt this is theologically important, but all too often what those with the power mean by 'unity' is that you have to agree with them, do it their way and, if you don't, you are somehow outside of God's purposes. In effect, you are socialized and spiritually bullied into compliance and conformity dressed up as unity. We need to set the bar higher than this and not settle for this diminished understanding of unity. Indeed, the word 'unity' is not explicit in the original Hebrew text – the word is about 'all-togetherness'. So, let's have togetherness, but let's have it focused on something aspirationally monumental like the Nazareth Manifesto, the Beatitudes and/or the Great Commission. Let's pursue the greater goals and possibilities of serving God, not the lowest common denominators that cause no offence to anybody. This means we have to deal with different views, perspectives and counter-arguments. We need to stand in the shoes of others and ask what the *missio Dei* looks like to them. We mustn't settle, accommodate and be reconciled just for the sake of it. We need adventure, pioneering and resolutionary approaches that engender change – unity and togetherness does not need to be dumbed down. If we are going to be a united people, let's do the word justice and unite behind a great cause.

No stake in society

I was really shocked. The poster in the Amsterdam city-centre shop window boldly stated (in English), 'Do Not Trust Anyone Under 30'. How dare they say this? I was appalled. It was only when I took a closer look at who ran the shop that I began to understand. The shop was the headquarters of a youth organization, and the poster was clearly designed to be provocatively ironic. Phew. Regrettably, however, there are those who don't trust anyone who is young. They might not say this explicitly, but this sentiment is communicated by all sorts of messages sent by adults about young people. For example, we don't let more than two young people into some shops. We get annoyed if they make noise in restaurants, become nervous if they gather in groups on the street, restrict what they can input into church ministries and, as noted, won't let them vote until they are adults. I even heard about a representative of one well-known Christian summer camp describing detached youth work as being for young people who don't like other young people or adults.

Society as a whole, the media, politicians and even Christians often marginalize young people in the way they talk about them, engage them and empower them to be involved in decision-making. Typically, adults – as the dominant group in society – decide what is best for young people and deny them the power to do so for themselves. They problematize the issue of youth, seeing young people as problems to be solved. Society only appears to acknowledge young people as a significant demographic when they have problems. Young people are often demonized, criminalized and excluded from many of the most basic aspects of life, community and decision-making in twenty-first-century Britain. The political (both macro and micro) outworking of these approaches is rooted in what is called a *deficit-based* approach. That is, it seeks to help young people and addresses their needs and problems, communicating that they are in some way lacking, failing, deviant, helpless, without aspiration and incapable of helping themselves. Adults create a dependency culture presuming young people cannot come up with solutions and responses of their own. Over time, the inevitable consequence of this approach is disempowerment. This has led commentators to declare that young people, particularly many marginalized and black young people, 'have no stake in society' – a phrase that came to the fore after the riots in England in 2011.[2] It is often politically expedient to marginalize young people in election campaigning by exaggerating their problems and poor behaviour, while appealing for the adult vote. Consequently, young people risk ending up disconnected, disillusioned and disenfranchised. Challenging these sentiments was behind the 'Labels R4 Jars' campaign I referred to in Chapter 3.

The phrase 'anti-social behaviour' has now become a common part of the English political language. Adult politicians vociferously campaign on the premise that they will crack down on such behaviour; with the target of their vehement agitations being, more often than not, young people. Once in power, politicians pass laws controlling and limiting the activities of young people. As noted, they then have to

2 See Singh et al. (eds) 2011; 2012.

continually remind us of the problems young people have, experience and are. They consequently keep them under surveillance, arguing they need to protect society from any evils that might possibly result from young people's behaviour and problems. This narrative has to be perpetuated by politicians so they are seen as the solution and young people the problem. They campaign on the basis they know the best *what*, *when* and *how* for young people. They electorally keep real power from young people because giving it up would potentially undermine this oppressive narrative.

The French philosopher Pierre Bourdieu called this type of oppression 'symbolic violence' (Bourdieu and Passeron, 1990). As the name suggests, symbolic violence is not actual physical violence. It is about how culture, language, socialization patterns and ways of doing things enable one group to have power over another. It is how relationships, systems and structures of power form, exist, are sustained and develop so one class or group of people dominates another to the point that the dominated group effectively (often unconsciously) becomes complicit in allowing themselves to be dominated. In effect, one group subordinates another with hidden agendas, cultural mechanisms and dominant narratives to the point where the subordinated group accepts these as normal, joins in being subordinated and takes their lot for granted. In short, adults with political power dominate young people, and the young people come to accept this as normal. Physical violence is not needed to ensure dominance, because symbolic power and societal structures convince the group being dominated that their domination is natural. One research participant commented on this regarding young people's awareness of what was happening to them regarding social policy: 'I think young people need to know how they are affected by legislation, so that they can be engaged. However, some young people live with a thought process that adults make decisions and they do "it".' This is where the issue of our philosophy, values and pedagogy are really important. If we get these dynamics wrong and don't address these barriers, we can misuse symbolic power and be symbolically violent towards young people.

We can see this type of symbolic violence at work in the story I told in Chapter 2 about the congregation that would not allow young people to become full voting members of the church. I am sure this church would have talked about being 'one body' (Rom. 12.5) and that everybody was 'created in God's image' (Gen. 1.27), but they had allowed adult dominance to become normal in their setting, somewhat undermining these prerogatives. I talked to some of the young people in the church, and some of them had got used to being subjugated. They had accepted they had no voice and behaved accordingly. They deferred everything to adults and saw it as a bonus if they were allowed to participate in a youth service or similar. The adults had effectively vanquished the young people and the young people became passively complicit in this.

I saw symbolic violence at work in my banking career. Men were in charge. All the bank managers and decision-makers were men; the men had the nice offices and the company cars; the women did the administration tasks, cashed people's cheques and answered the phones – usually passing on any queries demanding action to male colleagues. Both men and women accepted this was how it was. Male sexist attitudes asserted this dominance and the women were complicit in maintaining their subservient roles by seeing it as normal that they would make the coffee, do the filing, not take banking exams to empower themselves, and never aspire to become bank managers. In contrast, young men like me were pushed into doing exams and were fast-tracked to decision-making and managerial roles. Thankfully, towards the end of my career in the bank, this began to change. However, the violence continued during the period of change. I can sadly still remember accusations (mainly made by women) that the women who became managers had done so by 'sleeping their way to the top'.

Symbolic violence can be seen in community work where professionals or agencies parachute in to help 'at risk' communities and young people. They often label such communities negatively (by calling them, for example, a deprived area, sink estate, destitute or blighted) and the people in these communities embrace these labels and accept their lot as being what the label says. I witnessed this in my north Nottinghamshire work. These labels violate and denigrate people. They can be made to feel they need external professionals to support and sustain them. This undermines local relationships and community empowerment. These labels attract funding to these areas. The dilemma, however, is that the labels need to be maintained if the funding is to be maintained. Over time, the risk is these labels are normalized and symbolic violence becomes embedded in the culture. I witnessed this in the church I was part of. People from outside the area came into the area to help the 'poor and needy' local people. Local people were rarely empowered to become church leaders. I know this was the case because I was one of the people who parachuted in and (unwittingly) became complicit in perpetuating the violence. I wish I had known then what I know now.

Another research participant illustrated how this violence creates a dependency culture and oppresses young people: 'Most of the disadvantaged young people I work with have an entitlement mentality and feel they are victims of the system.' They then went on to talk about the challenges of trying to change this, noting that 'trying to instil a sense of personal responsibility into them regarding themselves is hard'. These comments act as powerful reminders that if change is to be realized, we need an approach that is centred on breaking the bonds of symbolic violence by focusing on empowerment and working towards the common good, rather than dependency and individualism.

Challenging symbolic violence in a culture that upholds it so vehemently is manifestly difficult. Christian-motivated workers need to create spaces and places enabling action to emerge, building shalom, not oppression. This will help the kingdom of God develop in those spaces and places. A participant in my research helpfully reminds us that 'everyone's born with potential and everyone's born with skills, you know, and everyone's born with the opportunity and can achieve something'. He contrasts this with a symbolically violent culture conspiring against young people 'as a vast part of society wants to write a lot of young people off'. If the symbolically violent culture is to be challenged, then youth workers need to promote the potential of young people and strive to combat any notion that writes young people off. This means challenging those with power and those who see everything in terms of money and economics. I recently met Father Tom Cullinan, an elderly Catholic monk from Liverpool. He was one of those people that oozed the presence of God – wisdom dripped from his being and nectar came out of his mouth. He said, 'If you are to be on the side of the voiceless, you must confront the vested interests of the rich and powerful who have constructed a justification for their wealth and power.' If Tom is right, then we need to do this for our young people and resist the pressures to conform to what powerful vested interests are doing to them.

Pressure to conform

The idea of 'paradox' appears frequently in this book. It is a word I find myself repeating to describe much of what is happening in our contemporary political and social policy world. In this section, I focus on one particular paradox that threatens the very existence of Christian-motivated workers. It is the paradox that in a world of perceived freedoms, unlimited potentials and vast individual choice possibilities, the pressure to conform to be and do what everybody else is being and doing is perhaps greater than it has ever been. The pressure might not be explicit or appear menacing, but it is pervasive, subtle and potentially disastrous.

I believe it is good to adapt, change and respond to the contextual environments we live and work in. Indeed, if we don't, we risk ceasing to be relevant. Throughout history, Christians have changed and adapted as they have sought God in the world. They have worked contextually, developed contextual theology and responded contextually to social, economic and political challenges. However, as we adapt and change we must ensure we do not lose sight of our core values, missional calling and kingdom ethos in any adapting and responding we embrace. If we get this wrong, we can quickly find ourselves in a place and position we never intended to end up in: what strategists call *mission creep*.

Liam Purcell works for Church Action on Poverty. He has written an evocative piece about poverty, illustrating how our values can so easily be corrupted and consumed by those values dominant in society.

Most people accept the powerful stories and attitudes about poverty which are reinforced every day by politicians and the media. They believe that people only end up in poverty by mismanaging their budgets; that there is widespread benefit fraud, and that benefits are generous; that work is an easy route out of poverty; or even that there is no real poverty in this country.

These narratives about poverty connect with people because they are all attached to a coherent worldview which promotes a particular set of values. They say that it is important to be self-reliant; that dishonest people will take advantage if we are too generous and trusting; that we should support politicians who will be cautious and prudent with public spending; that wealth and poverty are the natural results of moral or immoral behaviour. It's easy to promote these values because in recent decades our society has become more consumerist and individualistic, and tends to measure everything in terms of economic worth. (Purcell 2014)

Christian-motivated workers need to consider which narrative they are attached to and which particular values their world-view promotes. The challenge comes when we are seduced into compromising righteous values for those less virtuous. Some narratives appear to make sense on the surface even though deep down there is a suspicion they might be corrosive.

I accepted the invitation to speak at the headline Christian youth work conference, because it was what people who do what I do are supposed to do. It also pandered to my ego somewhat. I convinced myself that it would highlight the work I was involved in, add value to those present and further illuminate the focus of the conference. Deep down, I remained aware that keynote speaking is not what I am best at, and I don't think it particularly works as an educational tool or reflective practice process. It is certainly not very participative or empowering for those listening, when they have no right of reply. My input was satisfactory, but as soon as I had finished speaking, I knew I had compromised on what was important to me. I felt void because there was no chance to have audience questions and interaction; I despaired that there was no reflection time for people to weigh what I had said. The next keynote speaker was already introducing their talk before I had got back to my seat. I was full of regret. I had morphed into something I don't think I really am.

It was the late Tony Hart who made famous the plasticine animation figure 'Morph'. Morph is a figure who continually changes his shape not only to suit his environment, but also to become other characters and objects as well. He changes his profile and mimics other shapes and characters. He becomes whatever he wants to become. For those not familiar with Morph, an online search will tell you more and direct you to some television clips of him in action. I have seen lots of Christian youth work and ministry that has morphed. Sometimes this has been a genuine contextual response to a changing environment or need and sometimes a response to a move of God's Spirit or a new sense of direction and calling. However, I have also seen work morph for none of these noble reasons. I have seen work, and workers, morph for reasons to do with money, a need to survive, the distractions talked about in Chapter 2 and, regarding the specific context of this book, when political initiatives and social policy changes make it prima facie expedient.

I talked earlier about neoliberalism. This ideology and its outworking in policy has opened up opportunities for Christians to do more contracted work with young people, especially in local contexts. My research and work up and down the country has given witness to many Christian organizations and churches filling voids left by cuts in government spending. The general demise of youth work provided by local authorities and the move to more commissioned approaches has, in theory at least, provided greater opportunities for Christian-motivated workers to have more of a say in *what*, *when* and *how* youth work in local communities is done. Christian charities and churches can now operate services they could rarely run before. I have met workers whose organizations have purchased community centres for £1 because the local council can no longer afford to maintain and run them. I have met other workers whose churches now run the local youth centre on behalf of the community. One worker in my research captured both the opportunities and challenges presented by the current context:

> The reality is that lots of charities have suffered with the recent cuts so Big Society [a government initiative] offers opportunities but it also can push you in terms of where your mission is. So actually, 'Yes there's lots of opportunities for X, Y and Z, but does that still fit with your mission? . . . Who becomes your master then?' Actually what's quite nice about being funded by grants and churches is that you are able to stay true to that – that ethos and mission a bit more . . . If you're chasing the funding then that's a shame because you may end up in a place you didn't want to be. So I think . . . 'if I get in bed with these people what's it going to mean, what's it going to put on us as a charity, how's that going to be worked out?'

Long before the current political context emerged, two clever academics, Paul DiMaggio and Walter Powell (1983), took a science word, 'isomorphism', added another word to it – institutional – and applied it to the world. They determined that *institutional isomorphism* happens when one body, organization or company becomes a market leader, dominant influencer or recognized entity within a sector with the result that all other bodies, organizations or companies in that sector adopt similar practices in order to gain the same advantages as that leader. For example, over the last two decades, many supermarkets tried to become like Tesco because, at the time, they were the market leader and dominant force. Others have tried to emulate what companies like Apple, Amazon and Google have done, because they have each become the dominant force in their sectors, and their way of doing things has become the industry standard.

In the context of this book it is the social world of youth work that is being considered and it is the way government operates that has become the dominant standard. This is not necessarily because the government way is the best, or even most prolific; just the most dominant regarding expectations, approaches and services. Many bodies like charities and faith groups have adapted who they are, what they do and how they behave, in effect, to be like government wants them to be. It is argued this puts pressure on bodies like charities and churches to adopt certain ways of being to fit government values, methods, priorities and policy. Ultimately the constraints such bodies are put under means they risk losing their distinctiveness, ending up the same as other providers as they compete for resources and political power.

DiMaggio and Powell identified three distinct isomorphic threats. First, they said organizations risk being *coerced* into doing certain things in order, for example in Christian youth work, to get funding, profile and influence. Second, they might be seduced into *mimicking* and copying the behaviour of state and other institutional bodies. In Christian-motivated work, again for example, there has been a big drive to more formally evaluate services and measure outcomes, copying the shape of work done by local authority colleagues and funders like the Big Lottery. Third, they suggest that, over time, *normative pressures* impact what is done. In other words, the state sets the tone for what is considered 'normal'. Currently in youth work, government considers it normal for everybody to want to expand, scale up and replicate their work. They talk of financial returns and value for money and they zealously delineate between notions of success and failure. In my investigations these isomorphic threats were found to be commonplace. One interviewee went so far as to say, 'We just end up responding to other peoples' [that is, other organizations/policymakers] needs' rather than doing the type of work originally intended.

Based upon my own research findings, I consider there might be a fourth, or at least a significant extension of the third, isomorphic pressure. This involves the use of *presumptive language and ideology* whereby a dominant narrative is imposed and assumed as both the most positive and obvious way to proceed – a notion widely evident in current governmental rhetoric regarding the language of business and the market. In my recent work I have read many government documents, policy papers and consultations, where they tell me the world has changed. They talk about the need for charities and faith-based organizations to deliver government services. They presume charities will want to do this and impose a view that this approach is the only common-sense way of doing things. They continually talk about how in this *new changed world* the focus should be on business planning, cutting costs, trading, picking which competitor will get support, enterprise, contracting and greater competition. None of these things are why charities get involved in what they do. The interesting thing for me is that the world regarding these matters has changed, because the Government has changed it! They have imposed a presumptive ideology determining that this is the way of doing things. This threat is institutional isomorphism at its most stark. It also seeks to embed a new form of neoliberal marketization, and I fear those charities who succumb to it will lose sight of what they are all about.

In my PhD findings I discovered Christian youth work organizations with strong branding and public relations dimensions, competitive approaches to obtaining work, the desire to have political influence in order to enhance market positioning, with enterprising and philanthropic skills being employed and expansionist agendas seeking a greater 'market' presence. I discovered that some youth work organizations have fully engaged and are prospering in this new world. I also discovered that others have engaged, initially prospered, but then fallen by the wayside and subsequently closed as they fell out of favour or government priorities shifted, leaving them stranded. Getting involved in this new world and succumbing to institutional isomorphic pressures to conform may mean we end up being something we never intended becoming. One youth worker I met said she had 'sold her soul' in order to get funding. The warning signs are clear: don't be complicit with the agendas of those who may undermine what you are called to be and do.

Avoiding being part of the problem

Amy Hall is just about to complete her degree in youth work. She described the current approaches of government towards work with young people and communities as 'like trying to fix bone china with a hammer!' I thought this was a very apt description of the current socializing, symbolic violence, institutional isomorphic and policy threats to youth work and young people. If these threats are to be addressed, workers (and those organizations they volunteer or work for) need to take a step back and appraise what they should and should not be doing in the current context. They need to take steps to ensure they are not complicit in barriers, ideologies, policies and narratives that undermine what they seek to do. They need to avoid being part of the problem.

Pete Rollins is one of the deepest theological thinkers of our time. I repeat his words used at the beginning of this chapter, reflecting that if we are to remain loyal to our callings, stand up against those who oppress, then in all likelihood we will end up in conflict with the authorities.

For if I was really to take the teachings of Jesus seriously, would I not, sooner or later, find myself being dragged before the authorities? If I were to really live a life which reflected the subversive and radical message of love that gives a voice to the voiceless and a place to those who are displaced, if I were to really stand up against the systemic oppression perpetrated by those in power, then would I not find myself on the wrong side of the law makers? (Rollins 2008)

Our current political system means we might not literally be dragged before the authorities, but we are destined to be in conflict with power-holders and decision-makers if we address the barriers preventing effective work and politicking with and for young people. Andy Burns was one of the people who helped in my research. He is Chief Executive of East to West, an innovative Christian youth work organization. He is also a voluntary sector representative on panels that commission youth work for the local authority. After one such panel meeting, Andy was advised by a council colleague that by using the information gleaned in the panel meeting he 'could beat them [those currently bidding for work] by undercutting them in future years'. When Andy said these people were his friends and that he wouldn't want to do that, he was informed by the council colleague, 'That's the way the markets have done it for years.' This sentiment grieved my spirit and says so much about the selfish nature of our world. Andy went on to say that he had 'lost friends' as a result of the commissioning process. They have now become competitors fighting each other rather than colleagues who used to work towards the same objectives. He ended our conversation by saying he feared he could end up being something he didn't want to be if he became like them.

Andy's story illustrates how the policy context has changed of late. Where previously those youth workers across the community might have worked together for common good aims, they now compete against one another for funding and work. Andy chose not to get involved in this type of political process because he believed it contradicted his values. He was not open to the *what, when* and *how* being orchestrated according to such disingenuous values. He didn't want to be part of something he saw as highly problematic that was becoming a barrier in his relationships with colleagues. This has put him in conflict with those who hold power.

I admire Andy and think he has made the correct call. However, I am also aware that other Christians see the current economic context of cuts to youth and welfare services as a fantastic opportunity for the Church. This is what one worker from my research said:

> In the absence of government running things, funding things, getting involved in things at a local level, a vacuum will develop. What is going to fill that vacuum? If churches, you know, play this right, they could really, really fill that void and be the central focus of their community again, as historically they have been, but perhaps not so in recent times. There is a great opportunity for them to look at what has been taken away and see how they can fill that gap.

I am all for seizing the day, but I think we need to be cautious that we don't rejoice at the demise of other initiatives and of those who serve young people, and we don't become so opportunistic that we further erode common good principles. Andy's story and this youth worker's comment about 'playing it right' are illustrations of how the ever-increasing dominance of neoliberal ideology has gathered momentum and come to proliferate. Christian-motivated groups do not exist to deliver government policy. At times their aims might be the same as those of the state and therefore it might make sense to help deliver services. However, this should never constrain the prophetic call of God's people to challenge what is unjust in society and be an irritant to policy-makers acting in ways that undermine shalom. Those Christians who do venture out into the community and into the marketplace will be 'like sheep among wolves'. They will need to 'be as shrewd as snakes and as innocent as doves' (Matt. 10.16) as they encounter neoliberalism. I think this neoliberal barrier is one of the biggest facing Christian youth workers and those who work with young people; it is a barrier that is an affront to the values of the kingdom of God.

Neoliberalism has put a price on everything. Everything that can be commodified is. Commodification makes that which is up for sale vulnerable to exploitation. Recently, we have seen how a price is put on helping a young person find a job and a place in higher education. A new social construct has emerged predominantly seeing young people as economic units being prepared and educated for work. Branded goods and rampant commercial interests dominate the spaces and places young people occupy. From drinks machines to advertising banners, designer clothing to sponsored television programmes, we observe that consumerism is the god of the commodified landscape young people live in. In more extreme cases, we see how young people are trafficked for financial gain and have witnessed others being sold as slaves and for sexual pleasure. Young people should not be for sale. They are human beings with an eternal destiny, not economic units transfixed into being money-making zombies.

While there have been calls for a return to a philanthropic age, these have too often been presented in commodification rhetoric rather than compassionate concern. Philanthropy has become seen as a way to reduce bureaucracy and speed up response times, rather than challenge injustice and inequality. In Victorian times, philanthropy responded to destitution in the absence of any state welfare provision. This led to the development of a welfare state. However, we now see the beginning of the dismantling of this, which risks returning us to a position where the destitute are reliant upon charity – foodbanks being a good illustration. It appears inescapable that profits are coming before people, with society as a whole potentially paying the true and full social, environmental and spiritual costs of the future. Policy decisions are no longer based on compassion or made according to what is needed, but upon undemocratic ideology and the views of accountants.

In my view, turning young people into commodified beings and operating services for young people according to market-driven ideologies could not be further from the heart of God, a heart that sees each young person as uniquely precious and valuable, not something to be traded. Markets do not liberate people and bring political freedom. They enslave people. God does not enslave people. Markets do not bring about equality and develop the common good. They make a few people rich. They do not facilitate human flourishing, but rather engender a culture of individualism and greed that distorts and conspires against the collective whole. As I have shown in earlier chapters, this is not what God desires.

It might be argued that the market has worked in keeping food and fashion prices relatively low – although hard-pressed dairy farmers and those in the supply chains of Bangladesh, for example, might not agree. But the market has spectacularly failed regarding utility companies, train providers, care homes for the elderly, the 2012 London Olympic security arrangements, access to work providers and ensuring appropriate housing for everybody. The market here has failed to deliver on price, service and virtue. The market doesn't work when there are only a few providers present in the marketplace. Markets simply encourage a race to the bottom on price, as we observe in how youth services are currently being procured and put out to tender. In the marketized landscape, the agenda will always come back to what can be measured: what offers best value for money; how we can get more for less; and ensure a profit is made in the process. This might be acceptable for those making cars or televisions, but it is no way to treat human beings. Hardly a day goes by without news of some scandal, abuse of privilege, case of fraud, failure of delivery or simple incompetence and lack of public accountability by a neoliberal appointed service provider. Despite these failures, neoliberalists continue to idolize the market approach, seeing it through rose-coloured spectacles, or perhaps spectacles with pound signs on them.

In the national context I work in, I notice that fewer and fewer youth work providers are being awarded government and local authority contracts and work. The same names of organizations appear over and over again: the big organizations with high profiles and the people who 'play it right'. Increasingly, many of these organizations have no previous history of doing youth work, yet they get the grants, the work and the money. This is perhaps no surprise because this is what happens in the market; oligopoly and monopolies are the inevitable consequence of unrestrained capitalism. For many Christian organizations this is a barrier preventing them getting involved even if they wanted to. I recently applied for some grant money from a government scheme for some work with at-risk young people. I wasn't successful on this occasion. This was disappointing, but it happens. What was horrifying was to see the language used announcing who had been successful. These applicants were called 'winners'. I concluded I must be a 'loser' in what is becoming a neoliberal market-driven competitive nightmare.

If we are to challenge this barrier, perhaps we simply need to be even more counter-cultural than we are currently being. In FYT we try to be as generous as we can be with our time and resources. We often give things away or reduce the price of them to help others access them and do effective work with young people. We are not in it for the money. We seek to be a blessing not a barrier. We are aware that others share these values: we have to seek them out and work with them to counter market-driven ideologies that threaten to erode work with young people.

Andy Burns has stuck to his guns and he continues to do so. He seeks to work with others, Christians and otherwise, who share his values. Recently he told me how he engaged in a conversation with a school about a specific piece of work to help serve young people. He informed the school that he would walk away from the negotiations if the work compromised his organization's values. 'Principles', he stated, 'were more important than profits.' The school was taken aback by this. They told Andy how unusual this was in the modern era. They said this was not how many of the agencies they worked with positioned themselves. They also told Andy how delightful it was to talk about *values* rather than simply making money. They unreservedly gave Andy's organization the piece of work.

Shalom-makers in a military world

In Chapter 3, I referred to the Beatitudes. Space does not allow a full debate about the Beatitudes, but I consider one of them here because it particularly helps critique work currently done with young people. It is the one about being peace- or shalom-makers.

We live in a world full of conflict, violence and war; the world our young people grow up in and a world they participate in. How they perceive such conflicts and how they determine the best way to resolve them will be of significance to those of us who are getting older. There is a lot of rhetoric, propaganda, financial spending and cultural practice stacked against being a shalom-maker. This barrier against pursuing peace needs to be addressed if contemporary Christian-motivated work is to build shalom effectively. In the version of the Beatitudes in Matthew's Gospel, Jesus says 'Blessed are the peacemakers, for they will be called children of God' (Matt. 5.9). The sentiment here is that kingdom-builders will not only refrain from conflict and war, but actively seek to create peace and shalom. They will be shalom-makers. Contemporarily, some elements of the Church all too easily become complicit in endorsing a paradigm of God that supports militarism and war, especially if they can label it a *just war*. In this matter, it appears the politicized Christian youth work and ministry that does occur has little resonance with Jesus' ministry, but more to do with supporting nationalism and jingoism. This further illustrates the tensions Christian young people might experience between being citizens of the kingdom and citizens of the UK.

On one of the walls at the church I attend is a memorial to the fallen victims of world wars. It is headed up, 'For God, King and Empire'. I am very saddened that fellow believers have dovetailed the idea of war, royalty and God together and woven them into the psyche of their religious beliefs. I am doubly disturbed that this has been visually displayed for many decades, continually conveying this message to every young person who walks past the memorial. This approach is far from that set out in the Beatitudes.

This militarization of UK society appears to have accelerated after 9/11. In population size, the UK is only the twenty-second biggest country in the world yet the fourth biggest military spender. We spend more on defence than any of our European allies. We have regular parades of troops through our streets. Irrespective of how our soldiers morally behave, they are universally portrayed as 'heroes'. There is a growing militarization of young people in some schools and churches. In 2008, the UK Government published the *Report of Inquiry into National Recognition of our Armed Forces*. It said it wanted more young people to join military cadet forces in schools, saying, 'There needs to be a cross-Government consensus to ensure that as many children as possible can benefit from these opportunities' and that 'it should be a priority to do everything possible to encourage more Comprehensive Schools and City Academies to apply for their own Combined Cadet Force'

(Davies, Clark and Sharp 2008, p. 11). Government is now funding this expansion. The report went on to say that understanding of the military should be taught as an 'essential' part of the citizenship curriculum (p. 12), that serving members of the military visit the schools they attended, and that schools build links with senior military personnel. The National Citizen Service further extends the idea of regimented approaches to educating young people about citizenship. There is a multimillion-pound scheme to bring a military ethos to secondary schools and introduce a military-style discipline approach to education as more ex-soldiers are trained in the Troops to Teachers programme. These approaches do not sound much like shalom-making to me. They look more like an attempt to get our young people to sign up for the military forces. This was highlighted by one worker in my research who decided to speak out about this in their local context:

> We had guest speakers at an event to explore militarization in schools; as part of a pacifist church, young people can often feel isolated with the increasing militarization in schools. This session offered them skills and support in dealing with this issue.

Disempowered young people from poorer communities appear to be specific targets for military recruiters. Such young people are drawn to the military as they can 'hold guns', be 'seen as heroes', 'give up their lives for the country' and find purpose. This socializing rhetoric can be a way to make those that are marginalized feel empowered, but in reality it risks corrupting them, leaving them disempowered when they eventually leave the forces. I frequently witnessed this type of scenario in the former coal-mining areas of Nottinghamshire.

Young people are nearly always involved in Remembrance Sunday services and parades. Scouts, Guides, Boys' and Girls' Brigades and Cadet Forces often march into church on such occasions. I am sometimes disturbed by these services. We should remember the fallen and the sacrifices made, but not glorify war and our victories. We need to remember UK losses and the losses of others in equal measure, truly 'loving our enemies'. The Germans and Italians who died in the two world wars, the Argentinians we killed in the Falklands War, and the Iraqis, Afghans and Taliban we have killed in more recent times – all these people were part of God's created humanity. They were members of families too. If we are to honour what Jesus taught us and truly love our enemies, we need to pray for the families of our enemies as earnestly as we do those of our compatriots.

I am sure there is an argument to be made that a strong military presence helps support peacemaking, but we have had many decades, if not centuries, of strong military defences, and peace – let alone shalom – has not been realized. I find it hard to imagine the Jesus who told Peter to put his sword away, 'for all who draw the sword will die by the sword' (Matt. 26.52), would be in favour of, for example, unmanned drones firing Hellfire missiles at people, Brimstone missiles being launched at enemies and R36 Satan intercontinental missiles being aimed at us by Russia. I think there is a clue as to the spiritual source of these weapons in their names. I am also sure advocates of the militarization approach to work with young people point to team-work skills, personal discipline and fitness as the benefits. However, these outcomes can be achieved without the need to wear uniforms or carry guns. The type of shalom-making I think needs highlighting is that typified by the work of The Feast project I referred to earlier in Chapter 3.

The folks at The Feast have a concern for the peace and well-being of the communities they live in. They want to equip others to be shalom-makers. They work tirelessly to bring together young people from different faith backgrounds, especially Christians and Muslims. They do this by valuing the humanity of each and respecting different faith positions. This builds cohesive communities, reduces suspicion and develops a sense of mutuality and the common good. I have never really understood why Christians and Muslims do not work together more – they potentially have much more in common with each other than with their secular compatriots. No doubt extremists from both religions distort and undermine authentic expressions of the two faiths, but at the heart of both belief systems is the quest to be peaceful and to find peace. This quest needs valuing and embracing. Atrocities, terrorism, war and state-backed agendas dressed up as 'Muslim' or 'Christian' do not come close to representing the orthodox positions of either authentic Islam or Christianity. If we are to address the barriers of violence and conflict, shalom-makers like The Feast set a good example for this.

In the last 12 months, the Christian youth workers and ministers who took part in my survey work have run sessions about the local community (69 per cent), education (40 per cent), justice (37 per cent), racism (31 per cent) and the economy (27 per cent). However, only 11 per cent of them have run sessions exploring the subjects of defence, war or the military. I find this very surprising and politically alarming given the increasing militarization of work in our schools and the fact that we have continually been at war now for over a decade. It appears the vast majority of Christian-motivated workers are ignoring this subject.

Perhaps it is just too difficult to begin discourse on this topic for fear of what might result if we really started to unpack the implications of shalom-making for the UK, a country with such a long history of military conflict and violence with and against others. Notwithstanding this, I hope we at least attempt to get the shalom-making subject on the agenda and Christian-motivated youth work curriculum.

Can we 'do God' and politics?

I always find it interesting how a chance remark can become part of common use in a language. This is what happened in 2003 when Alastair Campbell, Tony Blair's then director of strategy and communications, told a journalist, 'We don't do God.' For those not familiar with the story, Tony Blair was being interviewed for a magazine article. During the interview the journalist asked Mr Blair about his faith. Mr Campbell, anxious to conclude the interview and avoid any discussion of the matter, interrupted the journalist and uttered the now infamous phrase, 'We don't do God.' The question about Mr Blair's faith remained unanswered. I have already highlighted some of the potential tensions between God and politics, especially regarding the idea of citizenship. In this section I seek to explore some wider questions about these two dynamics. I discuss how 'doing God' and 'doing politics' in youth work often conflict with each other, specifically considering how this can be a barrier to effective work with young people.

I would like to see the divide between secular approaches to youth work and faith-based ones close. If politicians don't or won't do God, then this divide can be a barrier. In order to overcome this barrier, attempts have to be made to build bridges with politicians and find common ground with them. This same reasoning applies to statutory or secularly orientated youth workers who might not find any sense of immediate resonance with those workers from a faith background. Neither faith-based nor politically located approaches need to be exclusive. We cannot afford to get bogged down in exclusive claims about faith, truth and dogma. I believe our response should reflect that of another research participant who said:

> There has to be at the centre of any religious engagement within politics [the belief] that 'loving our neighbour' trumps our desire to be taken as special or treated separately. We must engage within the acceptance of the UN Charter of Human Rights and realize others have the right to believe and live differently than we do.

Politicians, theologians and academics have been arguing of late about how welcome *people of faith* are in the public arena. There are those who argue we are now a secular society and, as such, religion should have no place – or at least no special place – in public matters. Others, like the highly influential German sociologist and philosopher Jürgen Habermas (2010), think that there is a growing awareness that something is missing in secular approaches and consequently suggest faith and religion might once again have a place in public discourses. People like Habermas say we are in a post-secular context, as people of faith and those who don't do God are more and more working together for the common good. This coming together of different political and faith-based groups is called rapprochement,[3] and it is about both sides *giving and taking* for the benefit of everybody.

Suspicions of, and a lack of understanding about, what Christian-motivated work is and does are widespread among those working outside a faith-based perspective. On one level, such suspicions are perhaps justified, given examples of poor practice, child protection scandals and concerns about the motivations behind faith-based work. This is a barrier Christians need to address if they are to engage with those not appreciating faith. Secularists and humanists might be confused over the words and language used to describe what work is undertaken; the confusion over what is meant by *youth work* and *youth ministry*, for example. We cannot ignore the fact that there are some Christians who are over-zealous about certain things and fanatical about particular issues. This can alienate secular colleagues. We are rightly accused of sometimes manipulating young people in our practice (particularly in evangelism and worship settings) and this raises ethical dilemmas for others. However, many of the problems (and perceived or actual deceitful practices) associated with the intentions of Christian-motivated work can be alleviated. Faith-based work appears more welcome in a post-secular context than it was. If these barriers can be overcome then I believe we can successfully work with those who don't do God as well as those who do.

Hopefully this will be a two-way process and those who share our passion for working with young people will do all they can to engage with Christians, even if they don't share the same faith beliefs. Christian-motivated workers might not always understand the language of the local authority, and secular bodies could do more to help here. I

---

3 For an academic discussion about rapprochement, see Cloke and Beaumont 2012; Cloke, Thomas and Williams 2012.

remember how confused and alienated I felt when I first got engaged with local authority politicking: trying to get to grips with all the acronyms, committee names, policy initiatives, outcome expectations and assumptions felt really bewildering. This barrier needs to be overcome if partnerships are to develop effectively. Those working from a secular perspective also need to acknowledge that faith is our primary motivation and driver. Faith can't just be a passenger as we travel together and work for the benefit of others. However difficult it might be for others, faith needs to play an active part in how we do politics, not just be a term used to describe the churches and organizations we work for.

Conversely, Christians might need to address suspicions they have of secular bodies, politicians and policymakers. My research indicates that there is a suspicion among Christian workers that they may be seen as a cheap alternative in challenging economic times. They suspect that while those in power perceive faith groups as having the ability to contribute to policy, community and social action agendas, they really want them to do such work because it costs less than the alternatives. This suspicion is often held by those of us who work in hard-to-reach communities. Christian workers often feel like a cut-price alternative to deliver work where others have failed. This politicking barrier needs to be addressed.

Furthermore, bad experiences of politicians can lead to cynicism and disillusionment among Christian-motivated workers. The following story from one research participant illustrates how barriers can develop and take hold:

> I got involved in a national flagship attempt to introduce localism into politics in an attempt to counter extreme disenchantment with politics at a Borough Council level. It gave an interesting insight into the way that councils act like ancient fiefdoms with elected and unelected and well-paid officials acting to maintain position against a national government scheme by denying us the majority of the funding that had been given to them to be allocated to the scheme. After many months of meetings, the withering contempt and deception of those who draw Council Tax payer's money as salaries became apparent to every one of the dozens involved and the scheme foundered.

Notwithstanding this, politicians and policymakers do often recognize the civic and civil value and resource of Christian-motivated social action work and welfare provision. The problem is they also recognize the potential for faith to cause social division and conflict. The more critical factions fear faith-based work will proselytize and promote narrow and restrictive pedagogies that counter social cohesion agendas and inhibit genuine partnership approaches. Christian-motivated workers need to work hard, both to alleviate concerns that they are simply out to indoctrinate young people, and overcome barriers that prevent joined-up working.

My opening comments of this book highlighted how we are schooled not to talk about religion and politics in the UK. I have noted how we tend not to focus much on politics in our work with young people. I have also noted in my PhD research how some Christian-motivated colleagues have become so accustomed to working with secular colleagues and young people that they forget to (or deliberately choose not to) talk about faith and God at all. The challenge here is defining what being 'Christian' and what 'doing Christian-motivated work' actually is. The danger is we can end up 'not doing God' either. No doubt this comes down to pragmatism and is perhaps an unforeseen consequence of the inevitably diminishing place of faith in the post-secular public space whenever rapprochement occurs. I am not saying we have to mention Jesus every 30 seconds or continually quote Scripture, but some passing acknowledgement beyond our good works might help young people and others connect with the God we serve in a more meaningful way. Maintaining a spiritual/secular divide in our work is a barrier to holistic work and this needs addressing if we are most effectively to serve young people while maintaining our own integrity.

Perhaps the fact that we have made religion such a private matter in the UK has made it harder to go public with our faith in a manner supportive of the common good approach. However, I believe we need to change this and find ways of being faith-filled, intelligent contributors to youth work policy and practice. Historically, Christianity has shaped British politics and society. Politics has also interfered with and shaped particular expressions of Christianity – we only have to look at how the Church of England is governed to witness this. Our laws, employment practices, health services, education policies, funding regimes, perceptions of royalty and general societal attitudes are all the product of this ongoing interrelationship. I believe Habermas is correct in thinking something might be missing if we just have a secular approach to public life. He didn't always think this and has fairly recently changed his mind over this issue. I suspect there will continue to be long-standing debates as politicians and predominantly secularly orientated governments try to shape faith groups to support their objectives and faith groups try to influence policies and government to dovetail with their aims. Hopefully, some common ground can be found as this process unfurls. In believing we need to stand up and change how things currently are, I am not arguing for Christianity to be a special case simply because our historical roots relate to faith. I am arguing for a level playing field and equal place at the politicking tables. My hope is that we are welcomed at these tables because we are good at what we do and because we effectively serve young people. The fact that we are Christians, or from any other faith background for that matter, should not disqualify us from having a place at the table, be this in local, regional or national contexts.

I think we can do God and politics. It would be naive to think this is easy, and many barriers still need to be overcome, but experience suggests it is possible. If some of us Christians can set aside our dogma, endless debates about gender and sexuality and practice more often that love we talk about, then maybe those who do not share our faith beliefs might be a little more inclined to value our work and be less suspicious and fearful of our motives. You never know, we might even learn something from this rapprochement. That would be a welcome outcome from doing both God and politics.

Things to think about

- In what ways have you been politically socialized? How has this impacted how you relate to politics today? Do you have the same or similar beliefs to the people who brought you up (parents, grandparents, step-parents, guardians) or are your perspectives different from theirs? In what ways have your views changed over time?
- The 'Things to think about' section at the end of Chapter 5 asked you to identify your own values. Some of Andy Burns' work and politicking values were 'non-negotiable'. He didn't necessarily seek to impose these values on other people, but they helped frame what work he undertook and how. Which of your values are 'non-negotiable' and how does identifying them shape your work?
- Is there any symbolic violence going on in your world where you are either a perpetrator or a victim? What can you do to address this and challenge it?

What can I do?

- Find some old birthday, greetings or Christmas cards and fold them inside out – so the picture can't be seen and you have a blank fold facing you. If you can't find any cards, simply fold a new piece of card in half. On each blank face of a card, write one of the barriers preventing you from realizing your politicking ambitions. When you have done this with as many cards as you require, line all the cards up on a table – so they look like an obstacle course. Now take a small teddy bear, action figure or other character and place this in front of the first card. This figure now represents you! With a colleague (or on your own if easier) determine how you are going to go through the obstacle course, addressing each barrier as you go. Make a note of what you need to do in order to overcome each of the barriers. When you have finished, look at all the notes you have made, prioritize them and turn them into an Implementation Plan so that over time you address the barriers identified.

- One way of bridging religious and secular divides is to get to know people who have other beliefs. Why not arrange to have a cup of coffee with an atheist, a humanist or a youth worker or politician from another religious background. Have no agenda other than relationship building and listening. I am an introvert and don't find this sort of thing easy to do, but during my PhD studies I did it several times and found it hugely rewarding. Enjoy, and see what God might do.

- Audit the work you do (or better still ask the young people to do it) and examine the extent to which it is 'peace- and shalom-making'. You could do this audit at a personal level (that is, do the young people and workers have a sense of peace?); a group level (is there peace and shalom to be found in the group of young people?); a community level (what about shalom between the young people and the local community?); and a global level (what evidence is there of peace- and shalom-making in your work that relates to the wider world?). Publish or present your audit report and raise action points to improve your shalom-making.

7

A Mandate for Future Work

We need to entirely reshape our society so it works for the common good, not just the interests of the 1 per cent, and we need to do this using just one planet.

Natalie Bennett, Leader of the Green Party

My starting point for politics is that whoever is in government, be it locally or nationally, should prioritize the protection and care of the vulnerable and weak in our communities. There is clearly a need for citizens to do this more for their own families and neighbours, but government ought to make sure no one is left uncared for.

Matt Perry, youth worker

Shaping principles

Having vision and dreaming dreams feature strongly in seeking and serving God. There is always the hope that God could, can, might and sometimes does make everything better. Believers have the certain hope that one day it will all be better (Rev. 22). In the meantime, we have to work with the reality that the world is not all it might be. In the waiting, the dreaming, the hope and the struggle we consider what we could do better, which of the many challenges we might seek to address and how we might prioritize our prayers, energy and resources. In this chapter, I set out principles to help Christian-motivated workers do politicking better; principles enabling better responses to those who need help; principles helping prevent future problems; and principles supporting a reshaping of society for the common good.

As already identified, we could do some things better and other things differently to improve our politicking. It is very easy in politics to criticize others: I have done my fair share in this book. The advent of social media mechanisms and online petitioning has added to this propensity. While these platforms have proved an effective way of venting frustration, there is a danger this is all they achieve. In essence these platforms risk making us commentators about – and consumers of – politics rather than active participants who offer genuine mandates and alternatives to those currently on offer. Most social media and online petitions are *one-way* means of communication. I seek in this chapter to clarify some of the more communal alternatives that I consider will help put right things that have gone wrong.

I describe what I try to do and encourage others to do. As an addition to the theological lenses I have already described, the principles discussed in this chapter are some of the propositions I passionately believe will help take Christian-motivated work forward into a more active, coherent and transformative politicking future. I establish how reading Scripture politically changes our understanding of God, the world and our response to it. I explore how shifting the emphasis of our work from an individual focus to a collective one helps ensure everybody is better off. I propose how adopting more collective principles and aspiring to the common good embed a more equitable and sustainable model for future youth work and ministry. Finally, in this chapter, I cement these mandates within the need to ensure young people are at the heart of all that is undertaken in ways that help their development and liberation.

Reading Scripture politically

The internet has opened up vast vaults of knowledge to aid our understanding; this is exciting. We can now read different translations of Scripture side by side without the desk collapsing under the weight of a dozen Bibles. We can examine the original Hebrew and Greek words used by the writers of the Bible at the click of a button and discover the subtleties of what the words originally used might mean. For people wired like me, this is exciting stuff, as it deepens understanding and knowledge of, and about, God. If we have the time and desire to go beyond English language translations of the Bible, we discover new nuances, different possibilities, challenging contexts and renewed convictions. I have endeavoured to highlight these throughout this book, embracing what the original writers said and might have implied, rather than simply conveying what translations communicate.

I suspect we all read the Bible in different ways and, at times, with different motives. We might read it as an historical document, instructions for living, or an account of God's character, values and way of being. We might read it systematically, critically, devotionally, for encouragement or in times of grief and anguish. We can read translations aspiring to be word-for-word accurate. We can also read translations that endeavour to capture the thoughts and intentions of the original writers of Scripture. We rarely read the Bible neutrally; it is almost impossible to do so. Academics call this process *eisegesis*; where the text is interpreted through one's own ideas, bias, presuppositions and agendas. If I have an eisegesis, it is to encourage people to read the text politically. However, I implore people to understand both the original words used and the thoughts and motives behind them.

I believe we need to delve into the text, understand the context and politicize – or more accurately, re-politicize – how we read Scripture. Our current orthodoxy has resulted because history has impacted and strongly influenced our understanding. Many writers in history have spoken on theological matters, but such ponderings have often gone alongside political insights and motivations. The political goals of people like Locke, Luther, Wycliffe, Hobbes, Machiavelli and the afore-mentioned King Henry VIII and Martin Luther King cannot be ignored. Some of these influencers have erred towards favouring the state as a means of supporting their own intentions and others towards more radical expressions of church as a challenge to the state. I think it is time we read Scripture politically for ourselves, and we need to do this at two levels. First, we need to grasp fully the significance, historical context and meaning of the political stories, illustrations, metaphors and prophetic words found in the Bible, rather than split out individual verses as weapons to be used selfishly. Then we need to contextualize these and ask what the contemporary political significance of the story, psalm, passage, parable or prophecy is.

For example, if we explore understandings of the parable of the talents (Matt. 25.14–30; Luke 19.11–27), we might be surprised by what we find. I have deliberately chosen this passage, because its meaning is contested. Convention suggests there are two principal interpretations of this parable. The most widely taught interpretation in western consumerist societies is that perceived through a capitalist lens. The basic analysis is: invest what you have and make more with it; use it or lose it. In other words, we must use what God has given us in ways that multiply our resources, gifts and talents for God. Then God will grant us a reward in heaven. The 'hero' in this interpretation of the parable is the servant who makes money. The 'villain' is the servant who does nothing with his money. The 'master' in the story is perceived to be God. Neoliberals like this interpretation.

The second interpretation is the contextual (and thus potentially more traditional) view. This interpretation argues that accumulation is wrong and no way to build honour in society, because any wealth is accumulated by taking it from others. The 'hero' in this interpretation of the parable is the servant who is happy with what he has and stays content. The 'villain' is the one who accumulates wealth. The 'master' (it is argued) is Archelaus, the son of Herod the Great, who was intensely disliked by the people (see Matt. 2.23). Advocates of this interpretation (and I would be one) argue it would be obvious to Jesus' audience that the parable was referring to Archelaus. He was a nobleman who went off to Rome on a journey to seek Caeser's support. He was a hard, exacting and unyielding nobleman/king (Luke 19.22), who had, according to the Roman historian Josephus, killed 3,000 people in the Temple. Advocates of this view argue the description and actions of the 'master' do not reflect the character and grace of God. They also argue that it is inconceivable that having commended and granted salvation to Zacchaeus for giving away his wealth (Luke 19.1–10), Jesus would immediately follow his encounter with Zacchaeus by telling people to go and acquire wealth and talents. Neoliberals are less inclined to like this interpretation.

If the first interpretation is correct, then Jesus contradicts all that happened regarding Zacchaeus. The second view is consistent with his Nazareth Manifesto and the teachings found in the Beatitudes; the first is not. Furthermore, Luke's account of this parable immediately precedes Jesus riding into Jerusalem. If the first interpretation is correct, it would not have been unreasonable to expect Jesus to have modelled the wealth-creation agenda of this interpretation. We might have expected him to have travelled into Jerusalem on an opulent golden chariot. He didn't. He got on a stolen – sorry, *borrowed* – donkey and rode into Jerusalem. Jesus turned what was expected upside down.

Reading Scripture in this contextual manner enables us to tease out original meanings of Scripture. We can also read Scripture politically by standing in the place of those in the text who are poor, powerless or marginalized. Imagine, for example, that Jesus was washing your feet (John 13.1–17); you were tempted to eat with the pigs (Luke 15.16); or you were destitute, ostracized and ill, but had the courage to touch Jesus' coat (Mark 5.21–34). Throughout this chapter I refer to other Bible passages we can read more contextually and politically. I believe this will increase our theological understanding. What we do with this understanding is perhaps the more important matter. I cannot help but conclude that reading Scripture politically opens up new vistas of hope and possibility: it confirms that God is a god of justice; it illustrates that Jesus was political, and portrays economic, social and counter-cultural ways of living. I also conclude that if this is the case, we are compelled to act and be in conflict with the visible, oppressive and dominant narratives and anti-kingdom forces at work in the world today.

Collective responses

The parable of the good Samaritan (Luke 10.30–37) has many overt political messages contained within it: community development, racial inclusion, dealing with political enemies, valuing ideological opponents, being good neighbours, and health and welfare service provision. My FYT colleague John Wheatley offers further reflections on this passage. He encapsulates the type of thinking I contend materializes when we read Scripture politically. Transposing the parable to a modern context, John wonders, 'Who then goes back after the mugging incident and petitions for more street lighting, regular patrols, more effective policing and additional ambulance services?' The rural area where I live is about 45 minutes from the nearest accident and emergency hospital. How does this parable speak to the political provision of health services in my area? If badly injured in my area, the victim in the parable might well die before he reached hospital. Would anybody set up a street pastors group to prevent possible muggings in the future? Would anybody think about employing a worker to do some preventative work with the local gangs and muggers? These are questions demanding not only individual answers but also collective responses. These types of questions arise when we read Scripture politically.

My dream is that we can respond to the challenges before us in a much more collective manner than we do currently. Ultimately, I dare to believe we can work towards realizing social conditions that do away with the need for 'good Samaritans'. This demands making decisions that benefit the majority more than happens currently. A new settlement is needed that works more effectively for the 99 per cent of society, not just the 1 per cent. Academic and theologian Chris Baker highlights how any new settlement necessitates a restructuring of how we do things so that we are not reliant upon organizations like the Church undertaking all the work. He says:

> I am not opposed to the flourishing of enthusiastic local groups caring for those less fortunate citizens amongst whom they live and work. But we also need to generate genuine alternatives to the way society is structured, and the distribution of wealth and opportunity. New affinities or alliances between progressive people of all religions and of non-religious beliefs can create a genuinely progressive shared . . . society. (Baker 2014)

I mentioned earlier how developing a sense of symbiosis was important in the work of the Christian youth work projects I investigated.

Symbiosis is the long-term mutually beneficial interaction between two or more individuals or organizations. One of the ways of realizing a new settlement and beginning to restructure society is to work more symbiotically. Symbiotic relationships can be found in nature, where there is a long-term association between two or more different species that benefit each other. My favourite example is found in the symbiosis between the crocodile and the plover bird. The croc needs to keep its teeth and gums healthy in order to stay an efficient killing machine. The plover bird needs to eat meat to survive. So, they have done an ecological deal. The crocodile allows the plover bird to eat the meat from between its teeth and keep them clean. In return, the croc promises not to shut its mouth on the plover bird as it is doing the cleaning. The crocodile gets free dental treatment, the plover a free meal.

Politicking in this co-dependent and mutually beneficial way can be done by Christian-motivated workers. A simple example is provided by a worker from my research who said: 'Most of our successes have been at a local political level. Our work with local councillors has led to the regeneration of open spaces in our community. This has transformed safety and play for young people.' I suspect most workers and ministers do this quite naturally, but perhaps it can be done more intentionally and pursued as a deliberate and preferred method in order to build a collective outcome. Ian Tannahill, Head of Youth Work Development at the Blend Youth Project in Derbyshire, told me, 'We deliberately geared our work in such a way that the projects can't maximize their potential and their full capacity without partnership working. That's in the design brief and the DNA of what we're about.'

I found this positioning highly courageous and incredibly encouraging. What might the world look like if everybody worked in this way? What if everybody positioned themselves to be symbiotically dependent upon someone else for their survival and success? We would have many crocodile-and-plover-bird type relationships rather than destructive fox-and-chicken ones. I suspect the world would look somewhat different from how it does today. In my research, projects like Blend have moved their partnership work into the realms of genuine reciprocal symbiosis and mutuality which at times has resulted in the development of close personal friendships and furtherance of all parties' work. I dream that everybody would embrace this type of joined-up, collective response rather than one that pits providers against each other, causing service fragmentation and an overemphasis on short-termism. If this dream could be realized, we might begin to develop more of a collective *what*, *when* and *how*, rather than an individually orientated and evaluated one. Metaphorically speaking, this would potentially render the good Samaritan redundant.

If it goes well for you . . .

Throughout my Christian life, I have continually heard people pray for the nation. I suspect most Christians in most countries pray similar prayers. We pray that our land will be healed (2 Chron. 7.14) and that if Britain is broken it will be restored. The challenge for me is not just about praying the prayers – although this is a good place to start – but more how the sentiment behind the prayers becomes reality. In Chapter 2, I highlighted the importance of what Jeremiah said in just one verse, 'Seek the shalom of the city where I have caused you to be carried away captive, and pray to the LORD for it; for in the shalom of it shall you have shalom' (Jer. 29.7, Hebrew Names Version). If we read this verse through a political lens, we glean further revelation about what *might be* regarding a future *what, when* and *how*. I do not believe we can stand idly by and expect God to do everything.

Over the last few decades many western Christians have followed societal trends and seem to have done the very opposite of seeking the shalom and welfare of others. We have become very focused on that unholy trinity of *me, myself and I*. I wonder if we have prioritized our own peace and prosperity, neglecting the welfare and shalom of others. Pursuit of individual and self-centred well-being risks making us all worse off. It appears anyone can be blamed for threatening individual welfare: immigrants, the poor, the unemployed, Muslims, Eastern Europeans, gypsies and, too often, young people. This has had the effect of distorting what people think of these groups of people. For example, we have done some research in FYT among adults, and they consistently think young people's anti-social behaviour and rates of teenage pregnancy are much higher than they actually are.[1]

I would like to suggest that a better way of seeking shalom for young people, and for others, is to see them differently. To see them through the aforementioned lens of *unconditional positive regard*, preferring them, and endeavouring to ensure in every way possible that the future goes well for them. To see them as God sees them. If we can think the best of young people – expect good things from them, value, endorse,

---

1 See 'Labels R4 Jars, Not Young People', 2007, http://www.fyt.org.uk/v2/wpcontent/uploads/labels-r4-jars-not-young-people.pdf.

support, speak up for and cherish them – we might catch a glimpse of something very special. Jesus is the embodiment of this message and models the way we might go about ensuring the welfare and shalom of others. He healed, restored, forgave. He offered hope and possibility to those scapegoated and discriminated against.

As I hinted earlier, much of this idea of preferring others and seeking *their* welfare flies in the face of modern society and its overemphasis on individualism. God seems to be saying something quite different through Jeremiah – it's not about *me* and *mine*, but something much broader. I consider it is the job of the Christian-motivated worker to help create spaces and situations reflecting this breadth: welfare where needed, support where required, compassion in every circumstance and a praxis supporting the ideals of the Nazareth Manifesto. One worker in my research captured this eloquently:

> The more I have worked with young people who are vulnerable or living in high-risk situations or coping with difficult circumstances, the more I have seen the need for structures to provide support and security for those who life is tough on.

This seems to reflect the words of Jesus in Matthew's Gospel. If we read the narrative about the sheep and the goats politically (Matt. 25.31–46) – as a benchmark for social policy, for example – we might begin to glimpse a heavenly understanding of what welfare is all about. What Jesus says here is not simply a list of minimum requirements to inherit eternal life. It is a mandate about how to live a life of love. It is a policy descriptor about caring for our neighbours. It is a picture describing how believers can be conduits of good news for the poor and the outcome of fulfilling the Nazareth Manifesto. It puts right the *what*, *when* and *how*.

It might seem a bit counter-intuitive, but helping individuals flourish happens best when done as part of a collective response. Currently, much politicking and political campaigning is designed to appeal to individuals. Personal wealth, security and comfort are offered as enticements for votes. For flourishing to take place effectively in a manner that supports collective well-being, politicking needs to consider the type of multiple bottom line embracing social, ethical, spiritual, physical, emotional, educational, economic and environmental considerations. Decisions should not be made on the basis of *what will benefit me and mine*, but *what will benefit us all*. This approach protects the most vulnerable in society and prevents benefits accruing to just a few.

Ubuntu is an ancient African word and concept. It refers to the idea that humanity is a quality shared between people and realized in the ideal that a person can only be fulfilled because of who everybody is: a person is a person through other persons. If we are able to grasp that our humanity – and who we are, what we do and how we do it – is indistinguishably bound up in the humanity, being, function and activity of others, we have an understanding of *ubuntu* and the beginnings of a revised way of co-existing. If we acknowledge that we are who we are because of who everybody else is, we might begin to do our decision-making and politicking on a different basis. We wouldn't oppress others, because this would oppress us. We wouldn't marginalize certain groups in society or blame them, because we would risk being marginalized and blamed ourselves. Jesus didn't use the *ubuntu* word, but in commanding us to do to others as we would like them to treat us (Luke 6.31), he seemingly influenced this ideal.

In political theory, many philosophers and thinkers have wrestled with the ideas behind *ubuntu*. They did not use the actual word, but discourses associated with human interconnectedness and how this might best work for all have been at the core of many political concepts. For example, Émile Durkheim talked about *social solidarity* and what holds society together. More recently, Pierre Bourdieu and Robert Putnam have highlighted the concept of *social capital*, discussing how relationships and togetherness matter in building strong societies. After the 2001 riots and disturbances in England, Ted Cantle discussed *community cohesion* and how having a common vision and shared sense of belonging in a diverse society was essential if that society was to flourish. As a mandate for future Christian-motivated work, I believe all these ideas are important. We need to move away from individualism to give sharper political and theological consideration to shared perspectives and understandings, so all goes well for everybody. We need to stop being self-indulgent. In view of this, I give further consideration to the common good principle as an aspirational goal.

Common good?

The people of the world have tried a number of ways of governing and organizing themselves. There have been empires, dictatorships, royal kingdoms, democracies and republics. We have tried feudalism, communism, fascism, capitalism and religious fundamentalism as ways of being organized. All have been found wanting in some way.

Commentators such as Anthony Giddens (1994), Phillip Blond (2010) and Jim Wallis (2014) have all argued that the politics of both the Right and the Left have contained positive traits within them, but have ultimately let us down. We need a new way of being and being governed. Or perhaps I should say a really old way, a way as in the beginning when everything was common to all and designed to work for all (Gen. 1).

Over time, new ways and new politicking models emerge. It has been a while since anyone came up with a genuinely new model of governance. It is as if we are in a state of suspended animation, waiting as we look for answers to the world's problems of food and water shortages, looming environmental disaster and gross inequality. Anthropologists call this transitional period where we wait for new thresholds a state of *liminality*: a period of ambiguity and uncertainty where we have the old present, but have not yet begun the new. Traditions are under threat, old structures and ways are beginning to be dissolved and things we once took for granted are no longer certain. Doubt pervades about what will happen next. We wait, betwixt and between macropolitical ways of being and models of governance.

Recently, the idea of the common good has re-emerged and come to the fore as a way of addressing these challenges. This ancient idea is now viewed as a possible means of taking us into the future. The common good is a contested and complex principle. It is concerned with economic aspirations, justice, equality, social responsibility, the environment, well-being, religious tolerance and educational considerations. It might be about a *quality* of existence or a *quantity* of wealth or resources. It is difficult to agree a universally acknowledged consensus regarding what common good entities might be made up of, let alone a collective agreement for all criteria.

The principle of the common good in the Christian faith tradition appears as early as possibly the first century. *The Epistle of Barnabas*[2] states, 'Do not by retiring live alone as if you were already made righteous, but come together and seek out the common good' (4.10); the sentiment of the original language being about common welfare, inquiry and advantage. However, it was thirteenth-century Catholic Dominican priest Thomas Aquinas who gave the common good focus. In simple terms, he argued that people flourish when pursuing God and that God is the common good of everything. This idea is no doubt

---

2 A text believed to be written between AD 70 and 130, but not included in what we now know as the Bible.

disputed by those who do not believe in God. Nonetheless, there appears a growing political sentiment that, setting the faith aspect aside, endorses the common good approach: an approach that is about how people flourish and live well in ways that contribute to others flourishing and living well.

For me, the common good is about realizing the best set of conditions that enable people to reach fulfilment in a just and equitable way. It is the best we can achieve at any one time that is to everybody's advantage. 'Together for the Common Good' is an initiative seeking to 'bring together a broad coalition between Christians of different traditions, fellow faith communities and secular allies, to re-imagine political life and commitment to the flourishing of all people'. They define the common good as:

> something that is revealed through the 'best possible conversation' using a clear set of rigorous theological principles centred around human dignity and care for creation. In effect it is about reconciliation between all parties concerned in a way that enables all to flourish.[3]

Of course, it is more than just a conversation. It is a process, a journey and a practice needing to be developed as lives, ways of being and embodied actions materialize. Jim Wallis says the common good is exemplified when we make 'every decision and action in the best interest of the people and the land, but always paying special attention to the weakest and most vulnerable creatures' (2014, p. 10). I believe the world would be transformed if we used the common good principle as the basis for our politicking. Christian-motivated work could use this ideal as a basis for doing politicking in the world. If such work took the principles of the Nazareth Manifesto, the call to be shalom-makers, and then used these common good definitions as a test to determine if something was worthy or not, we would all be better off. Work would mutually benefit everybody and, as already noted, individual flourishing would contribute to collective wholeness and blessing, rather than mere personal gain.

The common good is not simply about finding a way for people to live together. In the seventh century, Christians in what is now Syria had to pay half an ounce of gold to the Caliphate, the Islamic state ruling the area at the time. They had to do this politicking in order to

---

3 See http://togetherforthecommongood.co.uk. Quotation from Jenny Sinclair and Anna Rowlands.

be given the same property and legal rights as Muslims. While they were still seen as second-class citizens (known as *dhimmi*), they were allowed to practise their faith without persecution. If they didn't pay, they didn't enjoy the protection of the state and they either had to convert to Islam or take their chances (something similar has recently been imposed in parts of modern-day Iraq). This is not what I mean by the common good. It wasn't equitable, mutually negotiated; nor did it create safe space for people to flourish in. This approach was an abuse of power that worked against the common good. The type of common good I am advocating is based upon mutual trust, overcoming societal divides and working towards equality. If these virtues could be embedded in youth work and ministry we would all benefit.

I fully accept there are problems regarding the principle of the common good, let alone actually achieving it. Even something as simple as trying to get a youth group to agree on which DVD to watch at a social event can be a tortuous process. There are questions about what can ever be collectively achieved in such a diverse and plural society as the UK. Equally, the idealism might simply be unrealistic and unachievable. However, other notions such as freedom, equality, love and security are similarly illusive ideals. This does not invalidate their desirability or render pursuit of them redundant. I think it would be truly aspirational to seek the common good. Perhaps we might perceive it as an ongoing idealistic project that reaches into the future, while recognizing the challenges of the present. Given the failures of so many other ways of being, the common good approach warrants closer inspection.

Catholic social teaching

My PhD studies ended up in a place I had not anticipated. The more I studied, reflected and analysed, the more I was drawn to the idea of the common good as a model for contemporary faith-based youth work. The common good is inherently part of what has become known as Catholic social teaching (CST). I am not a Catholic and have never been one. If I am honest, I would have to admit that my early Christian influencers discipled me into believing Catholic believers were not *true* Christians. I look back on this input with significant regret and I am pleased to say my perspective has since changed. I have subsequently met many Catholics who have a much greater understanding of God and a stronger faith than I do. My history, however, has meant my understanding of Catholic ideas has been restricted. It was, therefore, a surprise to discover how much the (mainly Protestant) youth work and ministry I studied reflected CST ideas and provided a platform from which politicking could be developed. CST is not a statement of belief or a prescriptive response for every situation, but more a body of work and collection of themes. Space does not allow a full critique of all these themes here, but I will focus on CST ideas of *human dignity*, *solidarity*, *subsidiarity* and the already discussed *common good* as a mandate for future Christian-motivated work.

A belief in *human dignity* is based upon the idea that every person is important and valuable and has equal rights to respect, freedom, justice and peace. It considers individuals more important than things, profits, achievements and status in society. For me, this has to be the starting point not only for effective Christian-motivated youth work but also for any politicking. One research participant summed this sentiment up, saying human dignity is about:

> A belief in all young people . . . the idea that they might mess up on one session, but if they come in next time it's done, it's dusted, it's afresh . . . it's treating them like young adults, not children, not teenagers, not second-class citizens.

For another, this sense of preciousness was portrayed as 'seeing something in everything and everyone. There's always something to be had there, something good, some potential everywhere.' These sentiments create a grounding from which youth work and ministry can emerge. A place where young people are not seen as entities to be contained or problems to be solved, but as human beings who are in the process of potentially flourishing. This belief in human dignity contrasts markedly with the notions of symbolic violence, socialization, commodification and deficit-driven narratives highlighted in previous chapters. My default position is that young people have something positive to say and contribute to all things, including things about politics.

The practical application of a human dignity belief can be seen in how Pope Francis has taken the ideal, politically interpreted a biblical passage and re-contextualized it for the modern era. It has become a traditional Maundy Thursday papal act to wash the feet of men in recollection of Jesus' act of humility (John 13.1–17). In 2013, Pope Francis washed and kissed the feet of a dozen inmates at the Casal del Marmo young offender's institution just outside Rome. Two of the 12 young people were young women. In 2014, he washed and kissed the feet of 12 disabled people – several of them women and one a Muslim man. Previous Popes had only ever washed the feet of men. Francis can be seen simultaneously valuing all the people present, making a political statement about inclusivity, blessing others, being good news to the poor and revealing his own humility – it is profoundly challenging.

My research indicates that Christian-motivated work is committed to the CST idea of *solidarity*. This is a vital mandating principle for future politicking work. Solidarity is about sharing lives, developing social unity, building bonds that tie people together, and embracing the idea that 'we are members of one another' (Eph. 4.25 NASB). It is about living out the fact that we are connected with our neighbours and, as one research participant said, going 'the extra mile for a young person and for the community' (see Matt. 5.41). Solidarity was originally a nineteenth-century term that later became widely used following the uprising that led to the overthrow of Communism in Poland during the 1980s. The trade union movement leading the uprising was called *Solidarność* – meaning solidarity. The fact that in recent times the term has taken on such politicking stature suggests further connectivity between the CST idea and contemporary political imperatives. For another of my research participants, solidarity was about standing with young people, doing practical politicking and believing things can be better:

I think really serving the young people as best we can so whether it's . . . you know, supporting them, finding a job or with things that are happening at home. I always go back to, you know . . . raising aspirations and releasing potential. Encouraging them to get . . . out of their comfort zones and maybe out of the cycle they think they have to go through because that's what everybody else does.

Given the previously described propensity to demonize and exclude young people – especially the type of young people served by the work I do with FYT – such an approach is not without challenge. However, if it can be realized, I believe that shalom will be built and we will be able to call our politicking a success.

Subsidiarity is an ideal empowering people at a very local level:

Nothing should be done by a larger and more complex organization which can be done as well by a smaller and simpler organization. In other words, any activity which can be performed by a more decentralized entity should be. (Bosnich 1996, p. 9)

In my experience, most youth work is done at a local subsidiarity level. It is done in a community, village, estate, area of a town, suburb of a city, neighbourhood, school and/or skate park. It is often simply organized, independent of any centralized control, but connected to the grassroots of society. The projects I have researched all reflect the idea of subsidiarity. Nearly all the people involved in the projects lived in the communities they work in. As one commented, 'This is where I live . . . I wanted to work to make this place a better place, the best place it could be.' Thus, any successes in their youth work benefit not only young people, but also the community the workers are part of. I believe this is highly effective and enables the type of localism politicking that policymakers envisage.

In a youth wok context, subsidiarity does not just mean doing things to or for young people (although this has its place). It is about doing things at the most empowering level that enable young people to take responsibility for their own lives, becoming interdependent with those they share their lives with so that they in turn can become activists and advocates for others. Another research participant described this process as being:

> about journeying with young people . . . The idea is about coming alongside of the young person and journeying with them for a period of time. And you know supporting them and empowering them, so it's not doing it all for them but actually, 'what can we do to support you and help you . . . make good choices?'

This might mean intervening, supporting and responding to need for as long as required in order to enable a young person to progress to the next stage of their life journey. For many young people, this approach will take a lot of time, energy and resources. Helping damaged young people maximize their emotional, social, economic and politicking aspirations can be a demanding task. As Andy Burns, whom I mentioned earlier, commented, 'You can't put right 16 years of crap with a 30-minute chat and cup of coffee.'

Working at such a grassroots local level may not impact macropolitical dynamics particularly significantly, but it can have a great impact on micropolitical factors. If all these local initiatives can be perceived collectively, there can be a macro culmination of effort facilitating the common good. If Christian-motivated work can cherish common objectives rooted in a shared desire for justice, a more equal society, healing and wholeness, a common good and counter-cultural holistic expression of the world can emerge. Politically working for conditions that are just is very important. If the total conditions necessary for human fulfilment are to be achieved in work with young people, not only must young people's needs be met, but also the negative and demonizing societal context within which they live must be addressed. I mandate that it is time to start pursing the *good* in young people so that the *common good* is realized for all. The aspects of CST I have considered here provide a good starting point for this to happen, providing young people are put centre-stage in any politicking undertaken.

Young people's participation

Ansata lives in Senegal, and I have been sponsoring her for the last few years through World Vision. She and her family need some financial help to access everyday things like food, housing and education. I wish I didn't have to sponsor her. I wish she had enough money to have the basic things in life without the need for my support. I dream one day she will be free from the curse of poverty and liberated to access the things I take for granted. In the meantime, I am pleased to be able to help her development. I also dream that one day we will be liberated from the shackles of neoliberalism. While working towards this, many young people need developmental support. I hope Christian young people can be liberated from the constraints of institutionalized religion, but I recognize their development needs encouraging in the interim. Youth workers need to be liberated to be critical informal educators, but developmentally they often have to work within policy boundaries and cultural expectations. These two dynamics – liberation and development – need to co-exist when we do politicking. They need to exist in healthy tension not polarizing conflict. Politicking with young people is about both their development and their liberation.[4]

As discussed, finding developmental ways of helping young people participate in politics is a challenging process. As I travel up and down the country, I reflect on the progress we have made in helping them participate in church life, but, as already noted, there is still much work to be done regarding this. Young people need to be liberated from an *adult knows best* orientated world where those adults who have the power think they have a right to determine what everybody else should do. I mandate that liberation is best achieved by valuing young people in the manner I have described and creating space for them to prosper.

Malala Yousafzai is a remarkable young woman. She comes from Pakistan and advocates for women to go to school and be educated.

---

4 For a discussion about the theology of these two approaches, see Cooper 2007.

She politicks for this relentlessly. This contravenes the beliefs of Taliban Islamists. On 9 October 2012, a Taliban gunman shot her in the head. She nearly died, but made a remarkable recovery to become a global figurehead. *Time* magazine claims she is one of the most influential people in the world and in 2014 she became the youngest ever winner of the Nobel Peace prize – she is just 17. Stephen Sutton was another stunning young person. Stephen rose to fame because he had cancer and was dying. He only had a short time to live, so decided to make the most of it. He encouraged people to 'make every second count' and reminded people, 'We are on a journey together. This isn't about me; it's about helping others.' In 2014 Stephen died. He was 19. In his last few months of life, Stephen devoted himself to raising money for a cancer charity. He raised £5m.

Malala and Stephen are remarkable, but I think all young people are remarkable. What might the possibilities be if we gave all teenagers the same space and opportunity afforded to Malala and Stephen? Jim is not famous. Jim has autism, and because of his condition he finds it hard to relate to and communicate with other people. He sometimes gets very frustrated and lashes out. He has been excluded from school, but he is a fantastic young person: full of energy, questions and a love of football. Maybe we could give Jim some time, profile and space. Perhaps we could listen to what he has to say about the world, the changes he would like to realize and the campaigns he would like to support and politick about. All too often, it is only those eloquent, high-profile or media-appealing young people that we acknowledge. Young people need liberating from this culture.

American youth ministry expert Kenda Casey Dean talks about the need for faith to be 'consequential' (2010, pp. 45–60), something impacting and fruitful in the long term. If our politicking with young people can be developmentally liberating from the confines of contemporary culture, something more tangible and consequential can be realized. A youth worker who took part in my research did this with the group of young people they work with:

> We had a sleep-out to highlight the plight of the homeless. The young people then spent the following day delivering soup and sandwiches on the street. This had a huge impact on our youth, who continue to collect toiletries and clothing for the homeless.

It is this type of developmental, participative and prospective youth work and ministry that stands the best chance of changing our world and releasing young people to be the difference. The deficit approach doesn't really liberate young people. It might address some of their immediate problems (and this is often important), but does little to change the circumstances causing the problems in the first place. Both need to happen if young people are to flourish. I end this chapter with a further reflection on a political reading of Scripture illustrating this point.

In 1 Peter 2.11–17, Peter encourages the believers to behave well and submit to the king, governors and those in authority. He then goes on to issue instructions about servants, masters, wives and husbands. At the time this passage was written, the Jews were upsetting the Roman authorities. The Romans often associated the Jews and the Christians as one single cohort of religious people, rather than two distinct faith groups. My interpretation of this passage is that Peter was trying to put some clear water between the behaviour of the Jews and the Christians. If the Christians had a 'consequential faith' and stood out as good citizens (in contrast to the troublemaking Jews), the gospel could thrive, prosper and have more influence. Governments are ordinarily obliged to value the righteous and good deeds of citizens. I believe Peter's agenda was not simply unconditional submission to earthly authorities; it was an early illustration of activism and societal kingdom building, pragmatically responding to the painful consequences of not submitting. It was a developmental approach designed proactively to reorder society and promote liberation. It was, and is, an approach contemporary youth work and ministry could learn from as it seeks to help young people participate in a contested and diverse cultural context that all too easily labels them as troublemakers.

Things to think about

- What do you think about the mandates for future politicking work set out in this chapter? Do they resonate with your convictions? What additional mandates do you feel would make further positive contributions to young people doing politics?
- Consider what might happen if you stopped focusing your work on individuals and only worked in ways that benefited everybody. What would happen if all your decisions were made in the interests of the common good? How might your work be reimagined if you only made decisions that preferred people outside your church or organization?

- Bayard Rustin was an American civil rights leader. He organized the 1963 March on Washington, where Martin Luther
King delivered his famous 'I have a dream . . .' speech. As a
black and openly gay man in the 1960s Bayard encountered his
fair share of oppression and prejudice. He said, 'When an individual is protesting society's refusal to acknowledge his dignity
as a human being, his very act of protest confers dignity on him.'
What might you and/or the young people you work with protest
about in order to increase their sense of human dignity?

What can I do?

- As an exercise for personal reflection, youth work team
development or a session with young people, try rewriting
well-known pieces of Scripture so they have a very contemporary political emphasis. For example, you could take something
like the parable of the good Samaritan and change some of the
characters (for: a terrorist, Islamist, right-wing politician, East
European immigrant, young person, old person or atheist) and
context (for: your community, Downing Street, the church, the
mosque or the supermarket). What new insights and revelation emerge as you do this and reflect further upon it?
- *Subsidiarity* is a concept proposing that when a problem can
be better addressed at a more local level, then it should be done
at that level. When next planning a piece of work, give consideration to this concept. Deliberately choose to 'go local', if this
is possible. For example, could you achieve what you want to
achieve using local guest speakers, worship leaders, suppliers,
printers, booksellers and/or local banks/building societies?
- Talk to the young people you work with about *development
factors* and *liberation factors*. You might wish to use simpler
language and ask them about 'things they would like to grow
in, develop or try' and 'things they would like to be free from,
get out of their lives, or be less hassled by'. Work with the
young people to integrate what they say into your practice,
particularly your politicking practice.

8

Opportunities to Develop Work

It is better to debate a question without settling it than to settle a question without debating it.

Joseph Joubert, writer and moralist

I see my role as an enabler and facilitator – the views of the young people are their own and need to be heard and respected – even when I don't share them! They challenge me and help me understand and review what it is I believe.

Youth worker

From despair to where?

I recently delivered a lecture about the current state of youth work, young people and youth policy. Midway through the session I paused to ask if any of the students had any reflections they wished to share. Several did, including one who said she found my lecture depressing. I don't think she meant my delivery method was depressing (although she might have), but more that the content and context of what I was explaining was so challenging, so money-focused and so rarely good news for young people or the poor. I suspect she wanted to hear some good news, some uplifting narrative, perhaps something a little more in keeping with her particular view and hope of God.

I agreed with her; the situation was depressing. I find what governments have said and done to the poor, the disabled, youth work and those from other countries highly offensive and extremely ungodly. I added I was not overconcerned that she was depressed. I highlighted the fact that many books in the Bible (Lamentations, some of the psalms and Job, for example) can be seen as depressing. The situations these books reflect were very challenging. The writers can often be found pleading for justice, freedom and for God to do something. This is the place I find myself in today. I believe we often have to have a revelation about how bad things are before we start to do something about them. It is OK to be appalled by the terrible things happening in our world. All too often we simply live in happy-clappy Christian bubbles denying, or ignoring, the plight of those suffering in our world.

We need sobering up with reality, so we are spurred into action releasing the good news and the kingdom into the world. We must have passion and the joy of the Lord as our strength (Neh. 8.10), but that won't stop others being poor, destitute and marginalized. My hope is that our joy becomes theirs as we embrace the *missio Dei* and seize the opportunities before us. Throughout this book I have described methods, tools and processes that might effectively achieve this. In the rest of this chapter I set out some additional ways we might develop our politicking work to bring about a hope for a better future, a hope full of anticipation.

Developing awareness

If Christian-motivated workers are to move forward and seize the day regarding politicking work, we need to develop some strategies for doing this. I believe we need to develop our awareness of all things political and social. Workers and ministers appear to want to engage more effectively young people politically, but do we have enough knowledge about politics? However competent and experienced we are, I believe we need to enhance our understanding, increase our knowledge and improve the skills we have in working in these areas. Most importantly, we also need to help young people do this as well.

Workers can increase their knowledge by staying in touch with sector-specific policy developments, political news and theological discussion matters. There are no short cuts to ensure we stay up to date and on top of what is happening in the world. We have to do the groundwork: read, reflect and disseminate what is going on around us. Just like King David, we need people who have the spirit of the tribe of Issachar: people who understand the times, and know what we ought to do (1 Chron. 12.32). We need to develop a sense of mindfulness and perspective so that we avoid knee-jerk reactions and jumping to incorrect conclusions. We also need to be myth-busters, making sure we combat wrong information, misinformation and distorting spin emitting from unscrupulous politicians and sources. In John's account of Jesus turning over the Temple tables, we read Jesus prepared a scourge of cords in order to drive out the cattle and animals before turning his attention to the traders and moneychangers (John 2.15). Making the scourge would have taken time and preparation. This was not an uncontrolled knee-jerk act, but a considered response. Our politicking approach needs to be similarly considered and prepared.

I develop my knowledge awareness and undertake my politicking preparation by, among other things:

- Watching a diverse range of television and news channels such as Aljazeera (English version), Russia Today, CNN and other outlets offering a non-British-centric perspective.
- Reading different newspapers and magazines reflecting diverse political views. Many of these are now free online. I often read those I know I will disagree with.
- Scanning policy documents and critiques of them.
- Digesting the weekly bulleting from the National Council for Voluntary Youth Services – it contains a wealth of information and signposting to other sources of material.
- Looking at the electoral manifestos of the political parties. The Blend project I referred to earlier does this with the young people they work with. During election periods, they have the manifestos displayed on the youth centre computer screens and discuss the contents of them with the young people.
- Visiting museums, galleries, council offices and Parliament to see what goes on and what history can tell us. MPs and councillors can help with invitations to some of these establishments.
- Exploring our history through other people's eyes. For example, I have had the opportunity to go to Ireland and the USA and reflect upon our colonial enterprises in these countries. I consider some of what we did during these times shameful. We need to be aware of matters like these and learn from them.
- Subscribing to think-tank newsletters and journals to explore the latest in research and creative thinking by those better informed.
- Following lobbying, pressure-group and special-interest organizations who are experts in their fields.
- Scanning through social media entries, communications and blogs as political and youth-specific events unfold.

I improve my politicking skills by continually reflecting, critiquing and questioning what I am doing, what others are doing and what young people are doing. The sentiment behind the quotation from Joseph Joubert used at the beginning of this chapter helps illuminate so much for me. I genuinely believe, 'It is better to debate a question without settling it than to settle a question without debating it.' Praying about political matters helps develop our awareness. For example, praying for those who have no food might impact our behaviour. Facilitating some guided journeying about what it might feel like to be an asylum-seeker leaving your home country might raise awareness of the courage of those fleeing persecution.

A youth worker involved in my research uses debates to inform practice and develop awareness of the young people worked with:

> Debating with young people is exciting! We recently had a brief debate about paying tax at our film club – encouraging young people to explore a point from a lot of angles, even ones you don't agree with, trying to understand the reasoning another has gone through to get to a point of view, as well as being prepared to 'back down' or stand up for themselves in the face of those arguments. These are all skills valuable to them for their own political engagement – as well as for me when faced with my own responses 'in the heat of the moment'.

Followers of Marxist ideology might be aware of the idea of 'false consciousness'. This is where people's awareness and understanding of what is going on around them is obscured by those exploiting and dominating them. Such people fail to recognize what is being done to them and end up serving the values and pursuits of others rather than their own or what is good for everybody. What can happen in such circumstances is that a type of mob rule comes into play. Individuals have their world-views and lenses shaped by others and end up believing and acting in ways they would not otherwise do if left to their own devices. I think this is what is happening among some Christians when talking about immigration, gay rights, welfare and young people. I have lost count of the number of times well-balanced, considered, generous and otherwise godly people have made outlandish statements about people from other countries, homosexuals, the poor and teenagers. What they have expressed has been the very opposite of their core beliefs of love, compassion and acceptance. The mob rule of media hysteria and moral panics has impacted their world-view in a way they are completely unaware of. Jesus often challenged people to see past predominant world-views. American professor Jerry Maneker is a straight man who campaigns for justice for gay people. He describes the lack of awareness in his field most eloquently:

> This 'false consciousness' has most recently manifested itself in the diversion of most of the organized Church's reason for being: caring for the poor, speaking out for equality, dignity, and justice, speaking out against war, poverty, and inadequate education and health care, into it being obsessively consumed with rhetoric showing how

the Gospel of grace (God's unmerited favour) has morphed, in fact become perverted, into the false gospel of legalism, perfectionism, exclusion, and genital placement!

I am not asking us to take sides in debates of this nature, merely to be more aware of what we say and how we say it so that we do not fall prey to false consciousnesses that undermine our representations of God. I believe we need to be fully present in the *here and now*, seeing it how it is (which is often different to the mob's dominant narrative), telling it *how it is* and revealing what is really going on. We shouldn't be chasing political shadows, but seizing the sacrament of each and every moment so our awareness and consciousness levels are raised, thereby giving the common good every chance of success.

Increasing political attentiveness is a positive first step in developing awareness and calibrating our inner compasses. If we are in a setting or context, for example, that is perpetuating symbolic violence, we must challenge this: first within our own minds and spirits (so we are liber-ated to think more critically) and then in the cognitions and spirits of those we work with and for. I would not wish to dissuade anyone from politicking either because they felt they did not know enough about the subject matter they were entertaining or because they felt they did not have sufficient skills to engage with the matter in hand. Knowledge and skills are important, but it is more important simply to get involved. If we are not prepared to do this, no amount of awareness, knowledge and skills will make the slightest bit of difference. For me, the first steps in taking an opportunity are a willingness to have a go, being curious and developing critical thinking.

Promoting curiosity and critical thinking

I talked with a group (using the Gandhi quote) of young people about 'being the change they wanted to see', and I was surprised by their apathetic attitude. I think they felt they were unable to change things in their neighbourhoods and their world.

[Politics has] shaped my views by realizing how young people are a marginalized age grouping in society and they are often portrayed negatively by the media . . . I have been surprised how keen young people are to get involved on just about any issue; it is a way of them identifying/finding common ground with older youth workers.

These two comments are from different youth workers who took part in my research. In one sense they say the same thing, but in another they reflect very different points of view. Both consider ways young people can change the world against a backdrop of marginalization. However, one suggests being paralysed by apathy, the other motivated by enthusiasm. Politicking with young people can be a complex business and because youth work is a reflective and critical practice, perspectives continually emerge. It is reflective, in that it thinks about who *we* are as workers and what *our* role is; it questions why we do what we do; it looks back on what we have done, and forward to what we might do. It does this cyclically and repeatedly. Such work also needs to help young people reflect on what we do with them, and on what they do and who they are. It also needs to be critical so that both workers and young people develop an informed critical consciousness.[1]

Political youth work demands critical dialogue about important issues. This type of dialogue increases the likelihood of making those with power accountable. Critical engagement means power-holders can't just do what they want without recourse. Social responsibility, justice, equality and community can all be furthered, if we debate the issues. It is not that workers and young people have no critical consciousness about political matters, but it needs to be developed. It cannot be handed over for others to develop it, and it needs to be up-front, active and present in any rationale and decision-making processes. We need to embrace a curiosity that asks difficult and complex political questions as well as very simple ones, a holy restlessness that enables us to see things differently. Young people need the skills and knowledge to enable them to think deeply and critically. They need to be taught how to be reflective beings in a fast-moving world. They need to be supported so they learn how to develop the capacity to take responsibility, learn to care and rise to the challenges of doing politicking.

In recent decades, popular culture – particularly youth culture – has recognized the power of curiosity and critical thinking. Fads, fashions, movements and trends have continually asked questions of the Establishment. Musical genre from rockers, mods, punks, metal, new romantics, raves, gangster and a hundred other subdivisions have critiqued societal norms and what went before. Currently, artists such as Banksy are very popular. His confrontational, subversive street art challenges societal norms and dominant hegemony. He satirically disrupts,

---

1 For a broader discussion about this, see what Graeme McMeekin (2014) says about Stanley Hauerwas.

argues against and fights back against the ruling classes. He unsettles the status quo. Most youth workers I know revel in his work.

If we are to promote curiosity and critical thinking that develops politicking, I suspect we will have to be more disruptive. Politics, and the Church, need disrupting. God the Father, God the Son and God the Spirit are all disruptive entities. We serve a disruptive God: it is how he works. One immediate way of beginning to promote curiosity, develop critical thinking and be disruptive in a holy way is to introduce, or reintroduce, language that helps unpack what is happening in the world so that young people can name and respond to what is going on more consciously. Words and ideas associated with compassion, justice/judgement (same Hebrew word, *mishpat*), power, shalom, laying down, service, sacrifice, deferring gratification and abstinence (from consumption) need to be revisited, re-purposed and visualized for the modern age. Elected politicians don't often use these words. We need to give more thought to the significance of these words in our politicking work with young people.

When this has been done, or done some more if it is already being done, my second appeal is that we step into the stories of the poor, ostracized and marginalized. A research participant said, 'You can't make policies for people to care for each other, to look out for each other.' I suspect this is true. This means it is people like youth workers and ministers who have to do the caring, inspiring young people to do likewise. Catching a glimpse of how the world is by stepping into the world's stories is a powerful tool in helping promote the curious and the critical. We need to establish a dialogue between earth and heaven that goes beyond the immediate to discover the place within which our politicking should take place.

Stepping into the narrative of others increases our awareness, heightens our curiosity and prompts our thinking. Hearing, smelling, tasting, touching and feeling the experienced reality of others stimulates our politicking. It moves political possibilities out of theological, theoretical and policy realms and begins to allow what is happening on earth to touch us, while hopefully bringing a touch of heaven to earthly circumstances. Being present and getting our hands dirty impacts upon who we are and our response to situations. Sometimes what we experience will clearly resonate with our beliefs and hopes. At other times, we will be left theologically wanting. Such times will ask further questions of us and demand further reflection so we arrive in a new theological place, fit for purpose. Over time, everything should hopefully come together in a reflexive praxis that results in a continuum of new action, transformation, learning and reflection.

Practically, we can aid this process by literally engaging with the earth. For example, if we are politicking about the environment, take some young people and touch some soil; go out into the countryside and see the flowers, birds and animals; cover hands in oil or coal dust (risk assessments permitting); visit a power station or wind farm and watch and listen, and/or go to a landfill site and smell. If politicking about homelessness, talk to those without a place to sleep; get involved in a shelter supporting the homeless; smell the urine in street alleyways. Create opportunities to experience what is going on in the world and create space to reflect, develop curiosity and critique those experiences. As another research participant recalled, doing this can have lasting impact on young people: 'I once took two young people on an anti-nuclear demo at Faslane [a permanent peace camp set up outside a Scottish nuclear naval base]. They still recall it as memorable. I also took them on anti-war demos and it stimulated their political views.'

Informal education and discipleship

I am fascinated by North American Amish people. I have had the privilege of visiting where they live several times, appreciating their values and way of life. I find some of their practices unnerving and at odds with my own beliefs (especially regarding gender equality, being contemporary and contextual), but I am full of admiration for their simple and considered culture. Amish tradition is full of wise words and godly reflections. One of my favourite proverbs of theirs is 'put the swing where the children want it, the grass will grow back'. In our work with young people, I think we could focus more on what young people want and how they want it. As already mentioned, I am not advocating a self-centred and selfish cultural narrative, just one appreciating young people and pedagogically prospective and enterprising. Embracing the type of sentiment the apostle Paul uses when writing to the Philippians – 'do not merely look out for your own personal interests, but also for the interests of others' (Phil. 2.4, New American Standard Bible) – would be a good starting point. Let's metaphorically help young people play on the politicking swings they desire. If things don't quite go to plan and the metaphorical grass gets worn away or damaged, it is not the end of the world. Better to have set up and had a go on the swing than simply watched the grass grow longer from a distance.

Informal education is the process that I believe underpins youth work. It is 'a process that works through, and is driven by, conversation. It is spontaneous and involves exploring and enlarging experience. It can take place in any setting' (Jeffs and Smith 1997, 2005, 2011). Over the last couple of decades, government approaches to work with young people appear to have moved away from this *informal* approach. The emphasis has more been on targeted and prescriptive agendas, rather than voluntary participation and conversationally orientated pedagogies. Government has increasingly dictated where the swing should be put. I think this is regrettable. I believe the fundamentals of informal education need to be re-embraced, if youth work is to help young people do politicking. It is hard to imagine how targeted support work for young people would ever have the time, yet alone the inclination, to give young people the space required to do many of the things encouraged in this book. Asking the bigger questions about life is not something that can easily be performance managed and measured. Politicking cannot be contained within narrow *payments by result* type approaches. Any youth service having set outcomes attached to it or a profit element dependent upon it inevitably focuses on achieving targets and risks depleting spontaneous conversations and processes. My hope is that Christian youth work can rediscover what it means to do informal education and undertake this not only in Christian youth work settings but also in youth ministry discipleship settings as well. The worker quoted at the beginning of the chapter understood this strategy:

> I see my role as an enabler and facilitator – the views of the young people are their own and need to be heard and respected – even when I don't share them! They challenge me and help me understand and review what it is I believe.

Youth work stalwart John Ellis (1990, pp. 89–99) argues that Jesus was an informal educator who used the approach to great effect. While noting the dangers of confining Jesus to any one particular approach, he convincingly argues that Jesus practised informal education, indicating this had an intentionality to it that was specifically accessible to marginalized and uneducated people. Christian-motivated youth workers should embrace informal education principles if they want to be truly Christ-like in their work. Allegorically speaking, they might do well to have one eye on God and another on the things and themes really mattering to young people. Paulo Freire calls these 'generative themes' (1972, p. 97). These are cultural or political topics that matter to people, things they find of sufficient interest to merit starting a conversation about. It is from these points and places that we should begin politicking with young people. If we can create space for their generative themes to emerge, they may well play on these swings until the grass does indeed wear out.

Thinkers like Freire view education as a political act. I also think this is the case. Workers and young people need to be alerted to the politics involved in their education. They need to be mindful about what is happening as they create spaces allowing every voice to be heard, with each voice carrying equal weight. Ordinarily and without intervention, certain voices in a group of young people dominate. The more power-ful voices will take an upper hand if allowed to. Workers need to work hard to ensure all voices are heard and valued. Perhaps more signifi-cantly, there is sometimes an assumption that the worker (as educator) is there to tell the young people what to learn and how to learn it. In Freirean models of learning, the educator and learner are equal partici-pants in the process and engage in continual dialogue. This process is supported by what Freire calls 'problem posing' (1972, p. 85). Here, themes the young people feel strongly about emerge, challenging and changing perceived wisdom and bringing about new understanding. I believe it is this praxis that stands the best chance of being successful in both contemporary politicking and discipleship work. Youth workers learn to become true informal educators and young people learn to become critical thinkers as creativity, inquiry, invention and transfor-mation lead to positive action. As one research participant added, the

> best benefit [of this approach] is in enabling young people to see the possibilities and strengthen their ability to shape their own lives in the context of turbulent political activity . . . to enable young people to develop a renewed language to describe their world and, through description, act to adapt and change (sometimes collectively).

Training workers for transformative political action

I first met Rob Burns in a social policy lecture I was giving at the Oxford Institute for Children, Youth and Mission (CYM). Rob is a 20-year-old youth worker with a growing interest in politics. Rob was aware that a local conservative MP, Justin Tomlinson, had supported some work he had done previously with Swindon Youth for Christ. So, following the lecture, he arranged to meet with Justin. Rob told me:

> I met with Justin to look at the local/national government response to youth crime and informed him of the lectures that had taken place at Oxford CYM, and how this had opened up a lot of under the surface thoughts within me about how policy needs radical reform,

if we are to truly reach young people. Justin encouraged me to think about how I could get involved in political circles, as he says the Government are desperate for people who are on the front line of youth work to become involved in policymaking, as we are the ones who truly know what is happening on the ground. I informed him I was moving to Nuneaton to commence a new youth work job there and he has said he will put me in touch with the MP for Nuneaton so that I am able to start impacting things at a local level there.

I suspect I wouldn't share Justin's political views, but I greatly admire his encouragement and the help he afforded Rob. I also admire Rob for his passion and hope he continues to have a developing interest in politicking. I have wondered if this all would have happened if I and others hadn't done the social policy lectures. I am certainly not taking the credit for Rob's passion or Justin's encouragement, but I think I might just have been a bit of a catalyst in helping Rob and Justin get together and move things on. That is why I believe how and what we train people in is so important. If politics and policy are not on the training curriculum and agenda, we risk not animating and motivating people. We need to do politicking training.

I am encouraged that organizations like the Citizens movement, mentioned in Chapter 4, are beginning to train people in activism and community organizing. I am excited that youth workers have been interested in my research and are asking for more resources to assist their politicking. I am stimulated by the plethora of online petitions launched, as people decide they need to do something to combat perceived wrongs. However, too many expressions of Christians doing politicking remain on the margins of church and society. I believe we need to get these expressions into the mainstream by more effective training for youth workers and ministers.

Another youth worker who had the delight of attending one of my lectures said: 'It is quite mind-boggling sitting here listening to all of this, and I don't know what I think about any of it really.' I wondered why they didn't know what they thought about it. How had they managed to do three years of studying professional youth work without thinking about policy and political matters? If we are to persist with training leaders through accredited and professional courses, we need to get more politicking content on the curriculum – I am available at very reasonable rates to help with this!

We have made great strides in training Christian youth workers and ministers in recent decades. There are now more professionally qualified workers than ever before and there has been a steady rise in the number of practitioners obtaining degrees at master's level. However, if we are to make the most of these training and study opportunities, we not only need to study political and policy domains, we need to have expectations political action will materialize as a consequence of the learning. I acknowledge I am venturing into controversial areas, but the professionalization of Christian youth work risks reducing political activism rather than increasing it. Risk assessments, competence-based performance evaluation and academic rigor impinge upon radicalism. In short, trainee workers risk failing the courses they are on if they do some of the things advocated in this book.

As already noted, several workers in my research commented about how having responsibility in or working for a church restricts their political activity. I quoted earlier in the chapter a story about a worker who did some radical politicking. They ended their comment by saying it 'can be more difficult for me now as a church leader to do these things'. Rather than seeing church leadership as an opportunity for greater influence and politicking, this worker felt restricted by the office. I find this bizarre. We need to train our leaders to be radical, not conservative; more provocative, not less; and more willing to have courage and roar like the lion, not be timid and squeak like the mouse.

One worker in my research achieved this and was able to reflect back on their decades of politicking work with young people:

[I] have on several occasions worked with young people to lobby local councillors over community-specific issues relating to young people's resources; a particularly memorable one being a six-nation multinational camp wherein we were given the council debating chamber to meet with MEPs and local councillors to discuss European and local investment in youth work. It became quite heated in places but they ran the show without intervention from me during the debate, were greatly energized and keen for more. Most of the young people involved remain in faith groups to one extent or another and some have moved into other spheres of political activism. My political views have been shaped by working with young people as they have ever been the marginalized group with whom I have primarily identified during my career – not that 30 years ago I would have been able to express it in those terms. I'd never heard of liberation theology then!

This reflection brings together the facilitation, empowerment, participation, activism, community organizing and political theology skills I have referred to previously. These provide helpful summary headings around which other youth workers could be trained.

To end this section, I offer some training possibilities and narratives to prepare Christian-motivated workers do better politicking. I have phrased these as questions to consider because I think they need to be thought about and debated. If implemented, they need to be considerations that courses and ministry training are based upon rather than appendages to what is currently afforded.

- What would happen if we trained youth workers and ministers to (both metaphorically and actually) 'turn over the tables' in their churches and contexts?
- What would happen if we dispensed with hierarchical power structures in churches and instead trained ministers as facilitators and social pedagogues rather than conduits of power?
- What would happen if one of the competency tasks on youth work degree courses was to undertake a *political act*?
- How about setting a course assignment requiring the research, design, implementation and evaluation of a politicking campaign, rather than an essay, test or dissertation?
- What marks would a student get if they did some Alinski-style community organizing as part of, for example, a community work module? Would they get extra marks if they were successful regarding their campaign, were trending on Twitter, made the local paper and/or got arrested during the course of doing this?
- How would it go down if a student in a placement criticized any Pharisaical attitudes of people in their organizations? Would this be valued and applauded, or vilified and condemned?
- Would it be better to train political and community activists rather than people skilled to run youth programmes, church services and/ or pastoral initiatives?
- How might courses and training be designed so workers listen more to young people, enabling them, as one research participant said, to be 'heard in a way that will make a difference'?
- Could training sessions for volunteers be started with a worshipful reflection and prayer time about a political issue, politician or matter of justice, rather than a Bible verse, worship song or piece of liturgy?
- The rapprochement I talked about in Chapter 6 necessitates workers having the skills and knowledge relevant to secular landscapes. Should training undertaken primarily reflect this so workers can

effectively engage with policymakers and policy matters, seek the shalom of the secular community and serve others as a priority?

Finally in this section I suggest that if any training undertaken doesn't build shalom, then it should not be delivered. If it is not good news for the poor, it should be stopped. If it is not blessing people, something that is should be substituted for it. Academic courses and training for youth workers have rightly managed to embed within them imperatives regarding safeguarding young people, equality, participation and reflective practice. My hope is that politicking will be similarly embedded, be treated as a base-line learning outcome, and considered as a foundational component of contemporary Christian youth work and ministry.

Embracing change

I love the television programme *Top Gear*. It is funny, adventurous, risqué, at times ridiculous and controversial, and features some of the most amazing cars, as Jeremy Clarkson would say, 'in the world'. The show is now televised in over 100 countries, reaching an audience of 350 million people. I suspect I will never drive any of the super cars featured on the show. Nor will I drive a lorry through the jungle, a motorbike down a mountainside, race against a fighter jet or race a 200-mph car around a race track. The programme is built on a fantasy lifestyle and upon a largely out-of-reach paradigm of unrecognizable affluence, bearing no resemblance to most people's driving experiences. I sometimes wonder if our theology is a bit like *Top Gear*: it can sound good and is very engaging, but maybe it is unreal, only for those with money, disconnected, based upon fantasy rather than reality and focused upon matters most people never experience.

I have talked in my previous work about the end of Christendom.[2] Work undertaken needs to reflect this cultural and spiritual change avoiding delusional theology and past redundant understandings. In this new era, workers need to be trained to make the most of opportunities to embrace change in ways that emphasize the importance of their witness; not just for evangelism purposes, but by modelling a more just and equitable society. Change is important for growth and development. Churches and organizations need to embrace change, but they need to stay loyal to their values.

---

2 See Pimlott and Pimlott 2008.

Professionalism is not always the answer to adequately equipping workers to model this type of change. Sometimes a professional is the last person needed. In many communities professionals are seen as, and grouped and equated with, aloof politicians trying to be do-gooders. I have witnessed many times what happens when an earthy, common sense, grassroots voice comes to the fore and encapsulates what everybody else is thinking but never has the chance to say. Such occurrences wrong-foot professional politicians, negate the arguments of clever academics and portray powerful experience-based narratives that can't be contradicted – the weak shaming the powerful (1 Cor. 1.27). They are game-changers. We need ordinary, passionate, committed, change-makers and game-changers to be the difference – perhaps more bicycle, bus and Ford Fiesta type theologians than *Top Gear* Ferrari, Lamborghini and Porsche.

The Occupy Movement protest outside St Paul's Cathedral in London in 2011 drew attention to much of what is wrong in our world. The banners of the protesters were provocative: 'I threw out the money-lenders for a reason' and 'What would Jesus do?' were two regularly featured on news coverage of the protests. The Church initially welcomed the protests, but ultimately it couldn't cope with direct action on its doorstep. Accusations that the church authorities sided with the state, the corporate rich and the powerful and that they sold out the protesters were aplenty. Occupy has moved on since, but it does seem to have inspired something. It is perhaps not front-page news any more, but it ignited a conversation, helped move the goalposts and got the story of the 99 per cent into public consciousness. It changed things. The type of direct action Occupy engages in troubles some Christians. They might cite passages like Titus 3.1–11, imploring believers not to break the law, but instead comply with the demands of those in authority and 'be ready to do whatever is good' (3.1). My own upbringing has some sympathy with this paradigm – I was socialized into having respect for the law – but I do wonder where the paradigm begins and ends. This passage, like the others I have discussed concerning authority, is clearly written to tell us something. However, what it appears to say about being compliant citizens is contradicted by what Paul and the early disciples actually did. I think this is something we need to wrestle with further.

I do not believe Paul is telling us to blindly obey every statute laid down by government. We simply cannot do this if laws contradict our allegiance to God. If we read the text in the fuller knowledge of what the pagan Cretans and government of the time were like, namely, 'always liars, evil brutes, lazy gluttons' (Titus 1.12), we might conclude Paul was asking Titus and his compatriots to undertake something highly counter-cultural. Might the good deeds advocated be works designed to model good citizenship, where the believer avoided petty Cretan quarrels and stupid legal arguments, but more actively stood for what was right and lived counter-culturally to undermine the ethical dysfunction and immorality of Cretan society? If we can glimpse this meaning, movements like Occupy challenge our moral bankruptcy, becoming 'good deeds' and potential law-changers rather than law-breakers.

Of course, developing awareness, promoting curiosity, being better informed educators and ensuring training is fit for purpose will not alone maximize opportunities for Christian-motivated workers to help young people do more politicking. Social conditions have to be created whereby young people thrive and the collaborative good prospers. Karl Marx (1859) contended people need to change their situations in order to improve them. He said, 'It is not the consciousness of men that determines their existence, but their social existence that determines their consciousness.' In other words, he argued that how we see and define ourselves is shaped by our place in society and how we live. This is no doubt true, but I also believe what people *think* and how they *perceive* humanity shapes society. We need hope to *think* and *imagine* better existences and situations, so we experience a better, common good, changed reality. Young people need to *exist* in social and material conditions that help them, support them and create space and opportunities for them to flourish. However, they also need to *believe* the world can be a better place in order to begin the process of change. To use a biblical narrative (Prov. 29.18), if they don't have a sense of purpose and vision for something better, they may give up on hope, do their own thing and perish in any present-day malaise. If we want to realize change, we need to think opportunity, embrace change and act change. In effect, we need a cyclical process of methods to develop consciousness and awareness, resulting in action to change social conditions, further revealing and raising awareness of more social conditions that need changing.

Political activist Andy Flannagan reminds us:

In first-century Palestine . . . an oppressed people came looking for liberation. They were hoping for a mighty explosion of energy and light that would restore their status as God's chosen people. They came looking for fireworks, but they got a story about something practically invisible. What they got was a man who said, 'The Kingdom of heaven is like a mustard seed.' He said, 'This isn't going to be fast. This is going to be slow.' He said, 'This isn't going to start huge, it's going to start infinitesimally small.' We must not get sucked into the instant culture of the twenty-first century, where everything is about overnight sensations and next big things. Change in political thinking and practice is rarely fast, but we must believe the mustard seed will produce fruit.[3]

Change is often slow in politicking, but I am of the conviction there is currently a tremendous opportunity to begin, continue and develop work seeking change. It is not as if Christian youth workers and ministers are short of things to address. There is a place for what I have teasingly labelled '*Top Gear* theology' – especially if we want to dream big and fanciful ideas – but I also believe we have to stay practical, earthed and relevant in our approach. After the 'Things to think about' and 'What can I do' sections, I focus on some of the specific politicking issues youth workers face, offering a variety of practical ideas for consideration.

Things to think about

- Type the words 'Banksy images' into an internet search engine. Spend some personal quiet time reflecting on the images. What are they saying to you? What 'awarenesses' have they raised in your spirit? How have they prodded your curiosity and critical thinking?
- American writer Henry David Thoreau (1849) argued that unless individuals are prepared to stand up to governments they will become 'agents of injustice'. Spend a few moments considering when it might be acceptable to break the law of the land because of a higher set of moral beliefs or imperatives. Recently, anti-homeless spikes have appeared outside some buildings. These are spikes built into the fabric of buildings to stop people without homes sleeping in doorways and entrances. At one supermarket building, activists worked through the night and poured concrete on them to cover them up. The concrete didn't set properly, and it might be said the action didn't physically work, but the resultant publicity forced the supermarket to remove the spikes the very next day. Was this an illegal act of vandalism or a just redemptive act?
- Do you need more training to do politicking? If so, what do you need, and who might be able to meet your learning needs?

---

3 Extract of a speech given by Andy Flannagan at the launch of Christians on the Left, 5 November 2013.

What can I do?

- Which tables are you going to turn over? Which are the temples they are found in? Who are the modern-day Sadducees, craving power and influence, making money out of the gospel, conspiring with governments, working against the common good? Think about these questions both metaphorically and actually. Do you need to do something with your thoughts? What are you going to do, with whom, and when?

- If you feel short of knowledge, sign up to receive some information from an organization of interest to you. For example, you could start with Oxfam, Amnesty International, Christian Aid, Christians Against Poverty, Barnardo's. The websites of these charities will send you free emails/newsletters to help keep you better informed.

- Make the most of your skills, understanding and knowledge and mentor someone else in politicking. This could be a fellow youth worker or a young person. Simply make the most of what opportunities you have by meeting regularly with them to discuss a particular issue and/or implement some of the ideas contained in this book.

9

Practically Speaking

I have come to the conclusion that politics are too serious a matter to be left
to the politicians.

Charles de Gaulle, former French President

Whatever you do, work at it with all your heart, as working for the Lord, not
for human masters.

Paul, apostle (Col. 3.23)

A focus on practice

This last chapter is structured differently from the previous ones. Throughout, I have endeavoured to address theological, theoretical and philosophical matters as well as provide practical pointers and illustrations
to support daily politicking work with young people. In this chapter I
focus more deliberately on Christian youth work and ministry practice,
in effect devoting the whole chapter to 'Things to think about' and
'Things to do'. (For this reason I have omitted further end-of-chapter
suggestions.) I have taken some of the main politicking subject matters
already discussed and suggested how workers might practically address
these. To paraphrase the former French President Charles de Gaulle,
politics is far too serious a matter to be left to the politicians; youth
workers, ministers and young people need to do it too.

I identify some of the main issues associated with the subject matters
in question. I offer real-life practice stories illustrating how workers
have gone about their work and set out different ideas for practice. For
each subject matter, I do this in two sections: first, practice ideas for
Christian youth work; and, second, practice ideas for those more
involved in Christian youth ministry. I suggest a variety of session ideas,
strategic tools, things for churches and organizations to think about
and – most importantly – ways young people can play their part in politicking. Many of the activities can be used across all domains and are
interchangeable. In his letter to the church at Colossae, Paul encourages
believers to work for God, putting their heart, soul and every breath
they have into what they do (Col. 3.23). It is in this spirit that I hope

workers will engage in addressing these important subjects, outworking them in their practice.

Justice

The world is run by dominant institutions. The people who make the decisions in these institutions are very powerful individuals. Few of them have well-known faces. They are a small minority who control the world's finances and commodities and fund the elected politicians who serve us. The systems presided over are not designed to serve the poor of the world. Those with power lobby for policy initiatives that maintain their influence and wealth. They tell ordinary people like you and me that attempts at reforming or changing things risk upsetting global economic balances or ruining the economy. We are duped into inaction by arguments that some things are 'too big to fail' or 'the world is now so globalized we can't alter or influence it' and 'it needs to be done this way to preserve jobs'. These arguments keep the rich and powerful, rich and powerful, and condemn the poor to remaining poor.

Issues concerning wealth and power are often at the root of injustice matters. Those who have power can easily misuse it. One worker told me the following story:

> Young people were being harassed by the police: we discussed this with a Community Beat Officer (CBO) who was shocked at the treatment they were receiving. So we set up a meeting between the young people, the CBO, the Sergeant in charge in operations, which went some way to changing local policy. We have also stood alongside young people in not giving names to police [after particular incidents], which has at times put us in difficult positions.

Standing up for justice can put us all in 'difficult positions' sometimes. However, a quest for justice is part of our mission and calling. The following illustrates what I mean by this. At the Greenbelt festival, my FYT colleagues John and Debbie spoke about 'mission'. Mark, a youth worker, came along to hear what they had to say. Beforehand, Mark had asked what they were going to be talking about. When they told him they were arguing that youth unemployment was a *mission* issue, he seemed a bit surprised they saw a link. A couple of days after the session, John and Debbie facilitated a workshop on the same topic. Having heard what they had to say about the Church having a duty to respond missionally to the issue of youth unemployment, Mark came along. John and Debbie talked about the personal, psychological, emotional and spiritual impact of unemployment on young people. They also discussed the quality of support that young people felt they had access to and the fact their research into youth unemployment had found that young people's experiences of the Job Centre were almost universally negative. As a result of taking part in the workshop, Mark contacted his local Job Centre to explore setting up some kind of support/chaplaincy service to young people visiting there. He applied for and was awarded a grant for the project. A practical circumstance causing young people unjust and bad experiences was missionally responded to in a way that sought to change what was – compassionate politicking and transformative work at its most poignant.

The following practice ideas are designed to help Christian youth workers embed justice approaches in their work:

- Leaders are people with certain skills. This does not mean they are better people than others. When choosing youth work leaders and/ or promoting young people to leadership roles, ensure this is communicated to those who are not leaders. Young leaders need to be taught about power and mentored into not abusing it.
- The English language contains several phrases beginning with the word 'just': just war, just cause, just reason. Is it ever just, or right, that something *bad* is done to justify the realization of something *better*? Discuss this with the young people and debate the idea of what justice is all about. Ask them if they always act 'justly'.

Christian youth ministers could:

- Run a session exploring the causes of injustice. I recently had my hip X-rayed. The camera revealed what was beneath the surface. We often only see the surface consequences of injustice issues. If we are to stop injustices, we need to go below the surface and see the causes of the problem. I think this is what God does. Discuss with the young people what the causes are of: people going hungry; people being trafficked; immigration; climate change and/or homelessness.
- Illustrate unjust wealth distribution in the UK. Cut out of paper about 25 shapes of people. If you need help doing this, search on the internet for 'paper people cut-out'. I use some foam shapes of people I purchased in a craft store. On a table or on the floor, put one or two cut-out people at the top. Point out that these people

own the vast majority of wealth in the UK. Then put a few people in a row below them (symbolically, say, six to eight), indicating these people are quite well off. They have (or used to have prior to retiring) well-paid jobs, easily pay all their bills, holiday frequently and own their own property. Below these, put another row of people (again, say, six to eight). This group are in employment, might have some assets and just about make ends meet. Next, place another row (say, four to five people). This group of people might be in low-paid work or unemployed. They really struggle to make ends meet: their wages need subsidizing with welfare benefits; they go short of the things many take for granted and might have debt problems. Finally, add a row of people symbolizing those who can't make ends meet (say, three): they are in fuel poverty; have little food; no access to capital, holidays or private cars and/or have no prospect of breaking out of the cycles of deprivation they experience. Simply invite the young people/church to stand in the shoes of each group of people in turn. Role play each perspective, posing reflective questions to help people connect with the reality of wealth injustice: What is life like? What does the future look like? How do they feel about the other groups of people: the rich, comfortably off, struggling, poor? What, if anything, would they like to see change about their status and the status of other groups?

Equality

As highlighted, equality – or rather inequality – is one of the big issues of our time. I endeavour to pursue equality in all aspects of life and the work I am involved in. I seek to model it in the home, my family and my youth work. I need to be honest and say this is a work in progress, and I don't always get it right. Furthermore, I meet many Christians who have different views about equality. I observe some have a gender bias in their theology and practice. Others wrestle with issues like, for example, employing non-Christians in their projects. Debates about sexual orientation and same-sex marriage continue, and often I witness a disregard for equality laws and practices in churches and organizations. Fully inclusive ways of working remain elusive. People from black and minority-ethnic backgrounds remain poorly represented in senior leadership, academic and theological positions; those with mental health issues often get marginalized; and, as highlighted, young people have little say in governance matters.

If we are for equality, we have lots of politicking still to do. However, I believe progress is being made.

We have to continue to model what equality looks like in our work if we are to encourage others to emulate this. My PhD research indicated youth work projects were being inclusive in their practice. Several stories emerged from my research highlighting how young people were being treated more equally and inclusively. Sarah is a volunteer at one of the projects I studied. While an unhelpful label, in the past she might have been described as a 'marginalized' young person. However, through the work of one project she has flourished and fulfilled many aspirations. She has literally shared her life with the project: attending the project, working for them, gaining a youth work qualification and now serving the type of young people she once was. She commented:

> I think [the project] . . . sees good in young people. A lot of people tend to just brush young people off and think they're not worth the time of day . . . [The project] actually takes these young people and does see good in them, and they want them to have a positive future.

Other workers commented on how the work helped 'young people feel part of something'. Helping young people feel part of something is the first part of treating people inclusively. We then have to set about working to ensure they are treated equally. The following politicking ideas are some of the ways this can be undertaken.

Christian youth workers might:

- Organize a board games evening with a difference. Change the rules of the games to favour one group or person: load the dice; give people more chances; allocate them more money, points or cards (or whatever else relevant to each particular game); and make unfair rule changes as you go. Do this to highlight how inequality undermines fair play, opportunities and life chances, and causes arguments, conflict and unhappiness. Make sure a 'debrief' happens at the end to explain what has been going on.
- Watch a film (or part of a film) about inequality and discuss what happens in the film. For example, you could watch *12 Years a Slave*, *Amazing Grace*, *Schindler's List*, *Mississippi Burning*, *The Color Purple* or *Driving Miss Daisy* (this is a list of some of the most popular and readily available films, not necessarily most insightful). After watching the film, turn any reflections into actions: re-visit

youth club rules to make sure they are rooted in equality; review how people are treated so people are welcomed on an equal basis; and/or make sure language, attitudes and activities are appropriate to avoid alienating or demeaning any particular group of people.

Christian youth ministers could:

- Encourage young people to hold youth ministers and church leaders to account regarding their use of sexist and/or non-inclusive language and approaches.
- Use stories, pictures, videos, history and illustrations from a wide variety of ethnic and cultural traditions. Gale Richards, leader of the Baptist Union of Great Britain Racial Justice Group, says workers should:

> move away from a 'colour blind' approach to youth ministry/work. They need to know and acknowledge racial prejudice and discrimination exists in British society and beyond (just take a look at the shocking statistics on recorded levels of hate crime . . . if they have any doubt about this!). Acting as though racial prejudice and discrimination doesn't exist or being ignorant of its existence simply allows it to flourish. Thus, there is a need for youth workers as part of their practice to intentionally seek to source the stories, the images etc. they use, in a way that seeks to represent all regions of the world; so as to embrace and celebrate ethnic and cultural diversity.

- Workers could politically read Scripture through a 'black theological lens'. For example, read Luke 4.18–19 through the prism of an oppressed slave and discuss with the young people their resultant thoughts and feelings.
- Have a practical session orientated around the theme of standing up for those who might need some help and support in order to be treated more equally. Invite the young people to: stick up for someone they know is being bullied or rejected by their peer group; include someone who is often not included; and/or opt to forego their choices and preferences in order to allow others to choose activities, trips and things to do.[1]

---

1 Inspired by an original idea from *The Experiments: Leader's Guide*, Frontier Youth Trust, 2013.

Sex and gender issues

Christians doing politics made slavery illegal in the UK. The more enlightened have made gender bias a thing of the past and others are working towards making sexual-orientation equality a reality. In my experience, this generation of young people do not wish gender or sexual orientation identities to restrict who they are and what they do. Straight men like me (and the system we inadvertently represent) need to get to a place where heterosexual patriarchy no longer exclusively determines the *what*, *when* and *how*. This is a social justice issue and an essential requirement if everybody is to have the same chance of flourishing within pursuit of the common good. Nothing is more important than how we treat people and how we love them so they feel loved. If youth workers and ministers want young people to be involved in politics, they need to remove barriers relating to gender and sexual orientation that prevent young people participating. I appreciate some have a more conservative view on such matters, but Christians need to *do* the right thing (unconditionally love) as well as claim they *believe* the right thing.

During one field visit to a project I researched, I noticed a piece of artwork about a lesbian, gay, bi-sexual and transgender (LGBT) awareness week they were running. This was something I had never seen before in a Christian project. My practice experience suggests people often shy away from the subject given its polemic nature in the Church. I consider it encouraging that the project did this and addressed this subject with young people. An external stakeholder in the project declared that this approach had 'blown her away', saying she had 'witnessed gay young people . . . being affectionate with a partner and that being acceptable in [the drop-in centre] and that is gobsmacking! That is just fantastic! . . . Really deep respect for that.' As I have repeatedly mentioned, I am not seeking to be drawn into a debate about the issue, merely to reiterate that I believe we need not only to aspire to treat everybody equally in our work and politicking, but also send positively assertive messages ensuring our aspirations are supported by actions of hospitality, warmth and welcome. If we don't, or won't, I fear our views on other subject matters will never be taken seriously by those we are seeking to influence. Prior to being involved in this project, the external stakeholder was alienated from Christianity because of attitudes to homosexuality. Her experience in this project won her over and she began to see God and her people in a completely new and positive light.

Christian youth workers might:

- Undertake activities designed specifically for girls. 'Feminist Webs' is an 'online and real-world "women and girls work space"'. It has a 'bias toward work which encourages participation . . . from a perspective that focuses on women's rights and experiences'. Their online website is full of resources and ideas: www.feministwebs.com.
- Organize and have a LGBT week like the project I visited. Put up posters, have discussions and signpost specialist LGBT youth organizations supporting young people.
- Invite a politician to come and have a 'question and answer' session with the young people. Specifically invite them to talk about gender and sexuality issues in politics. They could be asked, for example: Does gender or sexuality have an impact on what it is like to be a politician in Westminster or on the local council? Why are there more male MPs than female? Does the way politics operates favour men over women? Should affirmative action or positive discrimination be practised to ensure the types of people who are MPs reflect the make-up of the population by, for example, having all-women shortlists for prospective MPs or councillors?

Christian youth ministers could:

- Do some feminist theology. Elisabeth Schüssler Fiorenza[2] encourages people to read Scripture in a number of different ways: suspiciously, believing men interpret things their way; in a way that sees women as victims of patriarchy who need honouring; and in a way that seeks to 'put back' women forgotten in all the stories and narratives. So, for example, ask provocative questions of young people: In the genealogies of the Bible (Matt. 1.1–17; Luke 3.23–38), where are the women? What were the women doing when Jesus fed the 5,000 (Mark 6.44)? Has history focused too much on 'evil' female biblical characters: Eve (Gen. 3); Jezebel (Kings 1 and 2); Delilah (Judges 16), for example? What would be your reaction if God turned out to be a Chinese woman? Were the writers of the Bible sexist, or simply reflecting the culture of their day? Part of reading the Bible politically (if you remember) is to wrestle with what was originally meant and the context it was written in. What

---

2 See Fiorenza 1994.

might some of the more sexist passages (1 Cor. 11.3; Eph. 5.22–25; 1 Tim. 2.12) read like if written today?

* Have a 'Hopes and Dreams' session where young people are invited to think about what they would like to do in life. As part of this, pose questions about roles, jobs and gender stereotyping. For example, ask: If you have children, should one parent stay at home and look after them – if so, which one? Is it acceptable that the vast majority of airline pilots, motor-racing drivers and celebrity chefs are male? It is right that the vast majority of primary school teachers, cooks and receptionists are women? Should we have more female and LGBT politicians?

Education

The sad fact about our current education system is that it doesn't really support the idea of social mobility. If children are born poor, they will likely grow up poor. While it is a noble idea to believe a good education and hard work will enable young people to progress in life, the reality is very few young people break out of the social conditions they were brought up in. Children of wealthy parents are likely to become wealthy. The UK has lower social mobility than most other developed countries. Four private schools and one elite college sent more students to Oxbridge over three years than 2,000 schools and colleges across the UK. Approximately 10 per cent of young people at the lower end of the socio-economic spectrum go to university compared with over 80 per cent of those whose parents are from managerial or professional backgrounds. While all the main political parties say they are committed to increasing social mobility, social background is still the most accurate predictor of what happens to young people in later life. This is tragic.[3]

If we believe in the idea of human dignity – where every life is equally important and precious – then we need to smash the shackles maintaining current inequalities. We need to create a new cultural paradigm: one that enables all young people to participate in politics, meaningfully influence society and one that passionately pursues the need for greater liberating education and higher levels of social mobility. I can find little solace in our existing system that encourages me to believe this will ever happen without fundamental change. Youth workers need to work to achieve this.

---

3 For a more detailed statistical analysis of Britain's social mobility, see www.sutton-trust.com.

As noted earlier, Jesus was in conflict with the ruling powers and classes of his day. I am in conflict with the powers of our day regarding how we educate our young people. Here are a few examples of how my narrative conflicts with the current ones. I would limit the choice of schools parents can consider. Building the local community, by attending and investing in local schools – rather than offering choice about schools across a wider area – would be my aspiration. I would ban private schools. I would put less emphasis on test and exam results, instead focusing on life-wide and lifelong learning achievements. I would not judge a school on what school inspectors say, but more on whether young people in the school flourish. I value music and art as much as maths and English. I consider kinaesthetic learning as important as cognitive development. I would teach young people to make a difference in the world, not just study hard in order to get a job. I could go on setting out my education manifesto, but space does not allow. I merely make the point that education is a widely contested issue and, once again, suggest that doing it Jesus-style might put youth workers and ministers in conflict with politicians, schools, teachers, parents and churches.

Christian youth workers might:

- Find out what young people think about current education policies. Young people will have experience *of* the policies, but they might not know *about* what they say and are intended to do. For example: What do they think about making exams harder? Educating people to get a job rather than for learning? Employing unqualified teachers to teach? You could design an online survey for young people to do. Keep it safe, simple and easy to use. Relay the results back to MPs and the like.
- Consider what learning is most important in life. Ask the young people what they think they need to learn about. You might need to prompt them to think about *all-of-life* issues: traditional education subjects; relationships; practical skills; setting goals; overcoming failure; social skills; handling money; how to be content; emotional skills and anything else you can think of. When they have come up with a list of things, work with them to see if they can put them in order of importance. Discuss the results with them and develop practice to reflect the outcomes.
- Invite the young people to get into small groups. On a series of pieces of paper, hand out to them a list of social and political issues. Make up others, but list things like: poor aspirations; living

in a deprived neighbourhood; substance abuse; learning difficulties; disability; poor mental health; family conflict; language challenges; racial and hate crimes; youth unemployment. Debate with the young people what they think about these issues and ask them to prioritize which should get most education resources to help empower people. Discuss the reasons for their answers.

Christian youth ministers could:

- Imagine learning in an ideal world. Have three empty cardboard boxes. Label them 'Ideal School', 'Ideal Youth Group' and 'Ideal Church' (you could add more boxes and have 'Ideal government, local council, youth parliament' etc.). Invite the young people to write or draw on pieces of paper or large post-it notes descriptions of their ideal *learning* factors. Animate them by asking them to think about: what people might learn; what they would be taught; what the learning environment would be like; who would do the teaching/facilitating; and how *success* would be measured. Work towards realizing these dreams in day-to-day youth ministry and/or do some politicking and report the findings back to school and church leaders.
- Organize a 'thank you' or 'support' evening for all those who work in schools: teachers, teaching assistants, governors, lunchtime assistants, school/youth workers, parent and other volunteers and specialist educational providers. Offer some food and drinks and have a nice welcoming atmosphere, just to show appreciation for all the hard work put into educating young people. Invite those attending to share their hopes, dreams, concerns and challenges, so these can be prayed about, acted upon and politically responded to as appropriate.

Money and welfare

In Matthew's Gospel (8.1–4) Jesus healed a leper – someone outcast, ostracized and in a social class at the bottom of Jewish society. Reflecting upon the account of what happened, I find myself feeling a bit sorry for Jesus – the leper seemingly 'dares' (Myers 2008, p. 153) Jesus to heal him. The man probably has nothing to lose, so he takes a chance, presents himself humbly before Jesus and gambles, 'If you are willing . . .' (8.2). Jesus has a bit of a dilemma here: walk away, or respond to the man knowing this would incur the wrath of the priests and make himself ritually unclean (Lev. 13). The story tells us what happened. I wonder if we would take the same gamble as the leper and *dare* Jesus to come and help us rediscover a political narrative that takes on the system and sees welfare, compassion and care for the poor as a Christian virtue.

The global neoliberal onslaught has often not been good news for young people. The problem is not globalization per se, but more the power the neoliberal aristocracy have over others. Economists and sociologists have begun to describe victims of neoliberalism as a *precariat*: a social class of people, including many young people, who precariously exist in society without any sense of security or predictable future.[4] It is argued living like this impacts material and psychological welfare. This precariat appears to live exploited and precarious lives, vulnerable to radicalization, political extremism and outbursts of pent-up anger. With around 1 million young people unemployed and many others working in low paid, low-skilled jobs on temporary or zero-hours contracts, it is perhaps no surprise money and wealth are big politicking challenges for this generation.

It appears the goal in life for so many is simply to earn money and then spend it on themselves. We need collectively to resist such selfish and seductive existences. All over the planet young people are beginning to protest about the world they exist in. Sadly, many are turning to extreme political and religious fundamentalism, because no one else is taking them seriously. I hope we can begin to take young people more seriously and rebalance how we perceive them, money and wealth.

Sarah is a young person who has been to prison. She came to FYT's young offender project lacking self-esteem and confidence. She had got herself into debt and had nowhere to live. When faced with difficulties, Sarah buried her head in the sand and hoped her problems would disappear. She might be said to typify the precariat previously described. Through practical support and guidance she has made progress and moved forward. She has undertaken one-to-one anger management and group self-esteem sessions. This has helped her cope with challenging situations and built her esteem. Sarah has now gained the confidence to start work, begin her own business and move into a flat. Sarah has joined a gym and is maintaining healthy living. She has been learning to bake cakes and is very enthusiastic to the point she bakes at every opportunity. She is caring enough to look out for others in need and often gives her cakes away. She also participates in cooking a weekly communal meal to share with her peers. Sarah has more positive friends now and has a stable boyfriend. She says she is happier than she has ever been and lives an independent life with a bit more security surrounding it.

---

4 For a discussion about the precariat, see Standing 2011.

Sarah's story is not an uncommon one: a young person with money troubles, nowhere to live, no job and a variety of personal circumstances to contend with. She needed some welfare, a fresh start and people to help support her. I am pleased to say FYT was able to provide all of these things. This costs money, but it costs less money than deciding not to help Sarah. If she returned to a life of crime, the outcome would have been predictable; she would have ended up costing the tax payer thousands of pounds. She is now beginning to flourish and contribute to the common good. This work is good news for the poor, the messy and maligned.

Christian youth workers might:

- Tell Sarah's story (or a version of it). Ask the young people to imagine they have unlimited means to help people like Sarah. What would they do to help change her *what*, *when* and *how* (you might need to explain this)? Now acknowledge that resources are limited, but things can still be done. What might these be and will the young people respond to the challenge and, where possible, begin to do them?
- A worker in my research said:

    Living and working in an economically deprived inner-city area has changed my political views, as I have sought to understand how God is at work here and in the world and sought to make sense of the deprivation that limits young people's life opportunities and God's agenda for justice.

    Do your political and theological views 'make sense' in your current work context and would they 'make sense' in other contexts? If not, what adjustments need to be made?

Christian youth ministers could:

- Turn a worship space into some shanty town houses. Use cardboard boxes, old tarpaulins and rubbish to build the houses and illustrate what living in destitution is like by showing images of global poverty. Ask the young people to go into the shanty town houses, experience what it might be like to live in one and invite them to pray for the world's population who live in such buildings.[5]

---

5 Special thanks to youth worker Robin Smith for this idea.

- Be very assertive in securing money from the Church to support work with young people. Church politics doesn't always work in favour of young people. An exciting vision, clear strategy, defined process and proposed work plan all need developing, along with a full costing for this work. This needs to be presented to stakeholders and the powers that be so money for young people's work is secured.
- In talking about money and economics, Fred Milson said, 'a church which has no quarrel with the world has no message for the world' (1980, p. 65). What quarrel and messages about money should the Church have in this era? How can these best be integrated into the values of the work done with young people? Is the quarrel/message reflected in the activities, processes and pedagogies present in youth ministry? If not, what adjustments need to be made? For example, young people could be encouraged to live and give generously or perhaps sacrifice their pizza night and make soup instead, giving away the money saved.

Community

A colleague recently met a young adult involved in a punk community in south-west England. This community were very opposed to the values of one of the more racist political parties campaigning in the area and so they went around taking down this particular party's campaign posters.

Rob Wardle, the worker I mentioned in Chapter 5, wanted to demonstrate the needs of the community from the perspective of the people living there. He asked the young people to make a film, interviewing parents and professionals delivering services on the housing estate. The youth workers' role in the film was to hold the camera and ask some of the questions. Importantly, the young people devised the questions and decided which questions were to be asked to whom. The result, Rob said,

was a 'community view' on what it was like to live on the estate, with some humour – an ingredient which always finds its way in when you let young people write the recipe. What was interesting was that we thought the film was just saying what we already knew – but the film seemed to be revealing something new and different to the professionals from the council and housing associations. This suggests young people can give a profound perspective on how things actually are; what reality is.

Both these stories illustrate young people doing politicking and taking responsibility for where they live. One approach was very confrontational, the other highly illuminating and impacting. It is my conviction that when communities do politicking together, it is more powerful. It brings people together, empowers them, motivates them, engenders mutual accountability and somehow carries more weight and attracts more attention. Both these groups comprise what I would call *common people*. I know the area Rob works in well, and I can imagine what a community of punk rockers resembles. They are both groups of common people. I mean no offence by using the phrase. I use it because it is the meaning of the Greek word (*ochlos*: the common people, as opposed to the rulers and leaders) Mark uses in his Gospel when reporting, 'the common people heard him gladly' (Mark 12.37, King James Bible). I believe common people coming together can be a powerful political force in the community. I hope youth workers and ministers can help communities come together to politick. I also hope that, in so helping, we will remember to be *common*, down to earth, understandable, and make the people glad.

Christian youth workers might:

- Strategically deploy the principle of subsidiarity (discussed in Chapter 7), so young people fully participate in the life of the local community. For example, if meetings are needed with stakeholders, let young people take a lead; if a community activity on the local park is envisaged, let the young people plan, organize and set it up; if your street, village, suburb or town is celebrating something, work hard to empower young people in the event design and delivery.
- Set up temporary respite centres. One of my research participants did this for the emergency services during the 2011 riots; they involved all ages from the community. Why not do something similar for local shoppers, visitors to the park or at a community event. This can be something simple that gives people drinks, snacks and an encouraging word to bless them on their way.
- Encourage young people to be accountable for their actions in the community. Some politicians have a reputation for being a law unto themselves. Work with the young people to be counter-cultural in their politicking.

Christian youth ministers could:

- Make sure, insist and demand that *all* young people and workers at *all* times are loved, accepted and welcomed into the community irrespective of their colour, religion, gender, sexual orientation, marital status and/or intersex status. Embed this into hearts, minds, policies and practices.
- Restore something lost or stolen. Restitution is a powerful political statement about community. With the young people, repair, restore, paint, grow and/or replace something in the community as a symbolic act and means of putting right something lost or stolen, or a past wrong. I have planted some flower bulbs in my village in a spot dominated by builder's rubble – I wanted to restore the landscape to something beautiful.

Young people's rights and representations

One project studied in my research had a specific Core Values document. It stated:

> Through putting . . . young people's needs first and not our own personal gain, we will be able to more accurately meet *their* needs, answer *their* questions and support them in *their* choices.

This is so important if young people's rights are to be upheld in a societal context that often conspires against them. I am not suggesting young people run riot without consideration of others, merely that the power balance is adjusted, so young people are more highly valued, respected and trusted. Sometimes this necessitates standing up for them and making political representation on their behalf. I politick in this way by writing letters to media outlets whenever I feel young people are not being valued and respected. Letters are sometimes ignored by media editors, but occasionally they print them and correct a wrong. I offer a couple of examples below of letters I have written to highlight how this key issue of lack of respect and misrepresentation might be addressed. I offer my own examples not as a way of magnifying my importance but simply as practice illustrations and examples.

This first letter was sent in response to an article in a newspaper weekend magazine supplement. The article, as the letter highlights, said some truly terrible things about young people – things society would not say about any other group:

[The journalist's] assertion that young people are 'bovine, useless, lazy-arsed, chlamydia-stuffed and good for nothing' is inaccurate, condescending and offensive. Perhaps she should get out more and visit the youth clubs and bus shelters she refers to and actually meet some young people. She might find them to be a generation that is academically high-achieving, concerned about the mess that adults have created and fed up with the ill-informed opinions of people like [her].

The second letter was written to a well-known 'rural issues' magazine. It was in response to a letter printed the previous month from an irate adult who took a swipe at all young people because of a bad experience with a handful of them:

I was sad to see the letter about young people littering and being abusive in a recent edition of your excellent magazine. I was sad on two levels. Firstly, as someone who has worked with young people for many years, I know they can be challenging and I was disappointed to hear of their behaviour on his occasion. However, I was doubly sad that you chose to print a letter that in one simple piece wrote off a whole generation!

While not excusing such behaviour, I can recount stories of how young people have been very considerate, served their communities, volunteered to help others and worked on projects to support the vast ecological treasures we have in this country. I can also recount incidents when adults have littered, been abusive and disrespectful to their environments. However, I wouldn't dream of writing them off with an over-generalization. The vast majority of young people behave well and grow up to be hardworking adult members of society like the rest of us.

Not only did this letter get printed, it won 'letter of the month', and I received a lovely hamper of wine and food goodies.

Christian youth workers might:

- Need to ensure that in everything they do, they fully consider young people's voting and decision-making rights. Be it choosing the new paint colour in the youth club, establishing membership criteria for the local community centre management committee, voicing opinions about the local council, and/or communicating and working with the community – young people have a right to have their say in what happens. Youth workers need to advocate and make sure this happens.

- Write a letter about one of the political issues important to the young people.
- Go through a selection of newspapers and identify political issues about young people. Discuss these with the young people and decide if any follow-up action or politicking is required.

Christian youth ministers could:

- Ensure young people's voices are heard in church decision-making. Establish, or develop, how young people are involved in church governance, so they have a say not only in decisions which impact them but also decisions about wider church life issues. For example, if they have grown up in the Church, they probably have great insight about the children's work they experienced; this could help shape future work.
- Make sure macropolitical issues affecting young people are brought to the attention of church congregations via regular communications.
- Establish processes to continually drip-feed stories about young people into the consciousnesses of people in the Church. This can be done in newsletters, personal testimony, via websites or social media channels.

Power

During the research for this book I engaged in a debate with my colleague Dylan Barker. Dylan suggested a youth worker may be highly politically engaged, but because of the nature of the work undertaken with young people the opportunity for encouraging political engagement with those young people might not be a priority. He suggested that the potential needs of the young people, especially if they were *at risk*[6] young people, needed to be responded to and met first. I suggested being political might be the priority for the worker because, if not, the young people will continue to have needs, unless they can be politically empowered (especially regarding social and economic political matters)

---

6 The term 'at risk' used here refers to social, personal, economic, spiritual and emotional needs, rather than being at risk in a safeguarding manner.

to change their world and social conditions for the better. In short, I contended they will remain victims of present politicking regimes and at the mercy of current power-holders unless their situation can be changed. We rested our debate, considering this was a classic 'chicken and egg scenario' as to what was most important – immediate help or long-term solutions.

Who has power, what that power is, where it emerges from, how it is exercised and to whom it is accountable are important questions in debates about the *what*, *when* and *how*. It is not possible to address all these questions in just one book. However, I wish to focus on one specific issue here. My hope is to create conditions that give young people more power. This gives them the opportunity to see our broken world with fresh eyes, respond to the challenges it presents in new ways and help mend it by ushering in the kingdom of God. A revolution of power would be nice, but I will settle for something smaller if it takes politicking debates forward.

> Recently we held a debate between young people . . . all about Scottish independence. Some politicians attended but they were not allowed to speak; but were there to listen to the young people debating. The young people then created a piece of art to represent their opinion which was then displayed in a gallery. This was then open to the public so that as many people [as possible] could hear/see what young people thought about the issue. The best thing to come out of this was that other young people came to the gallery who then started to talk about other issues they cared about.

This story from a research participant wonderfully illustrates how power can be used to engage others more effectively in politicking. I would encourage everybody to embrace this type of thinking about power. Ask those with it to be silent, and listen to those without it. Record in some way what is said and reflect upon what the powerless have said. Then invite others who are powerless to join and broaden the debate.

Christian youth workers might:

- Set up a 'Speakers Corner' in the youth club, local skate park or wherever else appropriate. Explain that this is an area where open public speaking, debate and discussion are allowed. Set up some ground rules (like no personal abuse of people or hateful language), invite the young people to come up with politicking topics they would like to speak about, support them in planning and delivering their speeches, and then *listen* to what they have to say. Debate and discuss speeches and, if they consent, video or record what is said for possible use in other contexts.

- Explore what the main political parties do regarding engagement of younger voters. Do an internet search with the words 'youth [name of political party]', or 'young [name of political party]' and you should find the relevant sites. Discuss with the young people their thoughts and feelings about these sites and what they say about people's power.

- Invite a guest speaker to the youth group who has undertaken an act of civil disobedience or done something politically 'dissenting'. Ask them to tell their story and hold a discussion about what they did and why they did it.

Christian youth ministers could:

- Explore the subject of 'power' in the Bible. Power can be seen to be used for good and bad in Scripture. Explore with the young people what biblical illustrations they can recall regarding *good* use of power and *bad* use of power.

- Pray and give thanks for those with power: MPs, MEPs, Prime Minister, council leaders, teachers, church leaders, business people, civil servants – anyone who has power. Pray they will lead and manage well and make just and godly decisions. Reflect upon the words of the prophet Zechariah (4.6), who says it is 'Not by might, nor by power, but by my Spirit, says the LORD Almighty'. What might this mean for people with power?

- Consider the idea that conformity can be a dangerous dynamic in both politics and Christianity. If malaise and tyranny are to be avoided, new ideas have to be pursued, tested out, refined and integrated into practice. In order to help develop this, hang around the 'right' people: nonconformists, risk-takers, reflectors, table-turners, peace-lovers, grace-bringers, shalom-makers and/or creative types!

Multiculturalism and immigration

Young people are growing up in a global world, the like of which has never been experienced before: their phones might come from South Korea; their clothes from Bangladesh; the trainers they wear from

China; the wood for their skateboards from Canada; the bus taking them to school from Germany (with components in it coming from Spain, Poland, Japan etc.); and the books they read from Northampton, invoiced via a company in Luxembourg. This global picture is now a familiar one. They will eat food originating from Asia, listen to music inspired by people from the Pacific Rim, potentially hear many different languages spoken in their schools, and some will inhale substances grown in South America. Yet, despite these global influences, the cross-pollination of cultures and fusion of ideas, UK society appears to be getting more politically insular, protective of its borders and more dogmatic about what it means to be British. The picture is a confusing one and the discourse contested.

At the macropolitical level, the politics of the Right are in the ascendancy. There are calls to restrict immigration and narratives stating (actually and metaphorically) that the time has come to pull up the drawbridges and protect that within the castle walls. Ongoing revelations of our institutional racist insularity and attitudes proliferate and assertions we are a Christian country continue to present as Islamophobic and imperialistic. Sleepy villages, thatched-cottage hamlets, green rolling fields and an ideal of an imagined countryside continue to be upheld as models of Englishness. Tourist brochures rarely exemplify the delights of Peckham, the plurality of Leicester or the diversity of Luton as places to be visited and emulated. This is the context, or rather the multitude of contexts, within which Christian-motivated work exists.

I mentioned previously my colleague Dylan. He wanted to address some of the issues around immigration in his youth work, so he set up the youth club as an immigration centre. The first few young people who arrived were asked to play wardens and guards and all other subsequent young people had to fill in a form in order to enter the club. With their completed forms, they were hauled in front of a panel and had to plead their case to be let into the youth club. Dylan had briefed the panel to intentionally discriminate against some of the young people. Afterwards everyone involved discussed what had happened and UK immigration policy.

Debates about multiculturalism and immigration are extensions of arguments about political power. The debates always involve a dominant group, a subordinate group, a perceived series of threats one group asserts about another, all usually underpinned by a gross lack of human connectedness and understanding. A more informed perspective influenced by *interculturalism*, I believe, would help the situation. At its most basic level, interculturalism is about enabling people to relate to those who are different from themselves in ways that focus on exchange and interaction. Interculturalism recognizes that people live differently, but accepts these differences with respect and appreciation, believing engagement with others is an opportunity to learn, rather than a threat. It demands a validation of other cultures, rather than a quest to change them. Interculturalism does not seek to assimilate those who are different into a predetermined way of being, nor expect a multicultural living of parallel lives. It sets the bar higher than this.

Good youth work and ministry should be intercultural. It should appreciate different cultures, engage with them, and work within them. Work seeking to impose or assimilate others into a particular way of being is based on an imperial colonial political mentality. I do not consider this has any place in contemporary models of mission. The gospel needs to engage with culture and allow an intercultural manifestation of the kingdom to materialize. Youth workers and ministers need to be prepared for the pioneering outworking and political consequences of this approach.[7]

Christian youth workers might:

- Organize a session like Dylan did. The youth club could be turned into an immigration centre or young people could be asked to take a citizenship test. You could make one up or search online for 'British citizenship test'.
- Remind young people we are all different yet the same. A famous fast-food outlet has restaurants in virtually every country in the world, yet it doesn't serve the same food in each. In different countries you can get shrimp burgers, lobster, fried brie cheese, seaweed-flavour fries, cold soup, potato and pea burgers, and even chicken porridge. Discuss how cultures are different – not *right* or *wrong*, but *different*. You could illustrate this by sharing or talking with the young people about food, customs, clothing, music, art, stories, TV programmes and/or family life in different cultures and how politics is expressed differently in different parts of the world.
- Make a piece of art to celebrate people diversity. Collect some old buttons (or anything similar) of different shapes and sizes. You will also need a piece of board or an art canvas and some glue. Explain that people are like the buttons – all different colours, sizes, ages

7 For a further discussion about these missional approaches, see Pimlott and Pimlott 2008, pp. 32–6.

and designs. Invite the young people to choose a few buttons each (adapt according to the numbers of young people) and then glue them on the board/canvas as a symbolic act to celebrate diversity. They could glue them in the shape of a person, heart, tree, question mark or anything else appropriate. Follow with a discussion about humanity, uniqueness and togetherness.

Christian youth ministers could:

- Set up an exchange event with young people from another part of the country, a different faith or a different ethnic background. The purpose would be to learn about each other, not determine if one way of being was better than another. A meal could be shared (taking special dietary requirements into account), a residential could be arranged or a visit to a different place of worship organized. Youth workers at The Feast have some excellent guidelines for doing this: www.thefeast.org.uk/resources/guidelines-for-dialogue.
- Gather a selection of old glasses, spectacles and sunglasses (people who wear glasses often have old pairs of these lying around at home). Invite young people to put the glasses on – just for a few seconds, so eye strain and headaches don't occur. The young people should notice they get a different view and perspective through different lenses; things get distorted, confused and blurred. Use this exercise as a way of introducing the idea of seeing things through different lenses. Follow it up by asking the young people how they might see the community they live in and their church, if they were: an immigrant just arrived from overseas; an asylum-seeker fleeing persecution in their homeland; unable to speak the language and/ or they were the only person of their race in the church/community. Discuss any resulting feelings, thoughts and actions.

War and conflict

Jodie Watson is a youth worker. She asked the Nottingham young people she works with what they would like to discuss. They said they wanted to talk about 'war and God'. Given the lack of attention given to this subject matter (see Chapter 6), I thought this encouraging. Jodie and the young people discussed the root causes of war and decided these were 'sin'. They looked at various Bible passages to arrive at this conclusion. They looked at how God tells people to deal with the wrongs done and explored issues like the armour of God, genocide, rape and world wars. They considered biblical characters like Joshua and looked in Deuteronomy at the conditions regarding the sending of people into war. One young person asked if soldiers would go to hell for fighting. They concluded that God does not condone war. However, in certain circumstances God appoints someone who will obey him to carry out judgement on his behalf.

This brief summary of what Jodie and the young people did is offered without critique. I simply retell the story to illustrate that young people are often interested in the big political issues of life and have many questions and insights about these. My appeal is that we follow the lead of workers like Jodie and have the courage to enter into an honest and open politicking debate about such matters.

As I write this, the country is once again discussing the issue of war and whether we should take military action in the Middle East. The military action being considered follows the previous military action which did not have the intended outcome for those who sanctioned it. Condemnations, debates, questions, accusations and counter-accusations rage about our recent military exploits. Space does not allow a full debate about this, but I simply observe that many have died, many young people have lost parents and we don't seem to have learnt much or made anybody's world a better place as a result. Blessed are the peacemakers.

Christian youth workers might:

- Organize a discussion about militarization in schools – as the youth worker mentioned in Chapter 6 did.
- Undertake a reflective exercise to help young people discover what they think about war and conflict. Divide a room into four zones, using strips of masking tape: Zone 1 means, 'I strongly agree'; Zone 2, 'I agree'; Zone 3, 'disagree'; and Zone 4, 'strongly disagree'. Then read out the following statements, pausing after each to ask the young people to move to the zone reflecting their opinion. After each statement ask a few young people the reasons for their choices; stress that you are after their honest opinion, not any one particular answer. Follow this with a discussion.

  o It is fine to go to war if it makes us richer.
  o The use of military force to prevent an even bigger military conflict taking place is acceptable.
  o Invading a country hundreds of miles away is OK if it protects our country from possible attack in the future.

- o Killing people is acceptable if it saves the lives of other people.
- o It doesn't matter how we use military force so long as we achieve what we want.
- o I would rather spend money on buying arms than on building better schools.

Christian youth ministers could:

- Run a session like Jodie did using the same ideas, Bible passages and reflections. Make a record of the discussion by creating a piece of street art, collage or graffiti so others can look at and reflect upon what the young people said.
- Explain, discuss with and invite young people to consider wearing white poppies during times of remembrance, rather than (or in addition to) the traditional red. White poppies have traditionally symbolized 'peace'. An internet search of 'white poppies' will provide further details and information.
- Organize a peace vigil. Work with the young people to determine where to undertake the vigil (military base, government offices, weapons manufacturer, for example) and spend time with them discussing what it is they want to achieve from the vigil, so they can clearly articulate what is motivating their politicking.

The National Youth Agency (2004, p. 6) has a set of ethical principles designed to ensure good practice for youth workers and good outcomes for young people. This commits youth workers to:

- Treat young people with respect, valuing each individual and avoiding negative discrimination.
- Respect and promote young people's rights to make their own decisions and choices.
- Promote and ensure the welfare and safety of young people, while permitting them to learn through undertaking challenging educational activities.
- Contribute towards the promotion of social justice for young people and in society generally, through encouraging respect for difference and diversity and challenging discrimination.

It is hoped the material in this book and the exercises and activities in this chapter will help realize these commitments and improve politicking work with young people.

10

Conclusion

I was in a kids' group at Spring Harvest when I first heard about trafficking and it changed how I saw the lives of other children my age around the world. My mum's friend works for the charity Love 146, and they organized a sponsored 14.6K event along our local sea front. I choose to cycle the 14.6K, because I believe all children deserve to sleep safely at night without fear of being taken and forced into a life they did not choose.

Even at my young age I can make a difference. It was a hard ride on the day, the wind was very strong and halfway through I wanted to quit, but I didn't! Children don't have a choice whether they are trafficked or not, but I had a choice whether I continued and I chose to push through the pain. I'm not going to lie, my bottom hurt for two days after the cycle, but it's nothing compared to the pain some young women my age are put through. Age doesn't stop you being able to make a difference.

George Dunning, aged 11

I have been inspired by the many people who have helped with the research, ideas, comments and actions contained in this book. No more so than by young people like George who decided she was going to make a difference in the world.

Thirty-five years ago, Fred Milson (1980, p. 63) wrote a book about education and politics. It was published, like this book, by SCM Press in association with Frontier Youth Trust. He said:

> The active involvement of Christians in politics is a matter of theology: in other words, it rests on what they believe God to be like as he has revealed himself in the Bible and supremely in Jesus Christ . . . The God of the Bible is involved in the affairs of men [and women, children and young people], opposing injustice of all kinds and working for social righteousness as well as individual goodness. His followers will join in the same struggle or they may find he is no longer in their midst.

I consider this is as true today as it was then. My research has uncovered a suspicion and cynicism towards national macropolitical representations. Many youth workers indicated an intention to leave national politicking alone and instead focus on politics and matters at a local level. While I understand the reasons for such views, I don't think we can do this. There is a Chinese proverb that says, 'The mountains are high, and the emperor is far away.' We cannot afford to take this attitude and let what is decided by politicians in London or Brussels become irrelevant to our local youth work practice. If we wish to continue faithfully to serve God, we cannot abandon national and international politics. Disillusionment abounds, but we cannot retreat – even if the system is broken.

Perhaps the experience of the 2014 Scottish Independence Referendum can provide some hope for those of us who are passionate about people doing macropolitics. When elections are about issues, rather than personalities and parties, people appear to engage more. When younger people have a vote they suddenly get attention from politicians. When lots of people participate and indicate they want things to be different, the Establishment gets worried. Perhaps Christian-motivated workers need to harness these dynamics and work extra hard at the micro level to help young people maximize the opportunities.

Notwithstanding this, we cannot ignore our role in establishing how the world has become. We have committed sins of omission, failing to do those things we know we should. We have also committed sins of commission, doing what we know to be wrong. I also believe we have committed sins of selectivity, picking and choosing which issues and wrongs to focus on, while ignoring others. I am probably guilty of doing this in this book, but I am convinced, like young George, that we have to get involved and struggle more for global justice, righteousness and goodness. As the Greek philosopher Plato very cleverly noted, 'One of the penalties of refusing to participate in politics is that you end up being governed by your inferiors.'

During the course of my writing, the world of politics and politicking has experienced many ebbs and flows. There is a continuing perception that party politics and elected politicians remain somewhat distant and detached from the electorate. The way we are governed has become dislocated from the *what, when* and *how* of the people. Simultaneously, social media and internet politicking appears to be growing in both volume and scope. Local activism is developing, particularly via the Citizens movement, and church-based activism has grown significantly. Elements of the Church continue to send mixed messages to society about politics. On the one hand, the Church is standing up against pay-day lenders, providing foodbanks and backing campaigns like the one George got involved in, yet in other matters it sides with those who hold power. A group of disabled people recently organized an 'occupy' protest at Westminster Abbey. They were campaigning to preserve services they rely upon and planned to camp out at the Abbey. The church and the police had other ideas: the police rushed to stop the protest and threatened those involved with arrest. This caused my good friend Al Barrett, Rector of Hodge Hill in Birmingham, to tweet, 'Yet again CofE's public face is that of the oppressive, defensive neoliberal state and not the vulnerable.' This is not good news, either for those in need of help or for the Church. It highlights that a lot of work still needs to be done if the Church is to embody the Nazareth Manifesto.

When I began my research, the idea of the common good was not a widely discussed principle. Now it is presented by academics, theologians, social commentators and politicians as an idea worthy of very serious consideration. I first started exploring the concept in 2010. It immediately resonated with my experience of Christian-motivated work and, when coupled with the idea of human flourishing, seemed to capture so much of what those of us who serve young people are seeking to do: help young people flourish and build a world where everyone can live life to the full. If you take nothing else from this book, I hope and pray you will embrace these dual ideas and make them a reality.

I decided to take no money from my publishers or my employers regarding the writing and selling of this book. I say this not because I am looking for accolades but because I wish what I have said to be as reflective of my beliefs, values and aspirations as possible. I don't want to be accused of making money out of a subject matter already far too tainted by allegations of misdemeanour and corruption. God, politics and the future for young people don't need any further recriminations from a cynical press or public.

We can change the future by helping our young people think about, critique and respond to the many ideas I have set out in this book. I don't ask you to agree with them all, but I do earnestly encourage you to think about them all. I am fully aware that other arguments and different perspectives to the ones I have presented exist. I would argue that these other perspectives tend to be held by people with money, power, influence, or all three. They may be right and I may be wrong. If that is the case I would love to hear their explanations as to why the world is like it is; why wealth and power are in the hands of a few privileged elite, and why so many remain poor and disenfranchised. If Scripture, history and experience are validating reference points, the current position cannot be what God wants.

Power-holders rarely encourage critical and reflexive thinking – they don't want those of us without power to do this because it might reduce

the power they have. The people of God need to speak truth and practise that truth towards the people with power. They also need to love
those in power – be they neighbours or enemies. The good news should
spur us on to love our neighbours *and* our enemies. The power-holders
and elites who might be said to run the empire all too readily identify
what is important. We need to change that. We need to change that
to avoid being culturally enslaved to an empire-based ideology alien
to that of the kingdom of God. I refuse to be despondent, in despair
and resignation. I am choosing to keep focused on the hope of a more
positive future – a hope ordained by a God who goes before us, who
has moved from forsakenness and now indwells among us as one of us,
Immanuel.

I always have hope, and I hope the books and youth work resources
I have written are helpful and make a difference to youth work practice
and outcomes for young people. I hope for no less with this book. For
me, this book is the most important resource I have written. It has been
a work of passion, motivated by a belief that God wants things to be
better and a conviction that they can be, so long as youth workers and
ministers take seriously the call to be *fully* Christ-like in their work.
We will never be Christ-like if we ignore the fact that Jesus did politics,
and did it in a highly charged and contested political context. We will
also never be fully Christ-like if our approach does not have a special
place for the poor, ostracized and marginalized of society: George
understands this – perhaps this is because her mum is a Christian youth
worker. There is another proverb, this time a French one, that says,
'There is no pillow so soft as a clear conscience.' I want to have a clear
conscience. I don't want to be the one who failed to politick, failed
to respond to the needs of the poor and marginalized and failed
to embrace the changes needed to build the kingdom of God more
effectively. As the proverb implies, I want to sleep at night, with a clear
conscience. My hope and prayer is that whatever your context, you
will embrace wholeheartedly the need to passionately do some politicking. This would make me very happy and help ensure we both have a
peaceful – perhaps even a shalom-ful – night's sleep.

Appendix

My Research

Doctorate research

My PhD explored faith-based youth work in a social policy context. The study developed an explanatory model for faith-based youth work and involved a scoping survey, focus group consultations and four case studies of Christian-motivated youth work projects. Data was collected from faith-based youth workers from a variety of backgrounds and practices to develop the model, which establishes the foundational ethos of faith-based work, the grounding upon which it is developed, the philosophical shape of how it operates and the pedagogical intentions of what it does as it supports transformation in young people. This research was undertaken between 2010 and 2013. My studies were funded by Staffordshire University, Oasis College and the Institute for Children, Youth and Mission.

Frontier Youth Trust research

This consisted of an online survey of Christian youth workers and ministers. One hundred and eleven workers participated in the survey, undertaken between December 2013 and February 2014. A variety of workers voluntarily took part. They were of mixed ages and genders, employed full time, part time, as volunteers and in a mix of roles. Some were professionally qualified, some had other qualifications and some had no qualifications.

Consultation Learning Day

Facilitated by myself at the Palace of Westminster in January 2014, this day was a joint venture between FYT and Worth Unlimited, sponsored by Gavin Shuker MP. Forty-five Christian-motivated workers from a variety of backgrounds took part, along with two MPs and a baroness. The day consisted of some short keynote inputs, a number of open discussions and times of reflection. Extensive notes of the conversations were documented to form a record of what was said.

Bibliography

Alinksy, S. D., 1971, 1989, *Rules for Radicals*, New York: Vintage Books.

Andrews, D., 2012, *Not Religion, But Love: Practicing a Radical Spirituality of Compassion*, Eugene, OR: Wipf and Stock.

Augustine, 2003, *City of God*, London: Penguin Books.

Baker, C., 2014, 'Never mind what Jesus would do: progressive atheism & the Big Society', William Temple Foundation Blog, Chester: William Temple Foundation, http://williamtemplefoundation.org.uk/never-mind-what-jesus-would-do-progressive-atheism-big-society/.

Balasuriya, T., 1978, 'Spirituality in politics', in A. Kee (ed.), *The Scope of Political Theology*, London: SCM Press, pp. 108–13.

Bartley, J., 2006, *Faith and Politics after Christendom: The Church as a Movement for Anarchy*, Milton Keynes: Paternoster Press.

Bentham, J., 1823, *Not Paul, But Jesus*, http://www.gutenberg.org/ebooks/42984.

Birch, S., Gottifried, G. and Lodge, G., 2013, *Divided Democracy: Political Equality in the UK and Why It Matters*, London: Institute of Public Policy Research.

Birdwell, J. with Stephen Timms MP (eds), 2013, *Exploring the Role of Faith in British Society and Politics*, London: Demos.

Blond, P., 2010, *Red Tory: How Left and Right have Broken Britain and How We can Fix It*, London: Faber and Faber.

Bonhoeffer, D., 1977, *Letter and Papers from Prison*, New York: Touchstone.

Bosnich, D. A., 1996, 'The principle of subsidiarity', *Religion and Liberty* 6:4, p. 9, http://www.acton.org/sites/v4.acton.org/files/pdf/rl_v06n4.pdf.

Bourdieu, P. and Passeron, J.-C., 1990, *Reproduction in Education, Society, and Culture*, London: Sage Publications.

Brierley, D., 2003, *Joined Up: An Introduction to Youth Work and Ministry*, Carlisle: Authentic Lifestyle and Spring Harvest Publishing Division.

Burridge, R. A., 2014, *Four Gospels, One Jesus? A Symbolic Reading*, 3rd edn, London: SPCK.

Cameron, C. and Moss, P. (eds), 2011, *Social Pedagogy and Working with Children and Young People: Where Care and Education Meet*, London: Jessica Kingsley.

Carter, W., 2006, 'The Gospel of John & empire: interview with Tripp Fuller', Homebrewed Christianity, http://homebrewedchristianity.com/2014/08/26/the-gospel-of-john-empire-w-warren-carter/.

Clark, R., 2007, *The Road to Southend Pier: One Man's Struggle against the Surveillance Society*, Petersfield: Harriman House Ltd.

Clifford, P. R., 1984, *Politics and the Christian Vision*, London: SCM Press.

Cloke, P. and Beaumont, J., 2012, 'Geographies of postsecular rapprochement in the city', *Progress in Human Geography* 37:1, pp. 27–51.

Cloke, P., Thomas, S. and Williams, A., 2012, 'Radical faith praxis? Exploring the changing theological landscape of faith motivation', in J. Beaumont and P. Cloke (eds), *Faith-Based Organisations, Welfare and Exclusion in European Cities*, Bristol: Policy Press, pp. 105–26.

Collins-Mayo, S. and Dandelion, P. (eds), 2010, *Religion and Youth*, Farnham: Ashgate Publishing.

Collins-Mayo, S., Mayo, B. and Nash, S., 2010, *The Faith of Generation Y*, London: Church House Publishing.

Cooper, T., 2007, *Controversies in Political Theology: Development or Liberation?*, London: SCM Press.

Davies, Q., Clark, B. and Sharp, M., 2008, *Report of Inquiry into National Recognition of our Armed Forces*, London: HM Stationery Office.

Dean, K. C., 2010, *Almost Christian: What the Faith of Our Teenagers is Telling the American Church*, New York: Oxford University Press.

Deutsch, K. W., 1980, *Politics and Government: How People Decide Their Fate*, Boston, MA: Houghton Mifflin.

DiMaggio, P. J. and Powell, W., 1983, 'The iron cage revisited: institutional isomorphism and collective rationality in organizational fields', *American Sociological Review* 48, pp. 147–60, http://www.ics.uci.edu/~corps/phaseii/DiMaggioPowell-IronCageRevisited-ASR.pdf.

Dinas, E., 2013, 'Why does the apple fall far from the tree? How early political socialization prompts parent–child dissimilarity', *British Journal of Political Science* 43:1, pp. 1–26.

Dustmann, C. and Farttini, T., 2013, *The Fiscal Effects of Immigration to the UK*, London: University College London, Centre for Research and Analysis of Migration, http://www.cream-migration.org/publ_uploads/CDP_22_13.pdf.

Ellis, J., 1990, 'Informal education – a Christian perspective', in T. Jeffs and M. K. Smith (eds), *Using Informal Education*, Buckingham: Open University Press, pp. 89–99.

Fiorenza, E. S., 1994, *Searching the Scriptures: A Feminist Introduction*, London: SCM Press, pp. 1–28.

Freire, P., 1972, *Pedagogy of the Oppressed*, London: Penguin Books.

Frontier Youth Trust, 2013, *The Experiments: Leader's Guide*, Birmingham: Frontier Youth Trust, http://www.fyt.org.uk/v2/wp-content/uploads/The-Experiments-Leaders-Guide-.pdf.

Giddens, A., 1994, *Beyond Left and Right: The Future of Radical Politics*, Oxford: Blackwell.

Gordon, C., 1991, 'Governmental rationality: an introduction', in G. Burchell, C. Gordon, and P. Miller (eds), *The Foucault Effect: Studies in Governmentality – with two lectures and an interview with Michel Foucault*, Hemel Hempstead: Harvester Wheatsheaf.

Habermas, J., 2010, 'An awareness in what is missing', in J. Habermas et al., *An Awareness in What Is Missing: Faith and Reason in a Post-Secular Age*, Cambridge: Polity Press, pp. 15–23 and 72–88.

Hansen, I., 2014, 'What happened during the European elections?', Fresher Perspective Blog, http://fresherperspective.tumblr.com/post/87622064467/what-happened-during-the-european-elections.

Havel, V., 1993, *Summer Meditations*, trans. P. Wilson, Toronto: Vintage Books.

Heywood, A., 2000, *Key Concepts in Politics*, New York: St Martin's Press.

Horvath, A. and Paolini, G., 2013, *Political Participation and EU Citizenship: Perceptions and Behaviours of Young People*, Eurydice and Policy Support Unit (P9) of the Education, Audiovisual and Culture Executive Agency, http://eacea.ec.europa.eu/youth/tools/documents/perception-behaviours.pdf.

House of Commons Education Committee, 2011, *Services for Young People: Third Report of Session 2010–2011*, Volume 1, London: The Stationery Office Ltd.

Imafidon, K., 2014, *The Kenny Report II: Is 'Politics' for Young People?*, London: Core Plan, http://kennyimafidon.com/wp-content/uploads/2013/10/The-Kenny-Report-2-Is-Politics-for-young-people1.pdf.

Ivereigh, A., 2010, *Faithful Citizens*, London: Darton, Longman and Todd.

Jeffs, T. and Smith, M. K., 1997, 2005, 2011, 'What is informal education?', *The Encyclopaedia of Informal Education*, http://infed.org/mobi/what-is-informal-education/.

Kallas, J., 1965, 'Romans xiii.1–7: an interpolation', *New Testament Studies* 11, pp. 365–74.

Knost, L. R., 2012, 'About the author', http://www.littleheartsbooks.com/about-the-authorillustrator/.

Lasswell, H., 1936, *Politics: Who Gets What, When, How*, New York: McGraw-Hill Book Company.

Lawrence-Lightfoot, J., 1997, 'On context', in J. Lawrence-Lightfoot and S. Hoffmann-Davis, *The Art and Science of Portraiture*, San Francisco, CA: Jossey-Bass, pp. 39–82.

Maneker, J., 2007, 'False consciousness in the church: my dialogue with a homo-phobic pastor', *Whosoever*, http://whosoever.org/v11i6/false.shtml.

Marx, K., 1859, *A Contribution to the Critique of Political Economy*, Preface, http://www.marxists.org/archive/marx/works/1859/critique-pol-economy/.

McMeekin, G., 2014, 'Christian youth work and the kingdom of God', in S. Nash and J. Whitehead (eds), *Christian Youth Work in Theory and Practice: A Handbook*, London: SCM Press.

Milson, F., 1980, *Political Education: A Practical Guide for Christian Youth Workers*, Exeter: Paternoster and Frontier Youth Trust.

Moore, T., 1832, *The Works of Lord Byron: With His Letters and Journals*, Vol. V, London: John Murray.

Morisy, A., 2009, *Beyond the Good Samaritan*, London: Continuum.

Myers, C., 2008, *Binding the Strong Man: A Political Reading of Mark's Story of Jesus*, Maryknoll, NY: Orbis Books.

National Youth Agency, 2004, *Ethical Conduct in Youth Work*, Leicester: National Youth Agency.

Nicholls, D., 2012, *For Youth Workers and Youth Work: Speaking Out for a Better Future*, Bristol: Policy Press.

Ortiz, I. and Cummins, M., 2011, *Global Inequality: Beyond the Bottom Billion: A Rapid Review of Income Distribution in 141 Countries*, New York: UNICEF.

Oxfam, 2014, *A Tale of Two Britains: Inequality in the UK*, Oxford: Oxfam, http://policy-practice.oxfam.org.uk/publications/a-tale-of-two-britains-inequality-in-the-uk-314152.

Passmore, R. and Passmore, L., 2013, *Here Be Dragons: Youth Work and Mission off the Map*, Birmingham: Frontier Youth Trust.

Pimlott, J. and Pimlott, N., 2008, *Youth Work after Christendom*, Carlisle: Paternoster Press.

Purcell, L., 2014, 'Are we losing the story war?', Manchester: Church Action on Poverty, http://blog.church-poverty.org.uk/2014/04/17/are-we-losing-the-story-war.

Rollins, P., 2008, 'No conviction', *Sojourners*, http://sojo.net/blogs/2008/10/14/no-conviction.

Shannahan, C., 2014, *A Theology of Community Organizing: Power to the People*, Abingdon: Routledge.

Sheppard, D., 1983, *Bias to the Poor*, London: Hodder and Stoughton.

Singh, D. et al. (eds), 2011, *Five Days in August: Interim Report of the 2011 English Riots*, London: Riots Panel.

Singh, D. et al. (eds), 2012, *After the Riots: The Final Report of the Riots Communities and Victims Panel*, London: Riots Panel.

Standing, G., 2011, *The Precariat: The New Dangerous Class*, London: Bloomsbury.

Thaler, C. and Sunstein, C. R., 2009, *Nudge: Improving Decisions about Health, Wealth and Happiness*, London: Penguin Books.

Thoreau, H. D., 1849, *Civil Disobedience*, http://thoreau.eserver.org/civil1.html.

Thornton, A., 2014, 'Citizenship education versus British values', London: *The Law Society Gazette*, http://www.lawgazette.co.uk/law/legal-updates/citizenship-education-versus-british-values/5042973.article.

Unwin, J., 2011, 'The Common Good – what does it mean for people and places in poverty?', The Ebor Lecture, 5 October 2011, York: Joseph Rowntree Foundation, http://www.jrf.org.uk/sites/files/jrf/Ebor-Common-Good-Lecture-series-JuliaUnwin.pdf.

Vatican, nd, *Catechism of the Catholic Church. Part Three: Life in Christ*, http://www.vatican.va/archive/ccc_css/archive/catechism/p3s1c2a2.htm.

Volf, M., 2011, *A Public Faith: How Followers of Christ Should Serve the Common Good*, Grand Rapids, MI: Brazos Press.

Wallis, J., 2014, *The (Un)Common Good: How the Gospel Brings Hope to a World Divided*, Grand Rapids, MI: Brazos Press.

Ward, G., 2009, *The Politics of Discipleship: Becoming Postmaterial Citizens*, London: SCM Press.

Wilkinson, R. and Pickett, K., 2010, *The Spirit Level: Why Equality is Better for Everyone*, London: Penguin Books.

Wren, B., 1977, *Education for Justice*, 2nd edn, London: SCM Press.

Index of Names

Index of Subjects